BRIDGE
ON
BRITISH
BEEF

66d

BRIDGE
— ON —
BRITISH BEEF

TOM BRIDGE

PIATKUS

This book is dedicated to the memory of
Jim Fitzpatrick,
and to
Jayne and Dr Mary Fitzpatrick

First published in 1997 by
Judy Piatkus (Publishers) Ltd
5 Windmill Street, London WIP 1HF

The moral right of the author has been asserted

A catalogue record for this book is available from the British Library

ISBN 0 7499 17512 (hbk)

Designed by Paul Saunders

Typeset by Wyvern 21 Limited
Printed and bound in Great Britain by
Butler & Tanner Ltd, Frome

Contents

✦

Acknowledgements *page vi*

Foreword *page viii*

Introduction *page 1*

Wine Suggestions *page 3*

Beef Essentials *page 4*

1. Stocks, Soups and Starters *page 12*

2. Roasts and Pot Roasts *page 41*

3. Casseroles, Braised Dishes and Curries *page 74*

4. Grilling and Barbecuing *page 120*

5. Pan Frying *page 154*

6. Pies, Puddings and Terrines *page 170*

Addresses *page 209*

Index *page 212*

Acknowledgements

✦

The last ten books that I have had the pleasure of writing have all started with 'I would like to thank…' But this book requires much more than just a word of thanks to the many people who have helped me put it together. I am very proud of the host of talented chefs and food experts who have supported a project very close to the hearts of all those involved.

Antony Worrall Thompson, chef and proprietor of many successful London restaurants and author of some wonderful cookery books, helped and advised and we kept in contact by every means of communication available 'except smoke signals' (the sign of a bad chef).

Derek Andrews, Catering, Development and Promotions Manager for the Meat and Livestock Commission at Milton Keynes – without his help and his knowledge of British beef I would not have finished this book. Mathew Done and Mark Bedrich – I know I was a pain but wasn't it 'worth it'? I also want to thank everyone at Euro-Toques, the organisation that promotes the use of fine-quality foods and the avoidance of convenience foods or products that have been adulterated or that are undesirable for consumption. Brian Sack MBE and Francis Coulson MBE – my two favourite people from The Sharrow Bay Country House Hotel in Ullswater – have also been enormously helpful.

Many thanks, too, to my dear friend Ted Weaver, from Makro, who has supported every one of my cookery books. The beef was provided by Anglo Beef Processors (otherwise known as ABP) and Mike Lees.

I also want to express my gratitude to Alistair MacDougall at PRIAM Public Relations Intercommunications and Marketing at Crowborough in East Sussex; Stewart Macphie and Mike Gibson at Glenbervie Aberdeen Angus Ltd, Glenbervie, Stonehaven, Kincardineshire; Steve Johnson; and everyone at Fairfax Meadow.

Grateful thanks to my Northern buddies and fellow chefs of repute: Paul Reed at The Chester Grosvenor Hotel; Adrian Park at Pubs Ltd; Nigel Smith at Holland Hall; and John Benson Smith somewhere in Yorkshire. Thanks also to Simon Whitney at Villeroy and Boch for the use of their classical plates, and to Phil Taylor (fruit), the man behind the horseradish.

Colin Capon, having toured the world, was rendered out of action for two weeks, but dragged himself from his sick-bed to write me three recipes. Veronica Shaw, commonly known as The History Woman, gave me back the seventeenth century. Acknowledgements are also due to Ron Maxfield from The Cliveden at Taplow, Berkshire, a place of astonishing grandeur; Steve Rowe from The Brewery Conference Centre in London; Peter Bourhill, Managing Director of Life Magazines in Preston; Bob Gledhill, *The Caterer and Hotelkeeper Magazine*, London; Peter (The Cheese Detective) Paprill; John Warmisham; Harry Yeung, the finest Chinese chef in Europe, from the Yang Sing Restaurant in Manchester; Mike and Woody and everyone at the Siam and Royal Orchid in Manchester; everyone at The Blue Elephant in Fulham Broadway; David Lidgate, the walking encyclopaedia on British beef; everyone at The Holland Hall Hotel, especially Tom and Lorraine Rathbone whose family of famous bakers inspired my Pie Society idea; and T. Frith Butchers of Parbold, Lancashire.

Sincere thanks, also, to Bibendum Wine Ltd., for providing wonderful wine recommendations

If I have forgotten anyone, it is not intentional. Very special thanks to The British Dietetic Association; The Family Heart Association; The British Nutrition Food Foundation; The Department of Health Nutrition Unit; and SHARP (**S**cottish **H**eart and **A**rterial disease **R**isk **P**revention).

Heather Rocklin, Philip Cotterell, Anne Black, Gill Cormode and Judy Piatkus at Piatkus Books – thank you for having faith in my work. Also Paul Saunders, for a great design job. And thanks to my Mrs Beeton, Kelly Davis, for all her help and advice.

Finally, Susan and Ed who are Transmedia, and everyone at Transmedia (UK) Head Office, thank you for all your support. The Transmedia card gives diners a 25 per cent discount in over 6000 restaurants around the world – an excellent investment for anyone who enjoys good food. (To become a cardholder or find out more, call freephone 0800 716 691.)

Foreword by
Antony Worrall Thompson

◆

I am giving my full support to this entertaining British beef cookery book by my friend and fellow chef Tom Bridge. In 1995, Tom was completing a tour of Britain with his *Bridge Over Britain* cookery book. During this tour, he came across a great many farmers whose livelihoods had been virtually ruined; honest farmers who had nothing whatsoever to hide…

Tom is a staunchly British chef who, throughout his career, has tried to use only British produce whenever possible. With this principle in mind, he has produced this medley of high-quality beef recipes.

There's no doubt at all that British beef is back – the tenderness, flavour, taste and texture of the best British beef is what makes for top-quality steaks, roasting joints and casseroles.

This cookery book is full of useful advice, with recipes from around the globe using only British beef, many of them contributed by Euro-Toques chefs. Veronica Shaw – whose restaurant Veronica's, in London, serves some of the finest traditional British food from previous centuries – not only came up with an inspired seventeenth-century British Hamburger recipe but a historical fact that is worth knowing. My own contribution extends further than the Foreword – try my four favourite beef recipes for Pickled Tongue; Baked Field Mushrooms with Bone Marrow and Taleggio; Spiced Mediterranean Burgers; and Beef and Cabbage Stuffed Latkes.

Tom also gives you tips on buying, freshness and storage; the different cuts of meat; healthy eating recipes; and classic recipes, like his Steak and Ale Pudding and his very well-known Beef Wellington, as well as curries and meat puddings.

All in all, this book is an A to Z of everything you always wanted to know about British beef. It's about cooking and eating *good-quality* beef, from animals that have had a good life and eaten from the best pastures. The former extensive demand for cheaper meat led to intensive farming methods – and the result of that was BSE.

We have to pay more for a quality product; the time has come to get back to traditional methods of farming. Your voice makes a difference. Only by consumers demanding 'real' meat can we stop farmers rearing animals in an inhumane fashion.

Tom has written an excellent book. It is a great step forward in our efforts to convince the Government that we, the public, need to know how our beef reaches the shops. Back British beef – it's the best!

Antony Worrall Thompson

Introduction

✦

I now have great confidence in the Meat and Livestock Commission, our British farmers and butchers. A year or so ago, the country was obsessed by BSE but it was minced beef that was the problem and not the main cuts of meat. Today, British Meat and the Meat and Livestock Commission are rebuilding consumer confidence by means of the quality mark (see page 5) which reassures the shopper that 100 per cent minced beef is made from regular cuts from prime cattle less than 30 months old and that it is offal-free.

Roast beef has been part of the British diet for centuries. It was popular in the past and is even more popular today – every traditional British restaurant serves roast beef and Yorkshire pudding.

There are many different cuts, from the famous Sir-loin (which was knighted in Lancashire) to rump, silverside, rib and topside. It was the knighting of the sirloin (p. 51) that marked beef's coming of age as the favourite dish of Old England. *The Cook and Householder's Dictionary* of 1823 contains the following advice:

BEEF. In every sort of provisions, the best of the kind goes the farthest; it cuts out with most advantage and affords most nourishment. The best way to obtain a good article is to deal with shops of established credit. You may perhaps pay a little more than by purchashing of those who pretend to sell cheap, but you will be more than in proportion better served.

They are still telling us today that you have to pay for high-quality cuts of beef. There is no such thing as a cheap cut!

When *The Forme of Cury* was compiled in 1430 by the master cooks of King Richard II, beef was called 'roast flesh' and continued to be called this until *The Castel of Helthe* was published by Sir Thomas Elyot in the sixteenth century. According to Elyot, *'here in England, grosse meates may be eaten in a great quantitie; and in a cholerick stomake biefe is better digested than a chykens legge'*. He also said that, *'Befe of Englande, to Englyshe-men whiche are in helthe, bryngeth stronge nouryshynge.'*

The only things that have changed since then are the price and the very high quality of British beef. After hundreds of years we are, without doubt, the finest producers of beef in the world. The only people who have made a mess of this are the cowboys in this industry and the civil servants and politicians who did not tell the whole truth. The fact remains that we have the finest pastures and a collection of traditional breeds throughout Great Britain whose flavour cannot be bettered. Talented people like Colin Capon, Paul Reed, Paul Heathcote, Adrian Park, Nigel Smith, Brian Turner and Anthony Worrall Thompson, some of the finest chefs on British soil, are constantly developing ways of combining new ideas in order to make the most of our British beef.

Putting aside my campaign banner for a moment, my main aim is that you should enjoy this collection of wonderful recipes which literally cover every aspect of beef. As for my personal preferences, although this book includes mouthwatering stocks, soups, gravies, casseroles, braised dishes, curries, pan-fried, grilled and barbecued dishes, roasts and pot roasts, I have to say that the pie section is incredible ...

Happy cooking!

TOM BRIDGE

Wine Suggestions

Most wine shops are able to give advice if you need help deciding which wines to serve with particular foods. To point you in the right direction and offer you some expert suggestions, I am delighted to be able to include here some excellent recommendations and notes from Willie Lebus, resident gastronome at Bibendum Wine Ltd, 113 Regents Park Road, London NW1 8UR. Enjoy!

Roasts and pot roasts

Calera Central Coast Pinot Noir 1994, California – One of California's greatest Pinots, this decadent plump red has a mix of farmyard aromas to support the hedonistic strawberry fruit which combines so well with a rare, succulent rib of beef, or indeed a pot roast.

Grills and steak dishes

Katnook Estate Coonawarra Cabernet Sauvignon 1994, Australia – What to have with well-hung steak? Answer: smoky, oaky 'Katnook Cab' with a stunning vanilla-scented bouquet which underpins spicy cassis fruit and some ripe tannins.

Lawson's Dry Hills Chardonnay 1994, New Zealand – With steak on the menu you could go wild with a rich, carefully oaked, tropical Chardonnay from Marlborough, New Zealand. Avoid serving it too chilled. You'll find the flavours are matched in heaven – particularly if you like your steaks rare.

Casseroles and braised dishes

La Rural Mendoza Malbec 1996, Argentina – A rich stew of beef and wine needs a nice spicy mouthful to accompany it. The La Rural Argentinian Malbec has rich, brambly flavour reminiscent of Cahors. Perfect glugging wine.

Beaumes de Venise Rouge Fenouillet 1995, Rhône – This opulent spicy blend of rich Grenache and Syrah complements the flavourful meat of rich casseroles and braised dishes, and is particularly good with oxtail.

Curries and sweet and spicy dishes

Grangehurst Stellenbosch Pinotage 1995, South Africa – What's needed for a delicious mix of sweet and spicy flavours is a redcurrant, beetroot and coffee-spiced wine. Grangehurst Pinotage, that unique South African star, fits the bill perfectly. Avoid too much fresh chilli or your mouth will be too cauterised to taste the wine!

Barbecues

La Serre Rosé de Syrah 1996, vin de pays d'Oc, France – A juicy, strawberry fruit rosé with zingy acidity is the perfect foil for smoky barbecue flavours.

Beef pies and puddings

Chianti Classico Riserva Borgo Scopeto 1990, Italy – Rich, nursery comfort food deserves a rich, smooth, warming red. This Chianti Classico has a herbal, nutty bouquet with a ripe, wild mushroom flavour and a hint of red pepper.

Terrines and meat loaves

Coteaux du Languedoc Rouge 1995, Domaine du Poujol, Languedoc, France – Garlicky terrines need determination! This *wunderkind* of a wine is made by an ex-Bibendum delivery boy turned winemaker! Plump blackberry and damson fruit – lovely and rich and with a structure to last for years to come.

Beef Essentials

◆

WHAT SHOULD YOU LOOK FOR WHEN BUYING BEEF?

Every chef who learns his trade in this country has to do some form of training in butchery. In the big establishments, this comes under the 'cold larder' (otherwise known as the *garde-manger*). And this was how I learnt about butchery.

When buying beef, these are the points to remember:

- Frozen beef is a *no-no*. Fresh is best and it should be slightly chilled.
- The meat should be red and quite firm, with flecks of creamy white fat.
- When buying joints, look for the best proportion of meat in relation to bone.
- The British Meat mark appears on most cuts. If it does not, only buy from a reputable butcher. *Never* buy beef from unknown market traders, car boot sales, etc. (The British Meat mark can be seen on the front cover of this book.)

WHICH CUT SHOULD YOU CHOOSE?

Do not be afraid to ask questions when buying any cut of meat. This will give you more knowledge of beef and stand you in good stead when cooking it. If I went through what to look for in every cut of beef this book would never be finished!

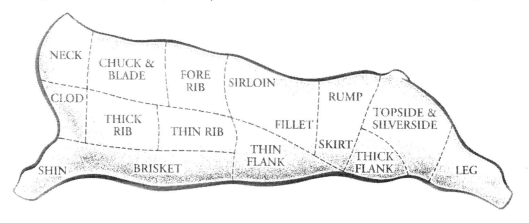

No matter what cut of meat you choose – whether it is a choice lean cut, or a cheaper cut from the leg or shin which has long, coarse fibres – if it comes from a reputable butcher and it is cooked properly, the flavour should remain.

Obviously, if you can afford to buy choice cuts, like fillet, sirloin, wing (thin) rib and fore rib, you will never have a problem, no matter how you cook them.

Middle (thick) rib is usually roasted on the bone; chuck and blade are used for braising; topside is roasted; silverside is usually salt-boiled; and top rump or thick flank are braised or pot roasted.

If buying mince, look for the Quality Mince mark (below), or choose a cut of beef and get your butcher to mince it for you (unless you have a mincer at home).

The cheaper cuts, like brisket, are used for pressed beef; and the flank (belly) for stews and braising. The skirt, which is the lower rump, is used in stews. Clod (neck), shin of beef and leg (hind and fore) are for stewing and soups only.

When buying any of these cuts in a supermarket look carefully at the label. It should tell you the country of origin and what the cut of meat is, the weight and cost per kg and, most importantly, the 'sell by' date.

WHY IS BEEF 'HUNG'?

The tenderness of beef is progressively improved the longer it is 'hung' in suitable conditions before cutting takes place. Tenderness is the most important single factor in eating quality, although flavour and juiciness are important considerations as well. The customer looks for eating quality, particularly tenderness, in the higher-priced cuts of beef which are traditionally cooked by dry heat (i.e. grilling or frying steaks and roasting joints). Shoppers are less concerned about the tenderness of the lower-value cuts which are stewed, boiled, braised or casseroled, as these wet cooking methods help to tenderise the meat.

So it is in the high-value, dry-cooked cuts that the benefits of properly controlled maturing or hanging are most apparent. Hanging has little effect on the tough connective tissue (collagen fibres); shin or leg of beef and similar cuts are therefore cooked by the use of moist heat, which tends to turn the collagen to gelatine.

I recently attended a lecture given by David Lidgate, master butcher, with other members of Euro-Toques (the organisation that promotes the use of fine-quality foods) at The Blue Elephant restaurant in London. To give you an insight into the activities of one of the UK's top butchers, this is what Henrietta Green wrote about him in her book the *Food Lovers' Guide to Britain*:

> David Lidgate is a man of vision, he leads the way in the butchery world; he was the founding Chairman of National 'Q' Guild of Butchers ('Q' for quality) and his shop is regarded as the benchmark to which butchers aspire ... Scrupulous in his inspections of farms and slaughterhouses, David hand-picks and visits all his suppliers in his never-ending quest for the best possible quality meat. He sees quality as a chain in which every factor – from breed, feed, age of the beast and finish to the method of slaughter, conditions and age of hanging and the art of butchering – must be taken into account. 'And every element in this chain must be right. It's no good buying organic meat if it's not well slaughtered or hung. For a good piece of meat everything must be right,' he insists.

HOW SHOULD YOU STORE BEEF?

Keep raw beef in a refrigerator, unwrapped and below 8°C. When you remove the meat from the refrigerator, allow it to stand for about 30 minutes to reach room temperature before cooking.

Cooked beef should always be allowed to cool naturally before refrigeration. Always ensure that it is kept away from raw meat and wrapped in cling film and cooking foil.

If you wish to freeze the beef, place a date in the wrapper and use within two months of freezing. Allow the meat to thaw naturally at room temperature. *Never* thaw meat quickly; always allow it to thaw for at least 8 hours.

Cooked meat should be used within five days and again it should always be wrapped

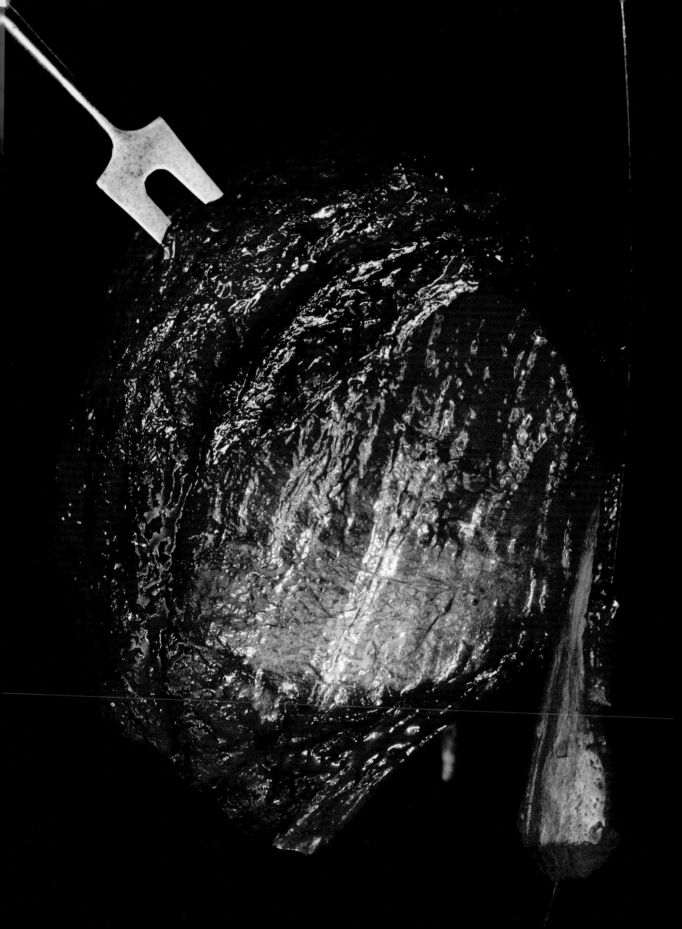

and kept away from raw food. Cooked meat should be placed on a separate shelf, with raw meats underneath the cooked. Always place raw meat in a deep tray so that any seepage stays in the tray.

Stewart Macphie runs Glenbervie, a small but very beautiful estate in the centre of Aberdeen Angus country, just south of Aberdeen, between the North Sea and the eastern edge of the Grampian mountains. The peaceful rolling farmland is ideal for rearing traditional pedigree Aberdeen Angus cattle. Glenbervie has benefited from 700 years of family ownership and enthusiasm for farming innovation, and Stewart was a British Academy of Gastronomy Grand Prix Winner in 1994. Stewart explains the Glenbervie philosophy:

Our Glenbervie grass-fed suckler herd of 200 pedigree Aberdeen Angus cows produce the very finest traditional beef: tender, succulent and full of flavour. This is made possible by total control through our specialist Aberdeen Angus Butchery on the farm.

Consumer demand is changing rapidly. Quality, not quantity, is the key. Clearly this requires the finest Aberdeen Angus developed by unswerving attention to detail by breeder, stockman, butcher and through the distribution chain. Total control by our Quality Assurance Manager is essential. Traditional standards and methods allied to the best modern hygiene practices are part of the total commitment.

- **Breeding** Both bull and cow really matter. We breed for our customers' needs, not for show – rosettes are indigestible.

- **Feed** The best-quality grass with a good clover content. The protein additions are entirely of vegetable origin. Turnips – yes. Barley – limited.

- **Animal Welfare** In Winter, straw-bedded airy courts with no overcrowding. Minimum stress.

- **Age and Type** All Glenbervie meat is from young (18–24 months-old) steers and heifers only. No bull beef.

- **Abattoir Standards** Vigorous control of hygiene and meticulous removal of all bovine offals etc.

- **Hanging** Back to tradition of 14–20 days under ideal control conditions.

- **Quality Butchery** Modest fat cover with essential marbling for flavour and succulence.

- **Distribution** Hygiene and temperature controlled.

OPPOSITE PAGE 6 A succulent joint of beef . . .   OPPOSITE Cold Spiced Beef Brisket (page 106)

HOW SHOULD YOU COOK BEEF?

Most of the recipes in this book assume that everyone likes their beef cooked to medium. If your tastes are different, you can reduce the cooking time of roasts by 10 minutes per 450g (1lb) for medium to rare; add 5 minutes per 450g (1lb) for medium to well done; or add 15 minutes per 450g (1lb) for well done.

It is safe to eat *very* rare beef as long as the cut is sirloin, fillet or rump. If you like your beef like this (often referred to as *saignant* or *bleu*) then reduce the cooking time of roasts by about 15 minutes per 450g (1lb).

It's not possible to be precise about cooking times for steaks, because so much depends on the thickness of the meat and the heat of your hob, grill or oven. You will need to check the meat frequently, by cutting into the thickest part and seeing if it is to your liking.

When roasting beef, remove the meat from the oven at the end of the cooking time and leave it to stand at room temperature for 10 minutes before carving. Cover it with foil (with the shiny side on the inside). This process further tenderises the meat.

Many of the recipes include beef dripping which should be available from your local butcher. If it's not available, you can substitute good-quality lard.

HOW DO I CHOOSE MY BEEF?

When it came to selecting meat for my beef recipes in this book, I wanted beef that had been matured on the bone and came from specially chosen beef producers.

First I contacted Ted Weaver at Makro's head office in Eccles, Manchester. I then saw some samples of beef which came from a meat company that is renowned for its quality. Anglo Beef Processors supply Scotch, Welsh and English beef to Makro and many other multiples, including top hotels, restaurants and supermarkets.

I found their beef extremely tender, because it is hung on the bone for a long period and totally matured under chilled conditions for several weeks before it reaches the consumer. During the hanging process, acids develop that soften the muscle fibres and this helps to make the meat tender. Years of research and development have enabled ABP to produce the best in British beef. Every cut, which has been matured in their own unique way, eats and cooks uniformly, giving a standard of taste, texture and tenderness which many of us chefs thought we would never see again.

Although the beef is produced in a modern ABP plant, the method of maturing it is very similar in principle to that used by the old school of butchers. The only difference is that modern controls have been brought in.

According to Mike Lees at ABP, they have 800 top beef farmers supplying them with cattle which are up to 30 months of age. They are all farm-assured (see below) and only eat grass and other vegetable products. ABP, and the other suppliers I have mentioned throughout this book, offer the finest-quality meat available on our shores. Their aim is to have naturally produced, humanely reared beef coming from the farm to our kitchens. And stress-free beef is tender beef.

The Government has introduced a Beef Assurance Scheme. This applies to herds which have had no history of BSE, have been reared mainly on grass, and have not come into contact with meat and bone meal. Cattle from these specialist herds can be slaughtered for human consumption for up to 42 months.

Ministry of Agriculture, Fisheries and Food

In the course of writing this book, I have talked to Derek Andrews of the Meat and Livestock Commission; Colin Capon; David Lidgate; Buccleuch Scotch Beef; Michael Gibson at Macbeth's; Ted Weaver at Makro; Mike Lees at Anglo Beef Processors (ABP); Stewart Macphie at Glenbervie Aberdeen Angus Ltd; and everyone at Fairfax Meadow. All these leading meat suppliers have a wealth of knowledge on British beef and I highly recommend their beef. (Their addresses are listed at the back of the book.)

Your local butcher will be happy to tell you where he gets his beef from. You only need to ask.

THE GUILD OF Q BUTCHERS

The Guild of Q Butchers represents the best of Britain's independent butchers – dedicated craftsmen determined to maintain and promote the fine traditions of top-class butchery. The Q stands for quality. Only those butchers who can meet the Guild's strict membership criteria can participate.

Every member's business must adhere to all current food safety and hygiene requirements, but to gain the coveted Q award, Q butchers have to demonstrate unsurpassed standards of meat quality, presentation, staff skills and knowledge, product innovation and general shop appearance.

Q shops are subjected to an independent annual inspection by British Meat Quality Assurance, with additional spot checks ensuring standards are maintained. The Q quality assurance scheme provides customers with the opportunity to purchase British meat and meat products at accredited shops nation-wide, each identified by the Guild's distinctive green and gold shield – the ultimate quality guarantee.

Q butchers have earned a reputation for excellence over the years, sweeping the boards at national and international food competitions. In addition, the Guild's own product evaluation events offer individual members the chance to gain recognition for their own outstanding products and new recipe ideas.

For a list of Guild of Q Butchers in your area contact the Secretary on 01908 235018

THE HEALTH BENEFITS OF EATING BEEF

Lean red meat is muscle fibre and tissue and is therefore an excellent source of protein and body-building food. For the past 30 years I have been cutting and cooking beef for kings, queens and even mad politicians but it was not the beef that drove them mad – it was the Opposition!

Here are some interesting quotes about lean red meat:

Lean red meat can be a nutritious part of a healthy varied diet.
British Dietetic Association

SHARP is pleased to endorse the message that lean red meat can be enjoyed as part of a low-fat diet.
Scottish **H**eart and **A**rterial disease **R**isk **P**revention

There are many misconceptions about meat, not least about its fat content. Lean meat is much lower in fat than many people suppose, but opt for lean cuts, trim any visible fat and use low-fat cooking methods. Lean meat (trimmed) typically contains less than 10 per cent fat, of which only half is saturated; the rest is largely monounsaturated plus some polyunsaturates. There are now many new lean cuts of meat on the market which contain even less fat – between 3 and 5 per cent.
Family Heart Association

Meat and meat products are a very useful source of some vitamins. They supply 50 per cent of the vitamin B12 and 33 per cent of the niacin content of the average UK diet. Red meat is a good source of iron which the body can easily absorb. It is also a good source of other important nutrients, such as zinc and protein, and it is reassuring to note that the fat content of red meat has reduced over the last few years.
British Nutrition Foundation

Eating lean meat is one of the easiest ways of helping to ensure that you get enough iron.
Department of Health Nutrition Unit

Yet, despite all this favourable expert opinion, market research indicates that many people are doubtful that red meat can play a central role in a healthy diet. They are particularly concerned about the question of fat. Even some health professionals are not aware that lean meat is significantly lower in fat than it used to be.

THE FACTS ABOUT MEAT

The facts about lean red meat show that the time is right to address the misconceptions about it and to promote the very positive benefits that come from making it part of a healthy, balanced, everyday diet.

The British Meat campaign does just that – giving the people of Britain the facts and giving caterers crucial support in making meat a central part of the menu – with rational messages that the consumer understands and appreciates.

The protein content of meat

Meat is a very important source of protein, essential fatty acids, B vitamins and minerals. The protein in meat is of a high biological value, because it contains all the essential amino acids in proportions ideal for human growth, repair and maintenance of bodily functions. Meat proteins are generally well digested and utilised by the human body. Meat and meat products provide 30 per cent of the protein in the British diet.

The energy content of meat

Meat and meat products provide on average only 15 per cent of our total energy intake. The amount of energy provided by each meat cut is largely dependent on the quantity of fat present.

This table shows the protein and energy content of a 100g (4oz) portion of the following cuts.

	Protein	Energy	
	G	KCAL	KJ
Grilled lean rump steak with no visible fat	28.6	168	708
Grilled rump steak with fat (89 per cent lean)	27.3	218	912
Roast lean sirloin with no visible fat	27.6	192	866
Roast sirloin with fat (80 per cent lean)	23.6	284	1182
Roast lean topside with no visible fat	29.2	156	659
Roast topside with fat (88 per cent lean)	26.6	214	896

All in all, on nutritional grounds lean red meat compares very favourably with many other foods. If we choose lean cuts, and cook them the right way, beef can even help us meet the Government's own Health of the Nation dietary targets for lowering total fat and saturated fat intake.

CHAPTER 1

Stocks, Soups and Starters

✦

This chapter is the basis for the rest of the book: the following stocks can be used in the casseroles, braised dishes, curries and pies. I cannot stress how important it is to have a good-quality stock; home-made stock is far superior to those convenient little stock cubes.

At the base of a really good soup there always stands an exceptionally good stock. There are two stocks for you to use throughout this book, a Basic and a Rich Stock. The Beef Soup with Sherry (p. 15) is a prime example of the importance of using a good stock. It makes all the difference to the flavour. And wait till you try my real Oxtail Soup with Tarragon Dumplings (p. 16). I know it seems easier to open a tin of oxtail soup or use those nasty packets, but once tasted your tastebuds won't forget the experience!

Master chef Paul Reed, from the world-famous Chester Grosvenor Hotel, has contributed his recipes for Basic Beef Stock (opposite) and Oxtail and Truffle Sausage (p. 23) – 'again, it is the strength and flavour of a good-quality beef stock that adds to the flavour of my oxtail and truffle sausage recipe,' says Paul.

During a recent lunch with Paul and other fellow chefs we discussed the catering industry today and we talked of the old school of cookery, but most of all we talked about the heritage of British food. For instance, at the moment oxtails are fashionable and so is beetroot, and it is to the advantage of the consumer that we chefs discuss these matters in great detail so that we are ahead of the industry and can keep traditional British food alive by combining the best of the old with the best of the new. I make no apology for the fact that every recipe in this chapter is time-consuming. Good food always is!

Although the soups and savouries in this chapter make ideal starters, by cooking in larger quantities and serving them with more substantial accompaniments, they can also make filling main courses.

Basic Beef Stock (Brown Stock)

MAKES approximately 1.2 litres (2 pints)

Paul Reed works extremely hard at the Chester Grosvenor Hotel to create very high-quality meals which have earned him praise from his clientele from around the world. The North-West of England not only produces good chefs but extremely good food. This stock is the one to use for soups and gravy. It keeps for four days in the refrigerator or up to two months in the freezer.

900g (2lb) beef bones	2 *bouquets garni*
450g (1lb) shin of beef, diced	6 black peppercorns
50g (2oz) beef dripping	2 bay leaves
2 leeks, washed and sliced	4 tablespoons white wine vinegar
2 large onions, peeled and sliced	a sprig of thyme
1 celery stalk, washed and sliced	salt and freshly ground black pepper
2 large carrots, peeled and sliced	(to taste)

1. Put the bones with the diced meat and dripping in a large roasting tin. Brown the bones in the centre of the oven for 40 minutes at Gas Mark 7/220°C/425°F.

2. Put the bones in a deep 3 litre (5¼ pint) casserole or pan, and add all the other ingredients. Cover with water and bring the contents slowly to the boil, remove any scum from the surface, and cover the casserole dish or pan with a tight-fitting lid.

3. Simmer the stock over the lowest heat for 4–5 hours to extract all the flavour from the bones and vegetables, topping up with hot water if the level of stock falls below that of the ingredients.

4. Strain the stock through a fine sieve, into a large bowl. Leave to settle for 5 minutes, then remove the fat from the surface by drawing absorbent kitchen paper over it. Correct the seasoning and the stock will be ready for use in the soup recipes that follow.

Rich Beef Stock

MAKES approximately 1.2 litres (2 pints)

I use this rich beef stock mainly for my consommés and pies.

450g (1lb) beef marrow bones, cut	2 *bouquets garni*
900g (2lb) shin of beef, diced	4 white peppercorns
50g (2oz) beef dripping	4 tablespoons white wine vinegar
2 leeks, washed and sliced	a sprig of thyme
1 large onion, peeled and sliced	1 bay leaf
1 celery stalk, washed and sliced	salt and freshly ground black pepper
2 large carrots, peeled and sliced	(to taste)

1. Blanch the marrow bones for 10 minutes in boiling water, then put them with the diced meat and dripping in a large roasting tin. Brown the bones in the centre of the oven for 30 minutes at Gas Mark 7/220°C/425°F.

2. Put the bones in a deep 3 litre (5¼ pint) casserole or pan, and add all the other ingredients. Cover with water and bring the contents slowly to the boil, remove any scum from the surface, and cover the casserole or pan with a tight-fitting lid.

3. Simmer the stock over the lowest heat for 5 hours to extract all the flavour from the bones and vegetables, topping up with hot water if the level of stock falls below that of the ingredients.

4. Strain the stock through a fine sieve, into a large bowl. Leave to settle for 10 minutes, then remove the fat from the surface by drawing absorbent kitchen paper over it. Correct the seasoning and the stock will be ready for use in a consommé or wherever rich beef stock is required.

Chef's Tip

To make use of the meat and vegetables, lift them out with a slotted spoon, put them through a blender and use them as a filling for a Cottage Pie (pp. 190–192).

Beef Soup with Sherry

SERVES 8–10

Should you wish, you can use a vintage port to make this soup that little bit richer and serve it with fresh croûtons.

50g (2oz) butter
1 onion, peeled and diced
1 carrot, peeled and diced
1 celery stalk, washed and diced
450g (1lb) rump steak (fat removed), diced
450g (1lb) any game meat (venison, rabbit, pheasant or grouse), diced
50g (2oz) plain flour

1.2 litres (2 pints) Basic Beef Stock (p. 13)
1 bay leaf
8 black peppercorns
a pinch of salt
3 tablespoons redcurrant jelly
150ml (5fl oz) cream sherry or vintage port

1. Melt the butter in a saucepan. Add the onion, carrot, celery, beef and game, cook slowly for 8 minutes, then sprinkle with the flour.

2. Cook for a further 3 minutes, then slowly add the stock, together with the bay leaf, peppercorns and salt. Simmer for 1 hour. Add the redcurrrant jelly and sherry or port, and let the soup stand for at least 4 hours.

3. Remove the bay leaf, and put the soup through a blender or liquidiser. Reheat and simmer for 10 minutes, and serve.

Traditional Scotch Broth

SERVES 8

A firm family favourite; the taste of shin of beef, barley, carrot, turnip, leeks and peas really makes you feel you're in the glens, watching the salmon jumping. This soup should be left for at least two days before being reheated and served with oatmeal cakes or bread.

50g (2oz) dried peas, already soaked for 6 hours or according to instructions on the packet	50g (2oz) barley, rinsed
	salt (to taste)
	freshly ground white pepper (to taste)
900g (2lb) shin of beef (fat removed), diced	1 large carrot, peeled and diced
	1 small turnip, peeled and diced
1.2 litres (2 pints) Basic Beef Stock (p. 13)	1 large leek, washed and thinly sliced
	1 red onion, peeled and finely chopped

1. Put the peas and beef in a large pan with the stock and 570ml (1 pint) water. Bring slowly to the boil and skim the stock as it boils, using a ladle.

2. When all the scum has been removed, add the barley and salt and simmer for 25 minutes.

3. Add the rest of the ingredients and simmer for 2 hours, skim and leave the broth to stand for at least 24 hours.

4. Reheat, adjust the seasoning and serve.

Oxtail Soup with Tarragon Dumplings

SERVES 6–8

This recipe is taken from my Heartbeat Country Cookbook which I wrote to go with the Yorkshire Television series and I am sure you will find it extremely popular with your family and friends. The combination of fresh oxtail and tarragon dumplings is something that every lover of good British food should experience. This recipe is made in two stages, but I am sure you will find it well worth the extra effort. Serve with plenty of home-made crusty bread.

For the soup

1 whole oxtail
50g (2oz) plain flour, seasoned
100g (4oz) butter
1 large carrot
1 celery stalk
1 onion
1 small turnip
3 tablespoons sunflower oil
100ml (4fl oz) claret or sherry
1 teaspoon dried thyme
1 bay leaf
salt and freshly ground black pepper
   (to taste)

1.75 litres (3 pints) Basic Beef Stock
   (p. 13)

For the tarragon dumplings

50g (2oz) self-raising flour
50g (2oz) fresh breadcrumbs
2 tablespoons shredded beef suet
2 tablespoons chopped fresh tarragon
2 tablespoons finely grated lemon rind
salt and freshly ground black pepper
   (to taste)
1 egg, beaten
a little milk
extra flour

1. To make the soup, chop the oxtail into pieces through its natural joints, coating lightly with the seasoned flour. Heat the butter in a large deep saucepan and quickly fry the oxtail until lightly browned.

2. Peel all the vegetables if necessary, and cut into 2.5cm (1 inch) cubes.

3. Add the oil to the pan and brown them together. Pour over the claret or sherry and add all the rest of the ingredients except the beef stock. Cook for 10 minutes, then gradually add the beef stock.

4. Simmer for 3 hours, skimming off any excess fat while simmering.

5. Strain the soup into a large clean saucepan and allow it to cool.

6. Remove the oxtail pieces, finely chop the meat and return it to the soup. Re-boil and correct the seasoning, and leave the soup to simmer while you make the dumplings.

7. To make the dumplings, mix together all the ingredients except the egg, milk and extra flour, in a large clean bowl.

8. Add the egg and blend in thoroughly. Add enough milk to make the dough moist, shape into small balls, roll them in a little flour and cook them for 10 minutes in boiling salted water.

9. Remove the dumplings carefully and add them to the soup. Cook for a further 12 minutes, and serve.

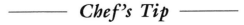

Chef's Tip

Take the left-over vegetables from the stock, mash them with a little butter and make them into small patties. Dip them into the left-over flour, fry them in butter and serve with your main course.

Dumplings – A Great British Institution

If you are on a diet you will just have to read (and not taste!) these recipes because dumplings are fattening but so enjoyable to make. I'm from the fun-loving North of England where we have what are known as homely cooks. My mother, being in that category, taught me the art of dumpling-making. Soup without dumplings is like Christmas without Delia Smith. No offence meant Delia! Loved her Christmas book...

You can use dumplings for practically anything. The Chinese fill them with prawns, beef and pork, and then steam them. The same mixture is used for Beef Roly Poly (p. 177). I have suggested some basic flavours and fillings to give you an assortment of dumplings, all of which go very well with soups, stews and casseroles.

Using the following dumpling recipe, you can add 1 level teaspoon of any of the following flavourings: mustard; crushed almonds; chopped nuts; ground ginger; curry powder; grated Parmesan cheese; crushed garlic; ground black pepper; chopped chillies; dried herbs (e.g. basil, parsley, mint, mixed herbs, fennel, tarragon or thyme).

If you wish to stuff the dumplings, you will need about 350g (12oz) of one of the following fillings: cooked minced beef, marrow, oxtail, kidney, game, lamb, pork or seafood, oysters, pâtés, stuffings, sausages or thick sauces; ham; cheese; apple; beetroot; chives; onions; shallots; leeks; garlic; fruit; any mixture of cooked chopped vegetables or fruit; cooked rice.

100g (4oz) self-raising flour
a pinch of salt
50g (2oz) shredded beef suet (fresh if
   possible)

4 tablespoons cold Basic Beef Stock
   (p. 13)

---

1. Sift the flour into a bowl, add the salt and 1 level teaspoon of any of the flavouring ingredients.

2. Then add the suet and sprinkle in the beef stock. Stir with a fork to form a soft scone-like dough.

3. Turn out the mixture onto a floured surface and divide into 12 small pieces. If you are not going to fill them, simply roll each one into a ball.

4. If you are going to use any of the fillings, first ensure that they are fully cooked; then chop, grate or shred them, as necessary. Roll the filling into small balls about 2.5cm (1 inch) in diameter.

5. With floured hands, flatten each dumpling into a small patty, place a ball of filling on it, and mould back into a ball.

6. About 25 minutes before the soup, stew or casserole has finished cooking, add the dumplings.

Curried Dumplings with Beetroot Filling

A classic combination of flavouring and filling. I always use Red Velvet beetroot because it is the only make of pre-cooked beetroot produced without any additives, and it retains all its colour and flavour. You can get it from Marks and Spencer's, Sainsbury's and other well-known supermarkets.

100g (4oz) self-raising flour	4 tablespoons cold Basic Beef Stock
a pinch of salt	(p. 13)
1 teaspoon mild curry powder	12 small rounds Red Velvet beetroot
50g (2oz) shredded beef suet (fresh if	
possible)	

1. Sift the flour into a bowl. Add the salt and curry powder. Add the suet and sprinkle in the beef stock. Stir with a fork to form a soft scone-like dough.

2. Turn out the mixture onto a floured surface and divide into 12 small pieces. With floured hands, flatten each dumpling into a small patty, fill with a round of beetroot and shape into a ball, ensuring that there are no gaps.

3. Add to your soup, stew or casserole about 25 minutes before it has finished cooking.

Beef Consommé

SERVES 6

This might sound snobbish, but it is not meant to. My mother does two world tours a year and when she stops off in Madeira I always ask her to bring me back a bottle of vintage Madeira wine especially for my soups and sauces. If you can't get hold of Madeira you can use port instead.

1.75 litres (3 pints) Rich Beef Stock (p. 14)	whites of 4 eggs plus the shells
150ml (5fl oz) Madeira	salt and freshly ground black pepper (to taste)

1. Place the beef stock and Madeira in a large saucepan and heat gently for 5 minutes.

2. Add the whites of egg and the shells to the beef stock, and whisk over the heat until the mixture begins to boil. When the mixture boils, remove the pan from the heat and leave it to subside for 10 minutes.

3. Repeat this process three times. This allows the egg white to trap the sediments in the beef stock to clarify the soup. Let the consommé cool for 5 minutes.

4. Carefully place a piece of fine muslin over a clean saucepan and strain the soup into it. Repeat this process twice, then gently reheat the consommé, season, taste and serve.

Rich Beef Consommé

SERVES 6

This is a very festive consommé and you can use whisky instead of brandy for a real flavour of Hogmanay.

1.75 litres (3 pints) Rich Beef Stock (p. 14)	whites of 4 eggs plus the shells
150ml (5fl oz) Madeira	6 tablespoons port
4 tablespoons brandy or whisky	salt and freshly ground white pepper (to taste)

1. Place the rich beef stock, Madeira and brandy in a large saucepan and heat gently for 10 minutes.

2. Add the whites of egg and the shells to the beef stock, and whisk over the heat until the mixture begins to boil.

3. When the mixture boils, remove the pan from the heat and leave it to subside for 10 minutes. Repeat this process three times. This allows the egg white to trap the sediments in the beef stock to clarify the soup. Let the rich consommé cool for 5 minutes.

4. Carefully place a piece of fine muslin over a clean saucepan and strain the soup into it. Repeat this process twice, then gently reheat the consommé, add the port, season, taste and serve.

Victorian Potted Hough

SERVES 6–8

*P*otted beef was very popular when I was knee-high to a grasshopper. This Scottish recipe dates back to the Victorian era, when food had to be preserved for longer periods of time. Serve it with toast triangles, a tomato salad and some Creamed Horseradish (p. 26). You should also try Steve Johnson's recipe for Potted Beef Terrine with Red Onion Marmalade (p. 210).

900g (2lb) shin of beef (hough)	freshly ground black pepper (to taste)
900g (2lb) shin bone	6 black peppercorns
1.75 litres (3 pints) Basic Beef Stock	a generous pinch of allspice
(p. 13)	1 bay leaf
1 teaspoon salt	

1. Place the meat and bone in a large pan and cover with the beef stock. Bring the stock to the boil, reduce the heat and simmer gently for 3 hours, until the shin of beef is really tender.

2. Shred the meat finely, including any meat from the shin bone, and set aside. Place the bone back in the pan, with the stock and the rest of the ingredients, boiling rapidly until the liquid has reduced by half. Remove the bones, peppercorns and bay leaf.

3. Place the shredded meat in a large basin or individual moulds, pour over the stock and leave to cool for 2 hours.

4. Place the basin or moulds in the refrigerator for 24 hours to allow the potted beef to set.

Olde English Potted Beef

SERVES 8–10

I created this recipe for Derek Andrews at the Meat and Livestock Commission, who very kindly arranged for all the photographs and provided a lot of the information in this book. This version of potted beef combines recipes from the seventeenth, eighteenth and nineteenth centuries. Serve it with my Creamed Horseradish (p. 26), some freshly baked bread and butter, and a generous glass of good claret. Enjoy...

900g (2lb) sirloin of beef
900g (2lb) shin bone, broken into pieces
450g (1lb) fillet of pork
1 litre (1¾ pints) Basic Beef Stock
   (p. 13)
1 bottle of red wine
150ml (5fl oz) port
1 teaspoon salt

freshly ground black pepper (to taste)
8 green peppercorns
450g (1lb) baking apples, peeled, cored
   and diced
5 anchovies (bones removed), pounded
8 cloves
¼ teaspoon allspice
1 bay leaf

1. Place the sirloin of beef, bone and pork in a large pan, and cover with the beef stock, wine and port.

2. Bring to the boil, reduce the heat and simmer gently for 2 hours until the beef and pork are really tender.

3. Shred the meat finely, including any meat from the shin bone. Set aside. Place the bone back in the pan, with the stock and the rest of the ingredients. Rapidly bring to the boil and simmer until the liquid has reduced by half. Strain through a fine sieve into a clean jug.

4. Place the mixed meats in individual moulds, pour over the stock and leave to cool for 3 hours.

5. Place the moulds in the refrigerator for 2 days to mature and allow the potted beef to set.

Oxtail & Truffle Sausage

SERVES 4

Paul Reed relies on quality of ingredients and highly professional execution for the impact of this very tasty recipe used at the Chester Grosvenor Hotel… pure class from the North-West of England. To serve, slice the sausages and accompany with creamy mashed potato, pouring the gravy over and around the serving dish.

250g (9oz) cooked chicken supreme
1 egg yolk, beaten
1 egg white, whisked until stiff
150ml (5fl oz) double cream
150g (5oz) braised oxtail meat, shredded
1 tablespoon chopped truffle

1 tablespoon chopped chives
1 garlic clove, peeled and crushed
salt and freshly ground black pepper (to taste)
caul fat or crépinette (available from your butcher)
150ml (5fl oz) Rich Beef Stock (p. 14)

1. Whiz the chicken in a food processor until smooth. Place in a bowl over a larger bowl containing ice cubes. Beat in the egg yolk and slowly fold in the egg white and cream, keeping the mixture stiff. Slowly fold in the shredded oxtail meat, truffle, chives and garlic.

2. Season with salt and pepper and leave to rest in the refrigerator for 15 minutes. Then place the mixture in a piping bag.

3. Lay out the caul fat or crépinette in 10cm (4 inch) × 20cm (8 inch) square pieces. Dry off any excess water. Pipe the mixture into a 15cm (6 inch) length and carefully wrap the fat around it to form a sausage. Repeat until you have about 8 sausages. Wrap them in cling film, binding and sealing the sausages at both ends.

4. Bring a pan of water to the boil, add the sausages and cook for 8–9 minutes until they are firm. Remove the cling film.

5. To make the gravy, heat the beef stock in a frying pan, add the sausages and braise for 5 minutes.

American Meatloaf

SERVES 6–8

*U*se only the best-quality minced beef for this recipe and serve it with the Waldorf Summer *Beef Salad (p. 39), omitting the beef from the salad.*

900g (2lb) finely minced beef	2 garlic cloves, peeled and finely chopped
450g (1lb) finely minced pork	
175g (6oz) fresh white breadcrumbs	2 celery stalks, washed and finely chopped
salt and freshly ground black pepper (to taste)	
	150ml (5fl oz) red wine
2 tablespoons best butter	¼ teaspoon allspice
2 tablespoons olive oil	1 teaspoon crushed fresh thyme leaves
8 shallots, peeled and finely chopped	2 eggs, well beaten

1. Put the minced beef, pork, breadcrumbs and seasoning in a large bowl and mix them together.

2. Heat the butter and olive oil in a large saucepan and cook the shallots, garlic and celery for 3 minutes. Add the red wine and cook for a further 3 minutes. Allow the wine mixture to cool slightly, then pour it over the meat and breadcrumbs. Sprinkle with allspice and thyme, add the beaten eggs and mix thoroughly.

3. Preheat the oven to Gas Mark 3/170°C/325°F and take a 1.8kg (4lb) loaf tin, butter it and line it with greaseproof paper. Pour the mixture into the loaf tin and leave it to settle for 10 minutes. Bake in the centre of the preheated oven for 1 hour.

4. Remove from the oven, baste with a little red wine and leave to cool. Refrigerate for 2 hours, then slice and serve.

Beef Cakes Cooked in Dripping with Creamed Horseradish

SERVES 6

Whenever I discuss British food with my fellow chefs we always agree that it should look robust and that the title should describe the food completely. Adrian Park, another Euro-Toques chef, and I debated this question and came up with this very British title for a very British recipe. For a healthier version, replace the dripping with sunflower oil and the butter with low-fat margarine. Serve with a light salad and small pots of fresh Creamed Horseradish (p. 26).

450g (1lb) boiled potatoes, warm
50g (2oz) butter, softened
450g (1lb) cooked silverside of beef, finely minced
50g (2oz) finely chopped onion
4 tablespoons finely chopped parsley
salt and freshly ground black pepper (to taste)

3 eggs
4 tablespoons milk
100g (4oz) freshly toasted white breadcrumbs
100g (4oz) beef dripping

1. Mash the warm potatoes with the butter, and blend in the beef, onion and parsley. Season well.

2. Beat 1 egg and add it to the mixture. Shape the mixture into 12 large balls.

3. Beat the other 2 eggs well with the milk and pour into a large saucer or flat dish. Put the breadcrumbs on a plate. Then coat each ball with the egg, roll through the breadcrumbs, and shape into cakes. Heat the dripping in a pan and fry the beef cakes until golden brown.

Creamed Horseradish

SERVES 6

This goes particularly well with Beef Cakes Cooked in Dripping (see p. 25) but it's also very good with Victorian Potted Hough (p. 21) and Olde English Potted Beef (p. 22).

150ml (5fl oz) double cream or crème fraîche	1 teaspoon dried powdered English mustard
3 tablespoons grated fresh horseradish	salt and freshly ground black pepper (to taste)
2 teaspoons white wine vinegar	

1. Simply whip the cream or crème fraîche and all the ingredients together to form a thick creamy sauce, place in 6 individual ramekin dishes and serve.

Beef & Cabbage Stuffed Latkes

SERVES 4–6

Another one of Antony Worrall Thompson's classic beef recipes. Use any cut of left-over beef, and serve the latkes with bread rolls and a mixed salad.

900g (2lb) floury potatoes, peeled	1 clove garlic, peeled and finely chopped
2 eggs, beaten	225g (8oz) cooked cabbage, chopped
salt and freshly ground black pepper (to taste)	350g (12oz) left-over boiled beef or roast beef, minced
2 tablespoons vegetable oil	1 tablespoon Basic Gravy (p. 43) or Beef Consommé (p. 20)
1 onion, peeled and finely chopped	flour
½ teaspoon fresh, soft thyme leaves	50g (2oz) butter
2 tablespoons chopped fresh parsley	
1 tablespoon snipped fresh chives	

1. Simmer the potatoes in boiling salted water until tender, drain and dry them. Mash the potatoes with the eggs, seasoning the mixture well.

2. Heat the oil in a frying pan and cook the onion, herbs and garlic until soft but without colour. Add the cabbage and season to taste. Combine this mixture with the minced beef and gravy.

3. Divide the potato into 8 even portions. Place each portion in the palm of your hand, spreading the potato out to form a flat circle. Place 2 tablespoons of the beef mixture in the centre and completely enclose with the potato. Push the ball shape down to form a patty or hamburger shape.

4. Dust each one with flour, heat the butter in a pan, and fry the latkes until they are golden on each side.

Roulades of Beef Stuffed with Anchovies & Onions

SERVES 8

*C*olin Capon's trademark is that he is **Professionally Different**. *Seeing him present a cookery demonstration, either at Hotelympia or at the BBC's Good Food Show, there is no starch, just honest to goodness cookery with a light-hearted attitude. The Meat and Livestock Commission use Colin's services for development work, presentations and specialist meat production. Why? Because he is* **Professionally Different**! *Just try this recipe of his for Beef Roulades.*

900g (2lb) finely minced beef	1 tablespoon chopped fresh parsley
400g (14oz) mashed potato, fairly dry	50g (2oz) arrowroot or cornflour
225g (8oz) onions, peeled, thinly sliced, and lightly fried in butter	about 15 tinned anchovy fillets, soaked in milk
75g (3oz) dried breadcrumbs	275g (10oz) white of leeks, washed and thinly sliced
450ml (15fl oz) double cream	50g (2oz) butter
salt and freshly ground black pepper (to taste)	150ml (5fl oz) Rich Beef Stock (p. 14)
2 eggs, beaten	25g (1oz) capers, roughly chopped

1. Put the minced beef, mashed potato, fried onions, breadcrumbs, 150ml (5fl oz) double cream, salt and pepper, eggs, parsley and arrowroot or cornflour into a large bowl. Blend them thoroughly and place in the refrigerator for 1 hour.

2. Remove the mixture from the fridge, place a layer of cling film on a large board and divide the meat mixture into 6 equal portions.

3. Moisten the mixture with cold water and spread into a 40cm (16 inch) square, about 0.5cm (¼ inch) thick. Divide the mixture again into 4 × 10cm (4 inch) squares. Then repeat the process with the remaining mixture. You should end up with 32 squares (to make 4 roulades per person).

4. Cut each anchovy into 4 strips. Then place a thin layer of finely sliced leeks on each square with 2 strips of anchovy. With a spatula and the cling film, carefully roll up each square to form a Swiss roll shape. Chill and repeat the method with the remaining mixture.

5. Heat the butter in a frying pan and cook the roulades, about 4 at a time, turning so they are evenly cooked all over, and keeping them warm.

6. When all the roulades are cooked, using the same pan, add the stock and boil until reduced by half. Then add the remaining cream. Gently bring to the boil and simmer for 4 minutes, add the chopped capers and a little seasoning, and serve with the roulades.

Creamed Strips of Sirloin

SERVES 4

For a Thai flavour, replace the cream with coconut milk and add 2 finely chopped chillies.

75g (3oz) butter	salt and freshly ground black pepper
450g (1lb) sirloin of beef, trimmed	(to taste)
and thinly sliced	2 tablespoons dry sherry
175g (6oz) button mushrooms, sliced	150ml (5fl oz) double cream
1 teaspoon mustard	4 slices hot toast, cut into triangles
a pinch of freshly grated ginger	a few sprigs of fresh parsley

1. Preheat the oven to Gas Mark 5/190°C/375°F.

2. Melt the butter in a large frying pan and gently fry the steak for 6 minutes. Remove the steak, using a slotted spoon, place in a serving dish and keep warm. Add the mushrooms to the frying pan, cooking them in the left-over juices. Add the mustard, ginger, salt and pepper.

3. Cook for 2 minutes, then add the sherry and cream. Cook for a further 3 minutes, and pour over the steak. Bake in the oven for 10 minutes.

4. Place the triangles of warm toast around the strips of beef, with the sprigs of fresh parsley, and serve.

Beef Olives

SERVES 6

In the eighteenth century Beef Olives were made in the following way: 'Cut some square steaks of beef, wash them with some egg, season them, lay on forcemeat. Role them up and tie them and either roast or stew them. Pour over them some good gravy with shallots, chopt fine in it. Garnish with pickles.'

Today this recipe is a little more refined.

6 × 75g (3oz) sirloin steaks (fat
   removed), thinly sliced
seasoned flour
25g (1oz) beef dripping
570ml (1 pint) Basic Beef Stock
   (p. 13)

For the stuffing
100g (4oz) fresh white breadcrumbs,
   toasted

25g (1oz) shredded beef suet
25g (1oz) mushrooms, minced or finely
   chopped
2 tablespoons chopped fresh parsley
salt and freshly ground black pepper (to
   taste)
grated rind of 1 lemon
1 egg, beaten

1. Preheat the oven to Gas Mark 2/150°C/300°F.

2. Flatten the steaks, using a steak mallet, and mix all the stuffing ingredients together in a clean bowl.

3. Divide the mixture equally between the 6 pieces of beef. Roll them up, folding in the ends, and tie each beef olive with butcher's string (available from your local butcher or supermarket).

4. Roll them evenly in the seasoned flour. Then heat the dripping in a shallow frying pan and fry the beef olives all over for 2 minutes on each side.

5. Place the beef olives in a deep casserole dish, cover with the beef stock and cook in the centre of the oven for 1 hour. Remove the beef olives from the casserole, remove the string, and place on a warm serving dish.

6. If you wish to thicken the beef stock/sauce, transfer it to a small pan, boil until reduced, and pour around the beef olives.

Meat Balls in Tomato Sauce

SERVES 4

There are two recipes for the meat ball appetiser. If you want to make a healthier version of this one, use a low-fat margarine and semi-skimmed milk, and replace the dripping with sunflower oil. Serve with bread rolls.

150g (5oz) brown breadcrumbs	1 tablespoon finely chopped fresh
150ml (5fl oz) milk	tarragon
25g (1oz) butter	salt and freshly ground black pepper
25g (1oz) wholemeal flour	(to taste)
200ml (7fl oz) Basic Beef Stock (p. 13)	1 large onion, peeled and chopped
1 × 400g (14oz) tin chopped	450g (1lb) minced rump steak
tomatoes	1 teaspoon paprika
2 tablespoons tomato purée	25g (1oz) beef dripping
1 teaspoon sugar	a few whole sprigs of fresh tarragon

1. Preheat the oven to Gas Mark 4/180°C/350°F.

2. Place the breadcrumbs in a bowl, add the milk and leave the breadcrumbs to soak for 30 minutes.

3. Put half the butter in a saucepan, add the flour and cook, stirring, for 2 minutes, taking care not to let the mixture burn. Stir in the beef stock and cook for a further 5 minutes. Add the tomatoes, tomato purée, sugar and chopped tarragon. Season well and simmer for 25 minutes.

4. Add the chopped onion, minced beef and paprika to the breadcrumbs, and mix thoroughly. Season with a little salt and pepper. Using floured hands, shape the beef into 14 large meat balls.

5. Heat the beef dripping and the remaining butter in a large frying pan, add the meat balls and cook until they are brown all over.

6. Place the meat balls in a deep casserole dish, pour over the tomato sauce, cover and bake in the centre of the oven for 25 minutes.

7. Remove the meat balls from the oven, allow them to cool for 3 minutes, garnish with the sprigs of fresh tarragon, and serve.

Meat Balls in Red Wine Sauce

SERVES 4–6

*H*ere's a healthier, low-fat meat ball recipe. Serve it with a pasta of your choice.

150g (5oz) white breadcrumbs
150ml (5fl oz) semi-skimmed milk
25g (1oz) low-fat margarine
25g (1oz) wholemeal flour
200ml (7fl oz) Rich Beef Stock (p. 14)
150ml (5fl oz) claret
4 tomatoes, peeled and chopped
1 tablespoon tomato purée

1 tablespoon finely chopped fresh basil
salt and freshly ground black pepper
  (to taste)
12 shallots, peeled and chopped
450g (1lb) minced rump steak
1 teaspoon paprika
2 tablespoons sunflower oil
a few whole sprigs of fresh basil

1. Preheat the oven to Gas Mark 4/180°C/350°F.

2. Place the breadcrumbs in a bowl, add the milk and leave the breadcrumbs to soak for 30 minutes.

3. Put half the margarine in a saucepan, add the flour and cook, stirring, for 2 minutes, taking care not to let the mixture burn. Stir in the beef stock and wine and simmer for 15 minutes. Add the tomatoes, tomato purée and chopped basil. Season well and simmer for 30 minutes.

4. Add the chopped shallots, minced beef and paprika to the breadcrumbs, and mix thoroughly. Season with a little salt and pepper. Using floured hands, shape the beef into 14 large meat balls.

5. Heat the sunflower oil and remaining margarine in a large frying pan, add the meat balls and cook until they are brown all over.

6. Place the meat balls in a deep casserole dish, pour over the red wine sauce, cover and bake in the centre of the oven for 30 minutes.

7. Remove the meat balls from the oven, allow them to cool for 3 minutes, garnish with the sprigs of fresh basil, and serve.

Lasagne

SERVES 4-6

Lasagne, candlelight, music and a bottle of good Italian wine – the perfect recipe for an evening with your loved one...

If serving as a starter, cut the lasagne into small portions and serve garnished with green salad. The meat sauce can also be used to make Spaghetti Bolognese.

2 tablespoons olive oil
25g (1oz) best butter
1 medium-sized carrot, peeled and
  chopped
8 shallots, peeled and finely chopped
1 celery stalk, washed and finely
  chopped
2 bay leaves
675g (1½lb) fillet or sirloin of beef,
  roughly minced

50ml (2fl oz) Marsala
100g (4oz) button mushrooms, wiped
  and sliced
1 quantity Italian Sauce (p. 34)
450g (1lb) dried lasagne
extra butter or oil
1 quantity Velouté (p. 34)
grated Parmesan cheese

1. Heat the olive oil and butter in a large saucepan. Sauté the carrot, shallots, celery and bay leaves. Add the beef and mix together, stirring and cooking for 5 minutes.

2. Pour in the Marsala and simmer until the wine has completely evaporated. Add the mushrooms and Italian Sauce, boil and then let the mixture simmer for 15 minutes.

3. Preheat the oven to Gas Mark 7/220°C/425°F.

4. Put the strips of lasagne in a large pot of boiling, salted water with a little oil. Cook until they are slightly soft, remove from the water and drain well.

5. Grease the bottom of a baking dish and cover it with a layer of pasta. Spoon over some meat sauce, then some Velouté, ensuring that the pasta is completely covered. Repeat the process until the dish is full, ending with the Velouté. Sprinkle the Parmesan over the top and bake in the centre of the oven for 20 minutes until the top is golden brown.

Italian Sauce

MAKES 570ml (1 pint)

As well as Lasagne, this Italian Sauce can be served with any pasta. Simply sprinkle 450g (1lb) cubed fillet of beef with some chopped fresh tarragon, pour over this sauce and cook in the oven for 40 minutes at Gas Mark 4/180°C/350°F.

25g (1oz) butter
1 tablespoon olive oil
25g (1oz) shallots, peeled and
  chopped
1 clove garlic, peeled and crushed
50g (2oz) mushrooms, wiped and
  chopped
50g (2oz) veal shank, ground
50g (2oz) finely minced beef

salt and freshly ground black pepper
  (to taste)
1 tablespoon red wine vinegar
1 clove
a pinch of thyme
225ml (8fl oz) Basic Gravy (p. 43)
100g (4oz) peeled chopped tomatoes
3 tablespoons tomato purée
some chopped fresh tarragon

1. Heat the butter and olive oil in a large, deep frying pan. Add the shallots and garlic, cooking gently for 2 minutes. Add the mushrooms, veal and beef, season with salt and pepper, and cook for 6 minutes.

2. Add the vinegar, clove and thyme, cook for a further 2 minutes and blend in the gravy, simmering for at least 20 minutes. Add the tomatoes, tomato purée and tarragon, and simmer for a further 15 minutes.

Velouté

MAKES 570ml (1 pint)

This is a basic white cream sauce which is used in Lasagne and several other dishes.

100g (4oz) butter
8 shallots, peeled and thinly sliced
100g (4oz) sifted flour, seasoned with
  salt
1 litre (1¾ pints) chicken stock,
  boiling

275ml (10fl oz) double cream
25g (1oz) mushroom stalks
salt and freshly ground black pepper
  (to taste)
freshly grated nutmeg (to taste)

1. Melt the butter in a saucepan. Cook the shallots in the butter without letting them colour. Add the sifted flour and continue to cook, being careful not to let the flour colour.

2. Stirring constantly, add the boiling stock and cream. Put in the mushroom stalks, salt, pepper and nutmeg and let the sauce simmer for 35 minutes. Strain through a fine sieve and serve.

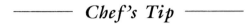

Chef's Tip

Velouté can also be used in dishes such as Chicken Supreme.

To make an Allemande Sauce, simply add egg yolks. The more yolks you use, the thicker the sauce. To reduce the sauce, keep adding cream.

For Mushroom Sauce, add 100g (4oz) sliced button mushrooms.

Drunken Beef Caribbean-Style

SERVES 8–10

*T*elevision chef Colin Capon has a CV that reads like a travel book. He has cooked around the world and served up his specialities for royalty, prime ministers, sultans and presidents. As a consultant for television and film companies, he works behind the scenes, producing modern and period in-vision foods. He recently worked on and appeared in Ivanhoe, produced by the BBC.

I value him for his kindness and keen spirit when it comes to him buying me a drink! When he faxed me his recipes he sent the following little note: 'Tom – Sorry for the delay. Having toured the world I came back with a bug that rendered me out of action for two weeks – adjust the recipes to your liking. Colin.'

Well, Colin, we are not going to get drunk on your beef! Only 75ml (3fl oz) rum for the marinade and 25ml (1fl oz) for the sauce... Now can you see why I remember when he buys me a drink? You can increase the quantity of rum in the marinade to 150ml (5fl oz) and rum in the sauce to 50ml (2fl oz) if you like. I do!

675g (1½lb) rump of beef, fat and
   gristle removed

For the marinade
75ml (3fl oz) Caribbean dark rum
25g (1oz) soft brown sugar
juice and zest of 1 fresh lime
1 hot red chilli pepper, chopped
2 cloves garlic, peeled and chopped
50ml (2fl oz) corn oil
a pinch of allspice
a sprig of fresh thyme

For the rice and garnish
560g (1¼lb) long-grain rice
275g (10oz) cooked kidney beans
150ml (5fl oz) tinned coconut milk

a pinch of allspice
a dash of hot pepper sauce
salt and freshly ground black pepper
   (to taste)
2 large mangoes, slightly firm, peeled
   and thinly shredded
16 spring onions, washed, trimmed and
   finely sliced

For the sauce
150ml (5fl oz) Basic Beef Stock (p. 13)
25ml (1fl oz) dark rum
1 teaspoon soy sauce
1 red pepper, de-seeded and finely diced
a little arrowroot

1. Place the meat in the freezer for 4 hours to firm up. This will allow you to slice it very thinly with a sharp knife or on a meat slicer. The meat should be sliced thinly across the grain, then arranged in the bottom of a high-sided dish, slightly overlapping.

2. Mix all the marinade ingredients together. Pour or brush the marinade over the surface of the sliced meat. Place a second layer of meat on top and repeat the process until all the meat and marinade have been used up. It is important that the meat is completely covered in marinade. Cover with cling film and chill for 4 hours.

3. Meanwhile, cook the rice and drain it well. While it is still hot, fold in the kidney beans, coconut milk, spice, hot pepper sauce and seasoning.

4. Combine the sauce ingredients, except the arrowroot, in a saucepan and gently bring to the boil. Thicken with a little arrowroot and keep warm.

5. Remove the meat from the fridge. Heat a griddle plate or large frying pan and quickly seal the drunken beef slices on both sides.

6. To serve the beef, place a portion of rice on a warm plate with 3–4 slices of beef. Garnish with the mango, spring onion and a dash of hot pepper sauce.

Baked Field Mushrooms with Bone Marrow & Taleggio

SERVES 4

This is one of Antony Worrall Thompson's recipes. Antony and I share a special love of an Italian cheese called Taleggio which is named after a small town near Bergamo and is made with unpasteurised milk. If you cannot find Taleggio, you can substitute Mozzarella.

4 tablespoons extra virgin olive oil

1 tablespoon soft fresh thyme
   leaves, finely chopped

4 cloves garlic, peeled and crushed to
   a paste with a little salt

8 large field mushrooms, stalks removed

50g (2oz) flat parsley leaves

2 tablespoons soured cream

150ml (5fl oz) mayonnaise

4 large 10cm (4 inch) marrow bones,
   soaked in salted water overnight

salt and freshly ground black pepper
   (to taste)

8 thin slices Taleggio cheese

1. Put the olive oil, chopped thyme and crushed garlic into a bowl and mix thoroughly. Allow the flavours to blend for at least 30 minutes.

2. Sprinkle the mushrooms with the flavoured oil and leave them to marinate for 60 minutes.

3. Whizz the parsley and soured cream in a food processor or blender and gently fold into the mayonnaise.

4. Preheat the oven to Gas Mark ½/110°C/225°F.

5. Blanch the marrow bones in boiling salted water for 2 minutes. With a very thin-bladed knife, cut around the inside of each bone and extract the marrow in one piece, if possible. Allow the marrow to cool.

6. Place the mushrooms on a baking sheet and cook in the centre of the oven for 5 minutes on each side. Season them well.

7. Carefully place a 1cm (½ inch) piece of marrow in the centre of each mushroom and top with a slice of Taleggio cheese. Return to the oven and cook for a further 5 minutes.

8. Serve hot, with a dollop of parsley mayonnaise.

OPPOSITE Roast Rib of English Beef and Yorkshire Pudding (page 52)

Waldorf Summer Beef Salad

SERVES 4

This recipe is for a dear friend, Julian Groom, who has supported all my books. Congratulations on your move to this wonderful hotel. I am sure you will be a huge success. This salad is also really nice with freshly grilled steak with Béarnaise Sauce (p. 157).

450g (1lb) red apples, cored, sliced and
    diced
3 tablespoons fresh lemon juice
150ml (5fl oz) light mayonnaise
1 head of celery
4 shallots, peeled and sliced
1 clove garlic, peeled and crushed

75g (3oz) chopped walnuts
560g (1¼lb) cold roast beef, cut into
    0.5cm (¼ inch) cubes
1 cos lettuce, washed and chilled
freshly ground black pepper (to taste)
some sliced apple and whole walnuts

1. Put the diced apples, lemon juice and 1 tablespoon of the mayonnaise in a bowl and leave for 40 minutes.

2. Slice the celery very thinly into horseshoe shapes. Add the celery, shallots, garlic and chopped walnuts to the apple. Mix together, add the rest of the mayonnaise, blend thoroughly and toss in the cubes of beef.

3. Line a glass salad bowl or serving dish with the washed lettuce, pile the beef salad in the centre, season with freshly ground black pepper and garnish with slices of apples and walnuts.

OPPOSITE Roast Peppered Rump Steak or Cajun Spiced Beef (page 45)

Proud to be British – Rare Beef Salad

Antony Worrall Thompson wrote this recipe for his Sunday Times *column and it is one of several really delicious dishes from his book* 30-Minute Menus, *published by Headline.*

Here's AWT himself, in fighting form: 'As a great supporter of the "Back British Food Campaign", I'm appalled at this country's continuing "foodie inferiority complex". It's about time we believed in ourselves and were proud of what we produce. The French buy our lamb, our shellfish, our game and even our sandwiches, and their food standards aren't bad, so let's put an end to the British disease of knocking everything we stand for.'

450g (1lb) Scottish rump or sirloin joint of beef

salt and freshly ground black pepper (to taste)

2 tablespoons lime juice

2 tablespoons *nam pla* (Thai fish sauce)

2 teaspoons clear honey

4 spring onions, washed, trimmed and sliced

1 cucumber, peeled and sliced into 2.5cm (1 inch) chunks

3 tomatoes, cut into wedges

3 teaspoons finely chopped fresh mint

assorted salad leaves

1. Season the beef with salt and freshly ground black pepper. Grill or pan-fry for 4 minutes on each side. Allow to rest for 5 minutes, then slice thinly across the grain.

2. Meanwhile, in a saucepan, combine the lime juice, fish sauce and honey. Cook for 2 minutes over a medium heat, then add all the remaining ingredients except the salad leaves.

3. Fold in the beef and mix well. Taste and season. Serve on dressed salad leaves.

CHAPTER 2

Roasts and Pot Roasts

✦

Those of you who know me will know that I am like 'a bull at a gate' ... and I admire people who speak their minds. Ron Martin, who lives in Somerset, sent me the following letter in October 1996, which I would like to share with you. It speaks volumes about the British beef industry.

Dear Tom

Your forthcoming book 'Bridge on British Beef', with which I wish you well, gives you a golden opportunity to promote what is 'the best' in British Beef and 'The Best' is, without any doubt whatsoever, obtained from Britain's Native Beef Breeds.

Though of slower growth and later maturity compared with the Continental Breeds, the British ones give the meat something that their European counterparts cannot and quite possibly never will, and that is 'Flavour'!! Nothing, I assure you, can taste better than a joint off a carcass of an Aberdeen Angus or a Devon, Hereford, Galloway, Sussex, Scotch Shorthorn, Red Poll or a South Devon.

Forty years ago Britain was looked upon as 'The Stud Farm of the World', a very proud title, which alas no longer applies, as it is now 'The Dumping Ground of Europe'. With the present beef crisis affecting much of the world and the British farmer's under-standable animosity towards certain European countries, your book gives you this golden opportunity to boost the confidence of the farming community by promoting the virtues of keeping British Native Breeds, which in some instances, alas, are almost extinct and are classified as 'rare' or 'protected' and in one or two cases as 'primitive'.

I look forward to the day when, once again, our Native Breeds monopolise the mead-owlands of this country and your book could help to do just that.

Yours sincerely

Ron W. Martin
Yeovil Cattle Market (1943–1991)   Secretary, Yeovil Fatstock Society (1968–1991)
Mid-Western Agricultural Society (1987–1990)

As Ron Martin says, I am fighting – with the help of Euro-Toques – to promote British beef again, to restore confidence in our great produce, and to bring it back to the dining rooms of our European neighbours.

ROASTING TIPS

There are very simple rules as to what cuts of meat should be used for roasting and pot roasting. For roasting, you should use thick flank, sirloin, rump, fore rib, middle rib, topside or fillet. For pot roasting, you can use topside, silverside, brisket, coast (rolled), and thick flank of beef.

Before you start any of these recipes, place all your ingredients in order of use. Prepare the joint as instructed, and place it in the roasting tin with the fat uppermost. This allows the joint to be basted with its own fat during the cooking process.

The oven temperature for most roasts is around Gas Mark 2–4/150–180°C/300–350°F. To test the joint, insert a thermometer into the thickest part. At 55–60°C it is under-done; at 66–71°C it is just done; and at 75–78°C it is well done.

The recipes in this chapter assume that everyone likes their beef cooked to medium. If your tastes are different, you can reduce the cooking time by 10 minutes for medium to rare; add 5 minutes for medium to well done; or add 15 minutes for well done. If you like your beef very rare, then reduce the cooking time by about 15 minutes per 450g (1lb).

When the joint has finished cooking, allow the meat to stand for 10–15 minutes, to tenderise it further. When carving, always slice the joint across the grain. A 900g (2lb) joint will feed 4–6; allow 1.3kg (3lb) for 8–10; and 1.8kg (4lb) for 12–14.

Every traditional roast should have a good gravy and roast potatoes so this chapter begins with recipes for these vital accompaniments.

'Real' Gravy

MAKES 570 ml (1 pint)

I have mentioned Francis Coulson, of the Sharrow Bay Hotel, Cumbria, on many occasions in this book and his immortal saying – 'Never decry the word gravy' – will live for ever! This recipe combines the talents of Paul Reed, who contributed the Basic Beef Stock (p. 13), and those of Francis Coulson, the father of real gravy. When roasting a joint don't waste the juices and goo that collect in the bottom of the tin – use them in your gravy. But if there is a layer of fat on top, pour this off first. If necessary, dislodge the cooked on sediment by adding hot stock or water and stirring and scraping it up.

2 rashers best back bacon, rind and
   gristle removed
50g (2oz) beef dripping
2 tablespoons medium British sherry
2 tablespoons red wine vinegar
50g (2oz) plain flour

570ml (1 pint) Basic Beef Stock (p. 13)
   and juices and goo from the roast
1 *bouquet garni*
1 tablespoon tomato purée
freshly ground black pepper (to taste)
a pinch of salt

1. Chop the bacon rashers finely. Melt the dripping in a heavy-based pan, add the bacon and cook for 6 minutes until light brown. Add the sherry and vinegar and cook for 3 minutes.

2. Blend in the flour, stirring the roux until it turns brown. Gradually add half the beef stock, stirring constantly until the mixture has cooked through and thickened. Add the *bouquet garni* and simmer for 30 minutes. Add the tomato purée, seasoning and the remaining beef stock and any pan juices from the roast, simmering and skimming for a further 45 minutes. Check and recheck the seasoning all the time.

3. Strain through a fine sieve, skim off any extra fat and serve in a sauceboat.

Madeira Sauce

SERVES 6–8

*T*his sauce makes a nice gravy for any beef dish.

a little butter
6 shallots, peeled and finely chopped
½ clove garlic, peeled and crushed
175g (6oz) button mushrooms, wiped
   and chopped
half bottle Madeira wine

4 tablespoons warm beef marrow
150ml (5fl oz) Basic Beef Stock (p. 13)
salt and freshly ground black pepper (to
   taste)
1 teaspoon chopped fresh parsley

1. Place a little butter in a saucepan, add the shallots, garlic and mushrooms and lightly cook.

2. Add the wine and boil until reduced by two-thirds. Add the beef marrow and beef stock. Season with salt and pepper, and simmer for a further 20 minutes. Add the parsley before serving.

Onion Gravy

MAKES 570 ml (1 pint)

This is a recipe that I have been using for years. Remember that the sticky goo at the bottom of the roasting tin is the most concentrated beef stock you are likely to get from any roast and it must be added to the gravy.

50g (2oz) beef dripping
2 rashers best back bacon (rind and gristle removed), finely chopped
2 large onions, peeled and sliced
2 tablespoons medium British sherry
2 tablespoons red wine vinegar
50g (2oz) plain flour

570ml (1 pint) Basic Beef Stock (p. 13),
   plus roasting juices and goo
1 *bouquet garni*
1 tablespoon tomato purée
salt and freshly ground black pepper (to
   taste)

1. Melt the dripping in a heavy-based pan, add the bacon and onions, and cook for 6 minutes until light brown. Add the sherry and vinegar and cook for 3 minutes.

2. Blend in the flour, stirring until the mixture is smooth and brown. Gradually add half the beef stock, juices and goo, stirring constantly until the mixture has cooked through and thickened.

3. Add the *bouquet garni* and simmer for 30 minutes. Add the tomato purée, seasoning and remaining beef stock, simmering and skimming for a further 30 minutes.

4. Keep checking the seasoning, then strain through a five sieve, skimming off any extra fat with a ladle. Add any extra juices from the roast beef and serve.

Perfect Roast Potatoes

Beef dripping and bacon fat are essential to the flavour of a good roast potato. I also roast my carrots, parsnips, onions and beetroot using the same method.

SERVES 4

75g (3oz) beef dripping
50g (2oz) streaky bacon, chopped
675g (1½lb) large potatoes, peeled and
   quartered

salt and freshly ground black pepper (to
   taste)

1. Preheat the oven to Gas Mark 7/220°C/425°F.

2. Heat the dripping and bacon in a roasting tin until smoking hot. Carefully place the potatoes in the hot fat, toss them around for about 3 minutes, season and roast in the oven for 60 minutes.

Roast Peppered Rump Steak (or Cajun Spiced Beef)

SERVES 8

A very simple recipe to start this section — one of my favourites which is popular with my guests when I entertain at home. It's really a Cajun recipe, known as Spiced Beef. Serve it with fresh, thinly sliced green, red and yellow peppers.

1.3kg (3lb) rump of beef	1 nutmeg, grated
150ml (5fl oz) Basic Beef Stock (p. 13)	1 teaspoon freshly grated ginger
3 tablespoons English mustard	2 tablespoons soy sauce
6 tablespoons green and black	2 tablespoons clear honey, warmed
peppercorns	salt (to taste)

1. Preheat the oven to Gas Mark 5/190°C/375°F.

2. Place a rack on top of a roasting tin, place the rump of beef on the rack and pour the beef stock over it. Then coat the rump with the English mustard.

3. Crush the peppercorns, using a mortar and pestle, and blend them with the grated nutmeg and ginger. Place in a mixing bowl, and thoroughly blend in the soy sauce, honey and salt. Completely cover the top of the rump with this mixture. Then roast for 2 hours, basting every 15 minutes.

4. Pour the left-over juices and stock from the roasting tin into a small saucepan and boil until reduced by one-third. Season, pour the sauce into a sauceboat, slice the rump and serve.

Roast Sirloin of English Beef Basted with Honey & Mustard

SERVES 4–6

Honey and mustard is a wonderful combination with roast beef. For a festive variation, you can replace the honey with soy sauce and the grain mustard with ground cinnamon.

Use the juices to make some Onion Gravy (p. 44), adding 2 bay leaves with the bouquet garni. Serve with Yorkshire Pudding (p. 53) and vegetables.

900g (2lb)–1.8kg (4lb) sirloin of beef	2–3 tablespoons clear honey, warmed
1 tablespoon coarse salt	2–3 teaspoons grain mustard
freshly ground black pepper (to taste)	

1. Preheat the oven to Gas Mark 8/230°C/450°F.

2. Place the sirloin in a deep roasting tin and coat generously with salt, pepper, honey and mustard. Cook in the centre of the oven for 20 minutes.

3. Remove the tin, pour off the liquid, and use it to baste the beef.

4. Place the beef back in the roasting tin, skin-side up. Reduce the heat to Gas Mark 4/180°C/350°F. Cook for 30 minutes per 450g (1lb), basting every 20 minutes. Allow the beef to cool slightly before serving.

Roast Sirloin of English Beef in an Overcoat

SERVES 4–6

Your local butcher will bone, trim and roll a sirloin for you; and most supermarkets have a butcher at hand to give you advice. Use the juices to make some Basic Gravy (p. 43) and serve with Yorkshire Pudding (p. 53) and vegetables.

1.3kg (3lb) sirloin of beef, boned, trimmed and rolled	1 tablespoon crushed fresh rosemary leaves
50g (2oz) butter	1 teaspoon coarse salt
100g (4oz) breadcrumbs	freshly ground black pepper (to taste)
175g (6oz) onions, peeled and chopped	1 tablespoon clear honey, warmed
1 tablespoon chopped fresh parsley	1 teaspoon grain mustard

1. Preheat the oven to Gas Mark 4/180°C/350°F.

2. Coat the beef with the butter and roast in the centre of the oven for 90 minutes, basting every 15 minutes.

3. At the end of the cooking time, mix the rest of the ingredients together and use to coat the sirloin. Return to the oven and bake at Gas Mark 6/200°C/400°F for a further 20 minutes, until the overcoat is crisp and brown. Allow the beef to rest for 10 minutes before you slice it.

Roast Sirloin of English Beef with Rose Petal Sauce

SERVES 6–8

Rose petal vinegar is made by my dear friend Sue Webb at Rotherfield Greys and is excellent in dressings for summer salads. There is no real substitute for rose petal vinegar but you could try using raspberry vinegar at a pinch. Serve this with baby roast potatoes and asparagus.

900g (2lb) sirloin of beef
1 teaspoon dried oregano
2 cloves garlic, peeled and crushed with
    1 tablespoon olive oil
150ml (5fl oz) rose petal vinegar
150ml (5fl oz) Basic Beef Stock
    (p. 13)

salt and freshly ground black pepper (to
    taste)
1 tablespoon clear honey, warmed
2 teaspoons grain mustard
a little flour
150ml (5fl oz) soured cream
1 tablespoon chopped fresh parsley

1. Preheat the oven to Gas Mark 6/200°C/400°F.

2. Put the sirloin in a deep roasting tin. Mix the rest of the ingredients, except the flour, soured cream and parsley, together in a bowl and coat the sirloin generously with the mixture.

3. Cover with foil, place the tin in the centre of the oven and cook for 70 minutes.

4. Remove the tin, pour off the liquid into a saucepan and boil until reduced by half. Meanwhile, place the beef back in the roasting tin, skin-side up. Roast for a further 30 minutes, basting every 10 minutes. Allow it to cool slightly.

5. Thicken the sauce with a little flour, add the soured cream and parsley, cook for 5 minutes and serve with the roast sirloin.

Jamaican Roast Beef with Guava Sauce

SERVES 6–8

This may sound unusual but guava juice and jelly are now widely available and the guava is a very healthy fruit. The jelly is sold in jars and tinned guavas are fine for this dish. Serve it with creamed potatoes and steamed mangetout.

1.3kg (3lb) sirloin of beef	freshly ground black pepper (to taste)
25g (1oz) butter	1 teaspoon freshly chopped ginger
150ml (5fl oz) Basic Beef Stock (p. 13)	1 teaspoon five spice powder
4 tablespoons dark rum	4 tablespoons guava jelly
1 tablespoon sea salt	3 guavas, peeled and sliced

1. Preheat the oven to Gas Mark 5/190°C/375°F.

2. Coat the sirloin with butter and roast in the oven for 25 minutes.

3. Mix together all the other ingredients, except the 3 sliced guavas. Coat the sirloin with the mixture and roast for a further 75 minutes, basting every 15 minutes.

4. Pour the left-over juices and stock from the roasting tin into a small saucepan, and boil until reduced by one-third. Pour the sauce into a sauceboat. Slice the beef, garnish with the guava slices, and serve.

Sirloin of Beef Lady Jayne

SERVES 6

I created this recipe for my wife on our wedding anniversary. Being a chef does have some advantages – it saved me a fortune on flowers and perfume. She was on a diet at the time, so we ended up eating most of the beef with our friends, who acknowledged how tender and sweet this recipe was. Just like my wife really! Serve this with new potatoes and fresh buttered asparagus.

1.3kg (3lb) sirloin of beef, trimmed
salt and freshly ground black pepper
  (to taste)
25g (1oz) beef dripping
a few sprigs of fresh basil

For the stuffing
150g (5oz) toasted breadcrumbs

450g (1lb) apples, peeled, cored and
  chopped
50g (2oz) chopped cashew nuts
1 tablespoon chopped fresh basil
2 tablespoons clear honey, warmed
3 tablespoons brandy
2 tablespoons dry sherry

1. Preheat the oven to Gas Mark 5/190°C/375°F.

2. Season the meat with salt and pepper. Heat the beef dripping in a roasting tin and brown the meat evenly on all sides. Remove from the tin and slice along the centre of the sirloin to form a pocket for the stuffing.

3. Place all the stuffing ingredients in a bowl and mix thoroughly. Fill the cavity in the sirloin with the stuffing and place it back in the roasting tin. Cover the sirloin with greased cooking foil and bake in the centre of the oven for 2 hours.

4. Baste the sirloin with the juices during the last 30 minutes. Then remove the foil and cook uncovered for a further 30 minutes.

5. Remove from the oven, carefully place on a large serving dish and slice the meat. Garnish with fresh basil and serve.

Lancashire Sirloin of English Beef Roasted with a Herb Crust & A Mustard Seed Yorkshire Pudding

SERVES 6

*W*hen Sir Richard Hoghton invited King James I for lunch at Hoghton Tower near Preston, he did not know that a new word was about to be added to the culinary dictionary. On that day of festivities a magnificent loin of beef was brought to the table. It so took the King's fancy that he knighted it there and then, saying 'Arise Sir Loin of Beef'.

Sir Bernard Hoghton still has the wonderful table at Hoghton Tower where the knighting of the loin took place and it is well worth visiting this historic house.

150g (5oz) beef dripping	a pinch of Madras curry powder
1.3kg (3lb) sirloin of beef	Yorkshire Pudding Batter (p. 53), with
75g (3oz) breadcrumbs	2 tablespoons mustard seeds whisked
2 teaspoons chopped fresh mixed herbs	into it

1. Preheat the oven to Gas Mark 4/180°C/350°F.

2. Melt 50g (2oz) beef dripping in a shallow roasting tin.

3. Trim the excess fat from the beef and cut in a little pocket. Place the beef in the roasting tin, on the melted dripping. Mix the breadcrumbs, mixed herbs and curry powder in a bowl and blend in a further 50g (2oz) melted dripping to make a paste. Cover the top of the sirloin with the paste, then roast in the oven for 70 minutes.

4. Increase the oven temperature to Gas Mark 7/220°C/425°F. Put the rest of the dripping in a large baking tray and place in the oven for 3 minutes until the fat is smoking hot. Pour in the Mustard Seed Yorkshire Pudding batter and bake for 30 minutes.

5. Remove both the meat and the Yorkshire pudding. Carve the beef, make some Onion Gravy (p. 44) with the beef juices and serve with the Mustard Seed Yorkshire Pudding.

Roast Rib of English Beef & Yorkshire Pudding

with Roast Potatoes, Carrots, Parsnips, Onions and Beetroot

SERVES 6–8

This recipe was created for the front cover photograph, taken by my favourite photographer David George who I have worked with on my last three cookery books. The rib was massive – over 4.5kg (10lb) in weight – and the Yorkshires a little bit bigger than normal. The vegetables were roasted with the rib of beef and it was cooked slowly on Gas Mark 2/150°C/300°F for 6 hours. The heat was then raised to Gas Mark 4/ 180°C/350°F for a further 3 hours. Here I explain how to cook a small rib.

100g (4oz) beef dripping
1.8kg (4lb) rib of beef, fat trimmed
8 potatoes, peeled
2 parsnips, peeled
8 small onions, peeled
8 carrots, peeled
salt and freshly ground black pepper (to taste)

2 packets pre-cooked Red Velvet beetroot (8 beetroot in total)
1 quantity Yorkshire Pudding batter (p. 53), and extra dripping or cooking fat for the Yorkshire Puddings

1. Preheat the oven to Gas Mark 4/180°C/350°F.

2. Heat the beef dripping in a large roasting tin. Seal the beef for 5 minutes on either side in the hot dripping. Remove the meat and put on one side.

3. Add all the vegetables, except the beetroot, and brown them in the hot dripping for 6 minutes. Place the vegetables on one side. Place the rib back in the roasting tin, leaving room to add the vegetables later. Season the rib all over with salt and pepper, cover with foil and roast in the centre of the oven for 2 hours.

4. Make up the Yorkshire Pudding batter (p. 54) and set on one side. Leave it to stand for 40 minutes before cooking.

5. Increase the oven temperature to Gas Mark 7/220°C/425°F. Carefully remove the cooking foil, add the vegetables, including the beetroot (drained), and roast for a further 45 minutes. Put the extra dripping in one large Yorkshire Pudding tin and place in the oven until smoking hot. Pour in the batter and cook for the last 30 minutes.

6. Remove the rib of beef, vegetables and Yorkshire pudding. Carve the beef, make some Onion Gravy (p. 44) with the beef juices, and serve.

Yorkshire Pudding

SERVES 4–6

I would have had my legs slapped if I had missed this section out, for my publishers at Piatkus warned me about a Yorkshire lass there called Heather Rocklin who loves Yorkshire Pud!

Nowadays it is made with milk and water to ensure lightness and crispness. For a crisp pudding, there must be no fat in the mixture. Other essentials for a good pudding are very hot fat and not too much of it, and a good hot oven.

It was originally eaten with thick Onion Gravy (p. 44) as a separate item before the main course. But it is now more usual to serve it as an accompaniment to roast beef.

In some areas, including the farms of East Riding, the Yorkshire pudding might be replaced by a suet pudding. Some were well seasoned; others filled with beef, pork, bacon, sausage, chicken and a variety of fillings which I have recreated for you, using the basic Yorkshire pudding batter below.

100g (4oz) plain flour	150ml (5fl oz) full-cream milk, mixed
½ teaspoon salt	with 150ml (5fl oz) water
1 large fresh egg	dripping or cooking fat

1. Sift the flour and salt into a large basin.

2. Break the egg into a saucer and then place the egg in the centre of the flour, whisking in enough milk and water to get a beating consistency. Beat well and leave to stand for 40 minutes.

3. Heat the oven to Gas Mark 7/220°C/425°F. For small puddings, use 6 × 2.5cm (1 inch) bun trays and put a knob of dripping into each indentation. Place the tray in the oven until the fat is smoking hot. One large tin may also be used.

4. Meanwhile, add the rest of the milk and water to make a batter. If making small puddings, take the bun tray from the oven and put 2 tablespoons batter into each indentation. Bake for 15–20 minutes. Or use a large tin, bake for 30 minutes, then cut the pudding into portions.

Here's to Yorkshire, my lads,
The Land of Good Cheer,
The Home of the Pudding,
Well known far and near,
Wed a lass who can make one,
Is the theme of my song,
But so long as she's Yorkshire
You cannot go wrong.

Take a quart of milk and five eggs, beat them up well together, and mix them with flour till it is of a good batter, and very smooth; put in a little salt, some grated nutmeg and ginger; butter a dripping or frying pan and put it under a piece of beef, mutton, or a loin of veal that is roasting, and then put in your batter, and when the top side is brown, cut it in square pieces, and turn it, and then let the under side brown; then put it in a hot dish as clean of fat as you can, and send it to table hot.

Hannah Glasse, *The Art of Cookery* (1796)

Yorkshire Pudding with Minced Beef & Onion

SERVES 4

I believe this recipe started its life with a mutton filling, then changed to rabbit. Now I'm using the finest-quality British beef. Serve this with Onion Gravy (p. 44) and vegetables.

25g (1oz) beef dripping
225g (8oz) best minced beef
1 onion, peeled and finely chopped

salt and freshly ground black pepper (to taste)
1 quantity Yorkshire Pudding batter (p. 53)

1. Preheat the oven to Gas Mark 7/220°C/425°F.

2. Heat the dripping in a large frying pan, add the minced beef and chopped onion, and cook for 12 minutes. Season well.

3. Pour the fat from the minced beef into a large baking tray and place in the oven for 3 minutes until it is very hot. The fat should be smoking. Pour in the batter and sprinkle with the minced beef and onion.

4. Bake for 30 minutes and serve.

Roast Rib of Beef with Rosemary Potatoes

SERVES 6–8

Nigel Smith, another northern chef (yes we do have chefs in the North of England and very good ones at that!), serves this traditional roast every Sunday lunchtime at Holland Hall in Lancashire. Place the beef on a large serving platter surrounded with the rosemary roast potatoes, Yorkshire Pudding (p. 53), green beans, baby carrots and fresh broccoli spears.

a little beef dripping
900g (2lb) small roasting potatoes, peeled
salt and freshly ground black pepper (to taste)
1 tablespoon fresh rosemary leaves, crushed

1.3kg (3lb) rib of beef on the bone
150ml (5fl oz) Basic Beef Stock (p. 13)
3 sprigs of fresh rosemary
25g (1oz) butter

1. Preheat the oven to Gas Mark 9/250°C/475°F.

2. Heat some dripping in a roasting tin, add the potatoes, and sprinkle with salt, pepper and rosemary. Cook and seal for 10 minutes.

3. Place a roasting rack in the bottom of another roasting tin. Place the rib on the rack. Pour the beef stock over the rib and into the roasting tin. Sprinkle the rib generously with salt and pepper.

4. Cook the rib for 20 minutes. Then reduce the heat to Gas Mark 7/220°C/425°F, and roast to your liking:
30 minutes for very rare
35 minutes for rare
45 minutes for medium rare
55 minutes for medium
60 minutes for medium to well done
70 minutes for well done
80 minutes ruined!

5. Roast the tray of potatoes with rosemary for 1 hour, and serve decorated with the fresh sprigs of rosemary.

6. Turn the meat and baste every 12 minutes at least, during the cooking time. Pour the juices from the beef into a saucepan, making sure you get all the goodness from the bottom of the roasting tin. Boil until reduced by one-third. Add the butter, whisking it in well, pour into a sauceboat and serve.

Roast Rib of Beef

with Stilton, Mushroom and Walnut Stuffing and Port and Cranberry Glaze

SERVES 6–8

*A*nother of my expensive recipes but the smiles and expressions of wonder are worth it.

1.3kg (3lb) rib of beef on the bone
150ml (5fl oz) Basic Beef Stock (p. 13)
salt and freshly ground black pepper (to taste)
25g (1oz) butter

For the stuffing
100g (4oz) fresh breadcrumbs
4 tablespoons finely chopped fresh parsley
50g (2oz) walnuts, roughly chopped
50g (2oz) button mushrooms, roughly chopped
50g (2oz) Stilton, crumbled
1 tablespoon port
salt and freshly ground black pepper (to taste)
1 egg, beaten

For the glaze
150ml (5fl oz) port
150ml (5fl oz) cranberry sauce

1. Preheat the oven to Gas Mark 9/250°C/475°F.

2. Place a roasting rack in the bottom of a large roasting tin. Place the rib on the rack. Pour the beef stock over the rib and into the roasting tin. Sprinkle the rib generously with salt and pepper.

3. Roast the rib for 20 minutes, then reduce the heat to Gas Mark 4/180°C/350°F for your calculated cooking time (see p. 55), minus 30 minutes.

4. Meanwhile, place all the stuffing ingredients in a bowl and mix together. Divide the mixture into 8 generous balls. Place the stuffing balls on a baking tray and cook for the last 20 minutes of the roasting time.

5. Put the glaze ingredients in a saucepan and bring to the boil. Simmer, uncovered, for 7 minutes. Remove the joint from the oven and brush the glaze all over the surface.

6. Roast for the remaining 30 minutes of the cooking time, brushing twice with the glaze. Pour the glaze and juices from the roasting tin into a saucepan. Boil until reduced by half, strain, whisk in the butter, and serve.

Roast Rib of Beef

with Curried Rosemary and Garlic Stuffing Balls

SERVES 6

*T*here is a restaurant in Bolton called Michael's and the chef Michael has a great love of beef, as shown by the quality of meat he buys. The inventiveness of the curried rosemary and garlic stuffing balls makes this a real northern signature dish.

1.3kg (3lb) rib of beef on the bone
5fl oz (150ml) Basic Beef Stock
(p. 13)
salt and freshly ground black pepper (to taste)
25g (1oz) butter

For the stuffing
100g (4oz) fresh breadcrumbs
4 tablespoons finely chopped fresh parsley
50g (2oz) calves' liver, roughly chopped

100g (4oz) button mushrooms, roughly chopped
2 cloves garlic, peeled and crushed with a little olive oil
1 onion, peeled and finely chopped
1 teaspoon mild curry powder
1 teaspoon fresh rosemary leaves, crushed
salt and freshly ground black pepper (to taste)
1 egg, beaten

1. Preheat the oven to Gas Mark 4/180°C/350°F.

2. Place a roasting rack in the bottom of a large roasting tin. Place the rib on the rack. Pour the beef stock over the rib and into the roasting tin. Sprinkle the rib generously with salt and pepper.

3. Roast the rib for 20 minutes, then reduce the heat to Gas Mark 4/180°C/350°F for your calculated cooking time (see p. 55), minus 30 minutes.

4. Meanwhile, place all the stuffing ingredients in a bowl and mix together. Divide the mixture into 10 generous balls. Place the stuffing balls on a baking tray and cook for the last 30 minutes of the roasting time.

5. Remove the joint from the oven and brush melted butter all over the surface. Cook for the final 30 minutes and present the joint on a large serving dish with the stuffing balls. Make some Onion Gravy (p. 44), using the beef juices, and serve in a sauceboat.

Roast Bombay Beef & Potatoes (or Rain Stopped Play)

SERVES 6

I had the idea for this recipe during a barbecue that was rained out. I had four full striploins of beef and about 100 baked jacket potatoes; with 35 to 40 guests due any minute, it was Ready Steady Cook *time! The Wilkinsons, Vickers, Lowrys, Elliots and the rest of the Newburgh families would have arrived come rain or shine. Fortunately they loved my Bombay potatoes. I had a little longer than the 20 minutes' challenge time, and this is what I came up with.*

50g (2oz) butter
4 tablespoons olive oil
25g (1oz) beef dripping
1.3kg (3lb) sirloin of beef
275g (10oz) smoked bacon, chopped
1 tablespoon fresh rosemary leaves, chopped
2 large red onions, peeled and diced
3 tablespoons mild curry paste
1 tablespoon mango chutney

½ teaspoon garam masala
175g (6oz) sultanas
3 large baking apples, cored, peeled and diced
12 potatoes, baked in their jackets and diced into 5cm (2 inch) cubes
salt and freshly ground black pepper (to taste)
a little arrowroot

1. Preheat the oven to Gas Mark 7/220°C/425°F.

2. Heat the butter, olive oil and dripping in a large roasting tin. Seal the beef all over by cooking for about 5 minutes.

3. Remove the beef and set on one side. Add the bacon, cook for 3 minutes, then add the rest of the ingredients, except the jacket potatoes, seasoning and arrowroot, blending the mixture together well.

4. Place the beef back in the roasting tin and cook all over again. Cover with foil and bake in the centre of the oven for 85 minutes, basting every 15 minutes.

5. Remove the cooking foil. Add the diced jacket potatoes all around the sirloin, covering them with the curry juices. Season with the salt and pepper and return to the oven for 50 minutes.

6. Remove the sirloin and the potatoes. Pour the sauce into a saucepan and thicken with a little arrowroot. Slice the beef and serve with the curry sauce and Bombay potatoes.

Roast Sirloin Stilton Steaks Garnished with Pears

SERVES 4

*S*tilton is a wonderful cheese to eat with roast sirloin of beef and I am sure you will enjoy this combination of flavours. Serve with potato salad and a glass of red wine.

225g (8oz) Stilton cheese, crumbled
25g (1oz) butter, softened
2 tablespoons port
50g (2oz) crushed walnuts
a pinch of salt

freshly ground black pepper (to taste)
4 × 275g (10oz)/5cm (2 inch) thick sirloin steaks, trimmed
2 pears, cored and thinly sliced

1. Preheat the oven to Gas Mark 7/220°C/425°F.

2. Place the cheese, butter, port and walnuts in a bowl and blend them thoroughly. Season them well with salt and freshly ground black pepper.

3. Using a sharp knife, cut a pocket the length of each steak and fill, using half the cheese mixture.

4. Place the steaks on a grill rack in a roasting tin, top each steak with the rest of the mixture, season again with pepper and place in the centre of the oven for 25 minutes.

5. About 10 minutes before the end of the cooking time, top each steak with a few slices of pear and return to the oven.

Roast Salt & Peppered Rump Steak

SERVES 6

Trying to give Ted Weaver cookery lessons is like trying to teach Henry Cooper to box. This is Ted's recipe. Thank you Ted, and everyone at Makro.

1.3kg (3lb) rump of beef
150ml (5fl oz) Basic Beef Stock (p. 13)
3 tablespoons English mustard
1 tablespoon sea salt
6 tablespoons black peppercorns

1 nutmeg, grated
1 teaspoon five spice powder
2 tablespoons dark soy sauce
2 tablespoons clear honey, warmed

1. Preheat the oven to Gas Mark 5/190°C/375°F.

2. Place a rack in the bottom of a roasting tin. Place the rump on the rack and pour the beef stock over the rump.

3. Coat the rump with the English mustard. Then, using a mortar and pestle, crush the salt and peppercorns and blend them with the grated nutmeg and five spice powder. Place in a mixing bowl with the soy sauce and honey, and blend thoroughly. Completely cover the top of the rump with the mixture and cook for 2 hours, basting every 15 minutes.

4. Pour the left-over juices and stock from the roasting tin into a small saucepan and boil rapidly until reduced by one-third. Pour the sauce into a sauceboat and serve.

Prime Beef Fillet with Hramsa Cheese

SERVES 6

Steve Johnson is a true Scot and he makes this dish with prime Glenbervie Aberdeen Angus fillet. Hramsa is a traditional garlic-flavoured Scottish cheese. Serve this with buttered new potatoes and green vegetables.

900g (2lb) prime beef fillet
4 tablespoons Hramsa cheese or soft garlic cheese
100g (4oz) calves' liver, sliced
12 rashers rindless streaky bacon
100g (4oz) beef dripping

2 onions, peeled and finely chopped
100g (4oz) button mushrooms, wiped
4 tablespoons red wine
2 teaspoons paprika
275ml (10fl oz) soured cream
2 tablespoons chopped fresh parsley

1. Preheat the oven to Gas Mark 6/200°C/400°F.

2. Cut the fillet in half lengthways and spread the Hramsa along it as if you were buttering a French stick. Place the calves' liver on top of the cheese, place the other half of the fillet on top and tie with butcher's string. Wrap the whole fillet with the streaky bacon, securing with wooden cocktail sticks.

3. Heat the dripping in a roasting tin. Sear the fillet in the hot dripping, place in the centre of the oven and roast for 30 minutes. Allow the fillet to rest for 5 minutes, then carefully remove the wooden sticks, bacon and butcher's string.

4. Fry the onions and mushrooms in the roasting tin juices. Using a slotted spoon, transfer the vegetables to a clean saucepan, add the red wine to the tin juices, and pour into the saucepan. Heat gently, add the paprika and soured cream, bring to the boil and simmer for 5 minutes.

5. Pour the sauce over the fillet, sprinkle with the chopped fresh parsley and serve.

Beef à la Mode

SERVES 4

I *had this dish in Caen in France and was taught to make it years ago, by a very wise old chef.*

100g (4oz) beef dripping	4 carrots, peeled and diced
2.25kg (5lb) beef sirloin, boned and rolled	4 onions, peeled and diced
4 × 75g (3oz) gammon rashers	225g (8oz) button mushrooms, wiped
1 calf's foot, chopped	4 celery stalks, washed and diced
1 shin bone	1 teaspoon freshly grated nutmeg
275ml (10fl oz) dry white wine	8 cloves
salt and freshly ground black pepper (to taste)	a sprig of thyme and a sprig of parsley

1. Preheat the oven to Gas Mark 2/150°C/300°F.

2. Gently heat the beef dripping in a large roasting tin until it becomes smoking hot. Carefully brown the sirloin on all sides. Repeat the process with the gammon rashers.

3. Place the gammon rashers in a clean roasting tin. Put the sirloin on top of the gammon rashers, with the calf's foot and shin bone at the side. Pour the wine over the beef, season well with salt and pepper, cover with foil and cook for 2 hours.

4. Add the vegetables and other ingredients and cook for a further 2 hours.

5. Remove the meat carefully, and discard the string, shin bone and calf's foot. Allow the meat to cool for 3 minutes, then slice thickly. Arrange the slices on a warm serving dish surrounded by the gammon rashers and vegetables. Strain over the juices, discarding the sprigs of herbs and the cloves, and serve.

Daube of Beef

SERVES 4–6

This recipe is very similar to the last one, except that the flavour of garlic is more prominent and we are using rump instead of sirloin of beef. We also have to let it stand for 24 hours before cooking. It is excellent served with a purée of garlic potatoes and toasted crusty French bread.

1.3kg (3lb) rump steak (fat and gristle removed), diced
100g (4oz) bacon, finely chopped
2 carrots, peeled and chopped
2 onions, peeled and chopped
1 celery stalk, washed and chopped
4 cloves garlic, peeled and crushed
570ml (1 pint) Guinness
6 cloves
1 teaspoon chopped fresh thyme and marjoram
50g (2oz) butter
25g (1oz) plain flour
grated rind of 1 orange
275ml (10fl oz) Basic Beef Stock (p. 13)
salt and freshly ground black pepper (to taste)

1. Place the steak, bacon, vegetables and garlic in a large casserole dish and cover with the Guinness. Sprinkle with the cloves and herbs, and refrigerate for 24 hours.

2. Drain the meat and vegetables from the Guinness. (Use the Guinness to make a sauce if you wish.)

3. Melt the butter in a large frying pan and brown the meat, sealing it completely. Add the vegetables, sprinkle with flour, add the grated orange rind and beef stock and season well.

4. Preheat the oven to Gas Mark 4/180°C/350°F. Transfer the Daube of Beef to a casserole, cover with a tight-fitting lid and bake in the centre of the oven for 2 hours.

To give you some idea of how the Victorians used to cook their meat, here is another original recipe from a book by Alexis Soyer. Anyone who read this young man's cookbook during that period would have found it difficult to measure whether the beef was done properly, for it was cooked in a coal-burning stove.

SPICED OR HUNTER'S BEEF

Serves 6

beef, a small round	pepper and common salt
nutmeg 1	forcemeat
cloves ½ oz	gravy 1 pint
a little saltpetre	butter

1. Take the bone from a small round of beef.

2. Salt it, using the nutmeg, cloves, saltpetre, pepper and salt.

3. Stuff the hole from which you took the bone with forcemeat.

4. Bind the round tightly with tape.

5. Put it in the dripping tin, that will just hold it.

6. Pour over it the pint of gravy.

7. Put a little butter on top.

8. Cover with a piece of greaseproof paper.

9. And then with several folds of brown paper, or a close-fitting lid.

The gravy in the pan is fine, and useful for flavouring soups and sauces.
If you don't want to keep the oven heated for so long, this joint will cook well in a fireless cooker, or over a low gas jet if the latter is first covered with an asbestos mat and the pot stood on it. An iron pot used for pot roasting can be either slung over a wood fire made on the hearth or placed on an open range or stove.

Isn't that beautiful...?

Tom Bridge's Hunter's Beef

SERVES 6–8

This is a more refined recipe than the Victorian one and I advise you to try and save a few slices and serve them cold with a simple asparagus salad

1.3kg (3lb) boneless sirloin of beef
3 tablespoons Worcester sauce
1 whole nutmeg, grated
1 teaspoon cloves, crushed
salt and freshly ground black pepper (to
   taste)
275ml (10fl oz) Basic Beef Stock (p. 13)

For the forcemeat
25g (1oz) butter
175g (6oz) mushrooms, wiped and
   finely chopped

1 onion, peeled and finely chopped
2 cloves garlic, peeled and crushed
50g (2oz) white breadcrumbs
1 tablespoon finely chopped fresh
   parsley
3 tablespoons ginger wine
2 tablespoons double cream
salt and freshly ground black pepper (to
   taste)

1. Preheat the oven to Gas Mark 5/190°C/375°F.

2. Make a long pocket in the sirloin by cutting along the back with a sharp knife about 7.5cm (3 inches) into the beef.

3. To make the forcemeat, melt the butter in a large frying pan over a low heat. Add the mushrooms, onion and garlic and cook for 4 minutes. Remove from the heat and stir in the rest of the ingredients, seasoning well.

4. Stuff the forcemeat into the pocket and secure with butcher's string.

5. Put the sirloin in a roasting tin, coat with the Worcester sauce, cover with the nutmeg and crushed cloves, and season with salt and pepper. Pour the beef stock into the roasting tin, cover with cooking foil and roast in the centre of the oven for 90 minutes. Remove the cooking foil and pour the stock into a saucepan.

6. Return the beef to the oven and roast for a further 30 minutes on Gas Mark 8/230°C/450°F. Meanwhile, boil the stock until reduced by one-third. Pour through a fine sieve into a sauceboat, remove the string from the beef, slice and serve.

Victorian Pot Roast Beef

SERVES 6–8

In days of old when knights were bold and cookers hadn't been
invented
They dug a hole in the middle of the ground and cooked their
hearts contented

This very ancient dish was copied by every Victorian cook and chef. Queen Victoria's chef Charles Elme Francatelli even claimed it was his own recipe. In 1862 it was called Braised Beef à la Polonaise aux Choux Rouges.

My version has been modernised a little, but the flavours and method are still Victorian and this dish is a regular feature on my dinner table.

1.3kg (3lb) topside of beef	a sprig of fresh rosemary
50g (2oz) butter	salt and freshly ground black pepper (to
20 shallots, peeled	taste)
4 large potatoes, peeled and quartered	275ml (10fl oz) Basic Beef Stock (p. 13)
2 large carrots, peeled and cut into	150ml (5fl oz) good-quality red wine
chunks	(not plonk)
2 parsnips, peeled and cut into chunks	2 tablespoons cornflour, blended with a
1 small turnip, peeled and chopped	little red wine
a sprig of fresh thyme	a few fresh thyme leaves

1. Preheat the oven to Gas Mark 4/180°C/350°F.

2. Quickly fry the beef in the butter, browning it well all over, then place on one side. Fry the shallots, potatoes, carrots, parsnips and turnip in the butter and beef juices. Then place the beef in a large deep casserole dish, surrounded by the vegetables. Add all the remaining ingredients except the cornflour and thyme leaves.

3. Cover with a lid or cooking foil, place in the centre of the oven and cook for 2 hours. About 30 minutes before the meat is cooked, remove the lid or foil to allow the meat to brown a little more.

4. Carefully place the meat and vegetables on a large serving dish, remove the thyme and rosemary sprigs and bring the stock juices to the boil. Add the cornflour blended with a little wine. Cook and simmer for 4 minutes, pour around the vegetables and serve, garnished with fresh thyme.

Pot Roast Silverside of Beef Seville

SERVES 6

I am a great lover of Spain, especially Seville and Marbella. Although this is a Spanish dish, the true flavour is obtained by using the best cut of silverside from British beef. Serve it with fresh asparagus.

1.3kg (3lb) silverside of beef, boned and rolled
seasoned plain flour
25g (1oz) beef dripping
4 cloves garlic, peeled and crushed
juice of 1 lemon
150ml (5fl oz) Amontillado sherry
salt and freshly ground black pepper (to taste)
1 cinnamon stick
100g (4oz) pitted green olives, washed and sliced
2 red peppers, de-seeded and sliced
150ml (5fl oz) Basic Beef Stock (p. 13)

1. Preheat the oven to Gas Mark 4/180°C/350°F.

2. Dredge the silverside in the seasoned flour, heat the dripping in a large frying pan and brown the meat all over. Place the meat in a large casserole with a lid. Add the rest of the ingredients, cover and pot roast in the centre of the oven for 3 hours.

3. Transfer the silverside to a warm serving dish and slice. Discard the cinnamon stick, spoon the juice and other ingredients over the beef, and serve.

Pot Roast Silverside of Beef Portuguese

SERVES 6

The sun shines through from the Algarve whenever I taste this pot roast. Serve it with rice.

1.3kg (3lb) silverside of beef, boned and rolled
seasoned plain flour
25g (1oz) beef dripping
2 cloves garlic, peeled and crushed
6 anchovies, crushed
juice of 1 lemon
175g (6oz) chopped tomatoes

1 tablespoon tomato pureé
salt and freshly ground black pepper (to taste)
100g (4oz) pitted green olives, washed and sliced
2 red peppers, de-seeded and sliced
150ml (5fl oz) Basic Beef Stock (p. 13)

1. Preheat the oven to Gas Mark 4/180°C/350°F.

2. Dredge the silverside in the seasoned flour, heat the dripping in a large frying pan and brown the meat all over. Place the beef in a large casserole with a lid. Add the rest of the ingredients, cover and pot roast in the centre of the oven for 3 hours.

3. Transfer the silverside to a warm serving dish and slice. Spoon the juice and other ingredients over the beef, and serve.

Pot Roast Rib of Creole Beef

SERVES 6–8

Try to buy a very hot spicy sausage for this recipe from New Orleans. Another method is to marinate the beef in all the ingredients overnight. Either way, you will enjoy it! Serve with pasta.

1.3kg (3lb) rib of beef, boned and rolled
seasoned plain flour
25g (1oz) beef dripping
3 cloves garlic, peeled
2 tablespoons chilli powder
1 teaspoon fennel seeds, crushed
1 teaspoon mild curry powder
2 tablespoons Vermouth

juice of 1 lemon
175g (6oz) spiced garlic sausage, diced
175g (6oz) shallots, peeled and sliced
1 tablespoon tomato purée
salt and freshly ground black pepper (to taste)
2 red peppers, de-seeded and sliced
150ml (5fl oz) Basic Beef Stock (p. 13)
4 tablespoons creamed coconut

1. Preheat the oven to Gas Mark 4/180°C/350°F.

2. Dredge the rib of beef in the seasoned flour, heat the dripping in a large frying pan and brown the meat all over. Place the meat in a large casserole with a lid. Add the rest of the ingredients, cover and pot roast in the centre of the oven for 3 hours.

3. Transfer the rib to a warm serving dish and slice, spoon the juice and other ingredients over the beef, and serve.

Italian Pot Roast Strips of Beef with Sweet Shallots & Brandy Cream

SERVES 4–6

This is really an Italian-style recipe without the use of basil. My cousin Lee, in New York, swears by a taste of Italian — she married one!
Serve this pot roast with fried rice.

675g (1½lb) sirloin of beef, trimmed and cut into strips
25g (1oz) seasoned flour
25g (1oz) butter
4 tablespoons olive oil
20 shallots, peeled
3 tablespoons clear honey
50g (2oz) leeks, washed and shredded
50g (2oz) carrot, peeled and diced

50g (2oz) celery, washed and diced
275ml (10fl oz) Basic Beef Stock (p. 13)
150ml (5fl oz) pure tomato juice
1 tablespoon tomato purée
50ml (2fl oz) good-quality brandy
200ml (7fl oz) crème fraîche
2 tablespoons chopped fresh parsley
salt and freshly ground black pepper (to taste)

1. Preheat the oven to Gas Mark 6/200°C/400°F.

2. Dredge the beef strips in the seasoned flour, shake off the excess flour and reserve. Melt the butter and olive oil in a large casserole and brown the sirloin strips for 3 minutes. Add the shallots and honey and cook for a further 5 minutes. Sprinkle over the leeks, carrot, celery and left-over flour, and cook for 3 minutes. Add the beef stock, tomato juice, purée and brandy, and cook for a further 6 minutes.

3. Cover and place the casserole in the oven for 45 minutes. Add the crème fraîche, parsley, salt and pepper, and serve.

OPPOSITE Beef Casserole with Leeks in Red Wine Sauce (page 82)

The Recipe
FOR Love

Slow Roast Beef with Lime & Coriander

SERVES 6

Lime is a great fruit to use with beef – the citric acid helps to break down the sinews in the meat. Serve this with roast potatoes and braised turnips with a mustard sauce.

1.3kg (3lb) rolled silverside of beef
salt and freshly ground black pepper (to taste)
25g (1oz) beef dripping
2 onions, peeled and thickly sliced
225g (8oz) carrots, peeled and thickly sliced

4 tablespoons lime juice
1 teaspoon ground coriander
200ml (7fl oz) Basic Beef Stock (p. 13)
200ml (7fl oz) Guinness
a little flour (optional)
a few fresh coriander leaves

1. Preheat the oven to Gas Mark 7/220°C/425°F.

2. Season the beef generously with salt and pepper. Heat the dripping in a large ovenproof casserole and sear the meat all over until it is brown.

3. Add the rest of the ingredients, except the flour and coriander leaves, and cook in the centre of the oven for 15 minutes. Lower the heat to Gas Mark 2/150°C/300°F and continue to cook for 3 hours.

4. Thicken the stock/sauce with a little flour if you wish, garnish with the fresh coriander leaves, and serve.

OPPOSITE Scottish Beef Sausage Pot and Scone Dumplings (page 97)

Pot Roasted Chateaubriand with Dijon Mustard & Herb Crust

SERVES 4

*P*aul Reed serves this dish at the Chester Grosvenor for the owner of this very prestigious hotel, the Duke of Westminster. He accompanies it with creamed parsnips, roast carrots and shallots and a Red Wine Sauce (p. 73). Make the Red Wine Sauce first and keep warm.

2 × 350g (12oz) Chateaubriand
3 tablespoons oil
1 large onion, peeled and chopped
1 leek, washed and chopped
2 carrots, peeled and chopped
2 tablespoons olive oil
4 large carrots, peeled and quartered
16 shallots, peeled
450g (1lb) parsnips, peeled and roughly chopped
150ml (5fl oz) double cream
salt and freshly ground black pepper (to taste)

For the Herb Crust
175g (6oz) chopped fresh mixed herbs (e.g. parsley, tarragon, rosemary and thyme)
3 tablespoons Dijon mustard
2 cloves garlic, peeled and crushed
175g (6oz) breadcrumbs
salt and freshly ground black pepper (to taste)

1. Preheat the oven to Gas Mark 7/220°C/425°F.

2. Seal the meat by browning it all over for 3 minutes in the hot oil in a roasting tin. Put the meat on one side.

3. Place the chopped onion, leek and carrots in the bottom of the roasting tin. Put the fillets on top of the vegetables and cook in the centre of the oven for 40 minutes, turning the meat every 10 minutes to ensure even cooking.

4. Heat the olive oil in a small casserole, add the quartered carrots and whole shallots and roast until soft.

5. When the meat is cooked leave it to rest for 8 minutes. Meanwhile, put the parsnips and cream in a saucepan and cook until the parsnips are soft. Remove the parsnips, reduce the cream until thick, season, and place in a warm serving dish.

6. Mix together the ingredients for the herb crust.

7. When everything is ready to serve, slice the steak into 4 portions, sprinkle with the herb crust mixture and brown under the grill.

8. Place the creamed parsnips on a serving dish, top with the steak and surround with vegetables. Pour over the Red Wine Sauce and serve.

Paul Reed's Red Wine Sauce

SERVES 4

I cannot emphasise enough that you must never use cheap wine when making sauces. Always *use a good-quality wine.*

15g (½oz) butter
25g (1oz) shallots, peeled and chopped
a sprig of fresh thyme
a sprig of fresh tarragon

75ml (3fl oz) red wine
450ml (15fl oz) Rich Beef Stock
(p. 14)

1. Melt the butter in a saucepan, add the shallots and herbs and cook for 2 minutes.

2. Add the red wine and boil rapidly, until reduced by three-quarters. Add the beef stock and reduce again by three-quarters, until the sauce can thinly coat the back of a spoon.

3. Pass the sauce through a fine non-metallic sieve and pour into a sauceboat, ready for use.

CHAPTER 3

Casseroles, Braised Dishes and Curries

✦

Beef

Hot on Sunday, Cold on Monday, Hashed on Tuesday,
Minced on Wednesday, Curried on Thursday,
Broth on Friday, Cottage Pie Saturday.

You can buy more economical cuts, like silverside and braising steak, for most of the dishes in this chapter, though if you have the money and the inclination, you can also make Fillet of Beef with Truffles and Champagne Sauce (p. 85)! But this chapter is really about the slow cooking and tenderising of meat.

It is important to brown the meat from the start. Do this in batches so that the temperature does not drop during the cooking process, causing the meat to boil rather than brown. And do not worry about how you thicken your casserole. Use cornflour or plain flour sprinkled over the meat after browning, and always check the seasoning before serving. Remember that you can put seasoning in but you cannot take it out. So *keep* tasting. When it comes to curries, do not be afraid to leave them to stand for 24–48 hours. This enhances the flavour and makes the meat even more tender.

If you don't have an oven, these dishes can all be made in a slow cooker or in a saucepan over a low heat. Make use of the section on Dumplings (pp. 16–19), and garnish your casseroles and braised dishes with Red Velvet baby beetroot or red cabbage. You can't beat mashed potato for mopping up the delicious gravy. Serve naan bread, chapattis, popadums and mango chutney with the curries and experiment with different herbs and seasonings. Food is to be enjoyed!

My favourite cookery authors from yesteryear are Florence White and Elizabeth David. To go back even further, there's Dr William Kitchiner (whose biography I wrote several years ago) and his wonderful book *The Cook's Oracle*, and Mrs Elizabeth Raffald whose book *The Experienced English Housekeeper* I treasure. Here are a few snippets on beef from these cookery experts of the past.

From Florence White, *Good Things in England* (Found in a Yorkshirewoman's scrapbook, 1931):

HOW TO COOK A RATHER COARSE PIECE OF BEEF

———— ◆ ————

Ingredients: Beef – any coarse piece cut into a neat slab, thick ribs or similar piece; carrots; peas; small onions; pepper; salt; hot water; lentil flour.
Time: About three hours.

1. Prepare the vegetables and arrange them as a thick layer in a fireproof oven dish with a lid.

2. Place the meat on the vegetables.

3. Season with salt and pepper.

4. Hot water just enough to cover the meat.

5. Cook slowly.

6. Pour off gravy.

7. Remove fat.

8. Thicken the gravy with the lentil flour.

9. Pour over and serve.

I think we have moved on a bit since this!

A WINE MARINADE FOR MEAT

———— ◆ ————

In a saucepan heat a wineglass of olive oil; when it is hot put in a sliced carrot, one sliced onion, and half a head of celery cut in inch lengths.

Let these vegetables brown lightly and pour in ¼ pint of white wine and a small glass of wine vinegar. Add 4 or 5 stalks of parsley, 4 shallots, 2 cloves of garlic, thyme, bayleaf, a sprig of rosemary, 6 peppercorns and salt.

Simmer this for 30 minutes. Leave to cool, and then pour it over your piece of meat.

Elizabeth David, *French Country Cooking* (John Lenman, 1951)

The following recipe for mincemeat is truly wonderful, and ought to be read by everyone who thinks that mincemeat comes out of little jars on supermarket shelves. This shows what real mincemeat was like, complete with actual meat.

This really is the recipe Dr Kitchiner wrote for mincemeat in 1827, from which we now omit the beef to make our Christmas mince pies.

MINCEMEAT

— ◆ —

2lb of Beef Suet, picked and chopped fine; 2lb of Apples, pared and cored; 3lb of Currants, washed and picked; 1lb of Raisins, stoned and chopped fine; 1lb of good Moist Sugar; ½lb of Citron, cut into thin slices; 1lb of Candied Lemon and Orange Peel, cut the same; 2lb ready dressed Roast Beef, free from skin and gristle, and chopped fine; the juice of six Lemons and their rinds grated; ½ pint Brandy, 1 pint sweet Wine.

Mix the Suet, Apples, Currants, Meat, Plums, and Sweetmeats well together in a large pan, and strew in the spice by degrees; mix the Sugar, Lemon Juice, Wine and Brandy, and pour it in to the other ingredients, and stir it well together – set it by in close covered pans in a cold place; when wanted, stir it up from the bottom, and add half a glass of brandy to the quantity you want.

NB: The same weight of tripe is frequently substituted for the Meat and sometimes the Yolks of Eggs boiled hard.

Obs: The lean side of a Buttock, thoroughly roasted, is generally chosen for Mince Meat.

Kitchiner refers to a citron which is a special variety of highly perfumed lemon, not usually eaten as it is. It is often preserved and used in confectionery. He also mentions 'Plums'. This is very precise usage by Kitchiner. Here it refers collectively to raisins, currants and grapes. 'Obs' stands for 'Observation'.

The above is taken from *Dr William Kitchiner, 'Regency Eccentric', Author of The Cook's Oracle* by Tom Bridge and Colin Cooper English

Elizabeth Raffald contributed a great deal to the food of Great Britain. Her most famous contribution was the Eccles cake. She was also one of the very first lady cooks to start a catering agency in Manchester in 1782. The letter 'f' refers to the letter 's' when it is printed in italics.

BEEF PORCUPINE

—— ✦ ——

To make a *Porcupine* of the *Flat Ribs* of *Beef*

BONE the flat ribs, and beat it half an hour with a paſte-pin, then rub it over with yolks of eggs, ſtrew over it bread-crumbs, parſley, leeks, ſweet-marjoram, lemon-peel ſhred fine, nutmeg, pepper, and ſalt, roll it up very cloſe, and bind it hard, lard it acroſs with bacon, then a row of cold boiled tongue, a third row of pickled cucumbers, a forth row of lemon-peel: do it over in rows as above till it is larded all round, it will look like red, green, white, and yellow dices, then ſplit it and put it in a deep pot with a pint of water, lay over a caul of veal, to keep it from ſcorching, tie it down with ſtrong paper, and ſend it to the oven; when it comes out ſkim off the fat, and ſtrain your gravy into a ſauce-pan, add to it two ſpoonfuls of red wine, the ſame of browning, one of muſhroom catchup, half a lemon, thicken with a lump of butter rolled in flour, diſh up the meat, and pour the gravy on the diſh, lay round forcemeat-balls; garniſh with horſe-radiſh, and ſerve it up.

Chefs today tell you how long it should go in the oven for, and note the use of horseradish with beef.

Creamy Moroccan Beef Casserole

SERVES 6

Try this recipe with a tablespoon of almond niblets and 150ml (5fl oz) coconut cream instead of double cream for a Thai taste. Serve it with saffron rice.

3 tablespoons cooking oil
900g (2lb) braising steak (fat and gristle removed), diced
50g (2oz) flour, seasoned
225g (8oz) button mushrooms, wiped and roughly chopped
350g (12oz) shallots, peeled
275ml (10fl oz) Basic Beef Stock (p. 13)
juice and zest of 1 lime

3 tablespoons honey
½ teaspoon ground ginger
2 teaspoons coriander seeds, crushed
10 strands saffron
4 tomatoes, peeled and chopped
salt and freshly ground black pepper (to taste)
150ml (5fl oz) double cream

1. Preheat the oven to Gas Mark 2/150°C/300°F.

2. Heat the oil in a large frying pan. Coat the meat in the seasoned flour and brown it all over, cooking for about 6 minutes. Lift the chunks of meat into a large, deep casserole.

3. Slowly fry the mushrooms and shallots in the steak juices. Add the beef stock, lime juice and zest, honey, ginger, coriander seeds, saffron and tomatoes. Taste, then season with salt and pepper.

4. Pour the sauce over the steak, cover the casserole with a lid or cooking foil, place in the centre of the oven and cook for a further 10 minutes and serve.

Seventeenth-Century Spiced Beef Casserole with Nuts & Grapes

SERVES 4–6

This is a very popular winter casserole served by Veronica Shaw at her restaurant, Veronica's, in London. Veronica combines four of Hannah Woolley's recipes from 1675 to make this rich, aromatic casserole which is good with wild rice or puréed potato.

3 tablespoons olive oil
675g (1½lb) braising steak, cut into 2cm
   (¾ inch) cubes
10 shallots or pickling onions, peeled
3 carrots, peeled and chopped
50g (2oz) ready-cooked chestnuts,
   peeled and sliced
50g (2oz) flaked almonds, toasted
½ freshly grated nutmeg
3 teaspoons ground cinnamon
275ml (10fl oz) red wine

275ml (10fl oz) Basic Beef Stock (p. 13)
175ml (6fl oz) red wine vinegar
1 tablespoon chopped fresh tarragon
1 tablespoon chopped fresh flatleaf
   parsley
1 tablespoon chopped fresh thyme
sea salt and freshly ground black pepper
   (to taste)
grated rind of 1 orange
1 tablespoon dark muscovado sugar
100g (4oz) black seedless grapes, sliced

1. Heat the olive oil in a large saucepan and fry the meat, onions and carrots for about 6–7 minutes, until browned.

2. Add the remaining ingredients (except the grapes) and simmer on a low heat for 3–4 hours until the meat is very tender.

3. Add the sliced black grapes just before serving.

Goulash 'My Way'

SERVES 6

There's Goulash, Hungarian Goulash and My Goulash. And my way really is better than any other for the simple reason that most goulash recipes use cheap cuts of Argentinian beef full of sinews. Using rump steak not only makes this enjoyable but gives it a taste you will never forget. Serve it with hunks of bread and a side salad.

900g (2lb) rump steak, cut into 2.5cm
  (1 inch) cubes
50g (2oz) flour, seasoned with salt,
  freshly ground black pepper and
  1 teaspoon paprika
2 tablespoons olive oil
25g (1oz) butter
1 onion, peeled and sliced
450g (1lb) shallots, peeled
1 red and 1 green pepper, de-seeded
  and chopped

1 tablespoon paprika
1 teaspoon crushed fresh rosemary
  leaves
4 tablespoons tomato purée
275ml (10fl oz) Basic Beef Stock
  (p. 13)
150ml (5fl oz) claret
1 × 400g (14oz) tin chopped tomatoes
150ml (5fl oz) soured cream
a sprig of parsley

1. Preheat the oven to Gas Mark 3/170°C/325°F.

2. Toss the meat in the seasoned flour, generously.

3. Heat the olive oil and butter in a flameproof casserole, and fry the onion, shallots and peppers for 3 minutes. Add the meat and cook for a further 4 minutes. Sprinkle with the paprika and rosemary, add the tomato purée, beef stock, claret and chopped tomatoes, cover and cook in the centre of the oven for 2 hours.

4. Remove the casserole from the oven and leave to stand for 4 minutes. Add the soured cream, garnish with fresh parsley and serve.

Jugged Steak

SERVES 6–8

In many of these recipes, the seasoned flour helps to seal in the flavour of the meat during the slow cooking process. The use of jugging started 200 years ago, when it was found that placing meat in earthenware jugs helped to marinate and preserve its flavour.
Serve this with creamed potatoes.

675g (1½lb) stewing steak, cut into
   2.5cm (1 inch) cubes
25g (1oz) flour, seasoned
25g (1oz) butter
2 tablespoons olive oil
450g (1lb) shallots, peeled and sliced
salt and freshly ground black pepper (to
   taste)
150ml (5fl oz) red wine

450ml (15fl oz) Basic Beef Stock (p. 13)
225g (8oz) Cumberland sausage meat
1 teaspoon chopped fresh mint
50g (2oz) fresh breadcrumbs
2 tablespoons blackcurrant jelly
75g (3oz) fresh blackcurrants, washed
   and stalks removed
a sprig of fresh mint

1. Preheat the oven to Gas Mark 3/170°C/325°F.

2. Toss the steak in the seasoned flour. Heat the butter and oil in a flameproof casserole, and brown the steak. Add the shallots and season. Add the wine and beef stock, stir and cover with a lid or cooking foil. Bake in the centre of the oven for 3 hours.

3. Blend the Cumberland sausage meat in a bowl with the mint and breadcrumbs, forming the mixture into 10 small balls.

4. About 30 minutes before the end of the cooking time, add the sausage balls and the blackcurrant jelly. Return the casserole to the oven, uncovered, to finish cooking.

5. Just before serving, garnish with the blackcurrants and a sprig of fresh mint.

Beef Casserole with Leeks in Red Wine Sauce

SERVES 8

*T*he combination of flavours makes this dish a wonderful winter warmer. This 'Recipe of Love' was seen on TV all over Britain in 1996 – this is a reminder of those wonderful advertisements for British meat. Serve it with rice.

675g (1½lb) sirloin of beef, trimmed and cut into thin strips
225g (8oz) rindless smoked bacon, chopped
3 large onions, peeled and sliced
2 cloves garlic, peeled and crushed
225g (8oz) small button mushrooms
3 tablespoons olive oil
25g (1oz) beef dripping

25g (1oz) flour, seasoned
salt and freshly ground black pepper (to taste)
275ml (10fl oz) good claret
150ml (5fl oz) Basic Beef Stock (p. 13)
1 teaspoon *fines herbes*
1 tablespoon tomato purée
450g (1lb) leeks, washed and roughly sliced

1. Toss the beef, smoked bacon, onions, garlic and mushrooms into a large bowl. Sprinkle with the olive oil and leave to stand for 2 hours.

2. Preheat the oven to Gas Mark 4/180°C/350°F.

3. Heat the beef dripping in a large flameproof casserole, add the steak mixture and brown for 5 minutes. Stir in the seasoned flour, and season again with salt and pepper. Add the claret, beef stock, *fines herbes* and tomato purée, blending them together thoroughly.

4. Cover the casserole with a piece of cooking foil and then a lid and cook in the centre of the oven for 2 hours.

5. About 30 minutes before the end of the cooking time, mix in the leeks and return to the oven, uncovered.

Polish Cassolette

SERVES 6–8

This is traditionally served with pickled cabbage, green beans and neat Polish vodka. I have added the Polish sausage to give the casserole extra bite.

900g (2lb) rump steak, cut into 2.5cm (1 inch) cubes
450g (1lb) Polish sausage, sliced
50g (2oz) flour, seasoned with salt, freshly ground black pepper and 1 teaspoon paprika
2 tablespoons olive oil
25g (1oz) butter
450g (1lb) shallots, peeled
1 red and 1 green pepper, de-seeded and chopped

1 tablespoon chilli powder
1 teaspoon crushed fresh rosemary leaves
4 tablespoons tomato purée
275ml (10fl oz) Basic Beef Stock (p. 13)
450g (1lb) tomatoes, peeled and chopped
150ml (5fl oz) soured cream
a sprig of parsley

1. Preheat the oven to Gas Mark 3/170°C/325°F.

2. Toss the beef and sausage in the seasoned flour, generously. Heat the olive oil and butter in a flameproof casserole and fry the shallots and peppers for 3 minutes.

3. Add the meat and cook for a further 4 minutes. Sprinkle with the chilli powder and rosemary, add the tomato purée, beef stock and chopped tomatoes, cover and cook in the centre of the oven for 2 hours.

4. Remove the casserole from the oven and leave to stand for 4 minutes. Add the soured cream, garnish with fresh parsley and serve.

Beef 'n' Beer

SERVES 8

I work a great deal on Victorian recipes and this is a really excellent one. It's even better if you have time to marinate the beef, onions and mushrooms in the brown ale overnight.

900g (2lb) rump steak
50g (2oz) beef dripping
4 large onions, peeled and sliced
275g (10oz) button mushrooms, wiped and sliced
25g (1oz) flour, seasoned
1 tablespoon soft brown sugar
2 tablespoons tarragon vinegar
1 *bouquet garni*

1 teaspoon crushed fresh thyme
275ml (10fl oz) Basic Beef Stock (p. 13)
570ml (1 pint) Newcastle brown ale
salt and freshly ground black pepper (to taste)
1 tablespoon English mustard
150ml (5fl oz) double cream
a sprig of fresh thyme

1. Preheat the oven to Gas Mark 4/180°C/350°F.

2. Cut the beef into large cubes, removing any gristle or fat. Heat the dripping in a flameproof casserole, add the beef and brown all over for about 4 minutes. Remove the meat with a slotted spoon and place on one side.

3. Add the onions and mushrooms and cook for 3 minutes. Return the meat to the casserole, sprinkle with the seasoned flour and cook for 2 minutes.

4. Add the sugar, vinegar, *bouquet garni*, thyme, beef stock and brown ale, stirring for 4 minutes. Season with salt and pepper, add the mustard, cover with cooking foil and then a tight-fitting lid and cook in the centre of the oven for 3 hours.

5. Remove the lid and foil, let the casserole stand for 5 minutes, then stir and pour a large swirl of double cream around the top. Garnish with a sprig of thyme and serve.

Fillet of Beef with Truffles & Champagne Sauce

SERVES 6–8

I have adapted this recipe from one that Mrs Agnes B. Marshall wrote around 1890, when truffles and champagne were often to be seen on high-class menus throughout Great Britain. Should you be able to afford this degree of luxury, enjoy! If not, try using sirloin, beetroot and cider in place of the fillet, truffles and champagne.

50g (2oz) butter
1 leek, washed and finely shredded
6 shallots, peeled and sliced
1 large carrot, peeled and finely diced
1 parsnip, peeled and finely diced
1 celery stalk, washed and finely diced
2 cloves garlic, peeled and roughly chopped
1.8kg (4lb) fillet steak or sirloin of beef, trimmed
salt and freshly ground black pepper (to taste)

450g (1lb) rindless smoked streaky bacon
25g (1oz) flour, seasoned
150ml (5fl oz) dry sherry
150ml (5fl oz) Basic Beef Stock (p. 13)
570ml (1 pint) champagne or dry cider
150ml (5fl oz) soured cream
1 large truffle or 2 large Red Velvet beetroot, cut into 12 diamond shapes

1. Preheat the oven to Gas Mark 4/180°C/350°F.

2. Melt the butter in a large pan and fry the leek, shallots, carrot, parsnip, celery and garlic for 5 minutes. Transfer to a large flameproof casserole using a slotted spoon.

3. Add the fillet or sirloin to the pan and brown it all over for about 2 minutes on each side. Season the meat well with salt and pepper and remove it from the pan. Wrap the bacon around the fillet or sirloin and place it on the bed of vegetables in the casserole.

4. Sprinkle the fillet with the seasoned flour and pour over the sherry, beef stock and half the champagne or cider. Cover with cooking foil and then a tight-fitting lid and place in the centre of the oven for 2 hours.

5. Carefully pour the stock and sauce from the casserole into a saucepan, and return the fillet to the oven, uncovered, for 20 minutes. Meanwhile, add the rest of the champagne or cider to the saucepan and boil the sauce until reduced by half.

6. Strain into a sauceboat through a fine sieve, add the soured cream, pour a little of the sauce over the fillet, garnish with diamonds of truffle or beetroot, and serve.

A Casserole of Oxtails

SERVES 6–8

*T*oday oxtails are a delicacy and are quite expensive. Ask for the thicker part of the oxtail, as it contains more meat. Always use fresh not frozen and boil them for 5 minutes before doing anything with them. When eating oxtails do use your fingers, and place a finger bowl of warm water with a few drops of lemon juice near each guest. Provide cloth napkins and give each person a soup spoon and fork. This is a recipe I have revised from an eighteenth-century manuscript.

50ml (2fl oz) peanut or sesame oil
2 onions, peeled and sliced
2 carrots, peeled and diced
1 small turnip, peeled and diced
1 celery stalk, washed and sliced
2 whole oxtails, chopped and blanched
   in boiling water for 5 minutes
450g (1lb) rindless, smoked streaky
   bacon, diced
50g (2oz) flour, sifted
570ml (1 pint) Rich Beef Stock (p. 14)
150ml (5fl oz) port

3 tablespoons soy sauce
2 tablespoons tomato purée
salt and freshly ground black pepper (to
   taste)
450g (1lb) parsnips, peeled
2 tablespoons olive oil
50g (2oz) butter
560g (1¼lb) potatoes, peeled and boiled
3 tablespoons cream
½ nutmeg, freshly grated
2 tablespoons chopped fresh parsley
3 tablespoons Madeira

1. Preheat the oven to Gas Mark 3/170°C/325°F.

2. Heat the oil in a large, deep casserole and cook the onions, carrots, turnip, celery, oxtails and bacon for 6 minutes. Sprinkle with the sifted flour and cook for 2 minutes.

3. Add the beef stock, port, soy sauce and tomato purée, bring to the boil and simmer for 5 minutes. Season well with salt and pepper, cover and place in the oven for 3 hours.

4. Meanwhile, boil the parsnips for 15 minutes, remove them from the pan, dry them well and coat them with a little butter and olive oil. About 1 hour before the oxtails are complete, put the parsnips in a roasting tin. Drizzle with the olive oil, dot with 25g (1oz) butter, season well and put in the oven.

5. About 30 minutes before the oxtail is complete, mash the potatoes with the cream, nutmeg and 25g (1oz) butter. Place the potato in a piping bag.

6. Using a very large, deep serving dish, pipe the potato around the edge, then place the oxtails on one side with the vegetables, and the baked parsnips on the other side. Sprinkle with the chopped parsley and Madeira, then serve.

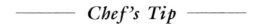

Chef's Tip

Sesame oil burns very easily so it's best to cook it over a low heat. Alternatively, you can mix it with an equal quantity of light olive oil.

Beef & Orange Casserole

SERVES 6–8

This is another combination of flavours that you would not normally think of – it has a semi-sweet orangey taste and goes very well with any type of rice or pasta.

900g (2lb) chuck steak, cut into 5cm (2 inch) cubes
25g (1oz) flour, seasoned
25g (1oz) beef dripping
2 onions, peeled and sliced
1 clove garlic, peeled and crushed
1 tablespoon soft brown sugar
275ml (10fl oz) fresh orange juice

275ml (10fl oz) Basic Beef Stock (p. 13)
salt and freshly ground black pepper (to taste)
3 tablespoons Orange Curaçao
segments and zest from 4 large Jaffa oranges
1 large green pepper, de-seeded and sliced

1. Preheat the oven to Gas Mark 3/170°C/325°F.

2. Toss the steak in the seasoned flour, then heat the dripping in a flameproof casserole with a lid. Brown the floured beef in the dripping for 3 minutes, add the onions and garlic and cook for a further 2 minutes.

3. Sprinkle with the brown sugar and pour over the orange juice and beef stock. Cook for 10 minutes, stirring all the time. Season again with salt and pepper, place a piece of cooking foil over the casserole and then the lid, and cook in the centre of the oven for 3 hours.

4. About 45 minutes before the end of the cooking time, add the orange liqueur, segments, zest and green pepper, blending them into the casserole thoroughly. Cover and return to the oven. Turn up the heat to Gas Mark 4/180°C/350°F until the casserole is cooked.

OPPOSITE PAGE 86 Carbonnade of Beef (page 95)

OPPOSITE Top to bottom: Persian Royal Beef Korma with Rice (page 119), Indian Fillet Steak with Corn and Rice Fritters (page 152)

Twentieth-Century Beef

SERVES 6–8

This is what I will be serving at my Millennium party – with rice.

900g (2lb) rump steak	1 teaspoon crushed fresh thyme leaves
50g (2oz) beef dripping	275ml (10fl oz) Basic Beef Stock (p. 13)
450g (1lb) shallots, peeled	275ml (10fl oz) champagne
275g (10oz) button mushrooms, wiped	salt and freshly ground black pepper (to
25g (1oz) flour, seasoned	taste)
1 tablespoon soft brown sugar	1 tablespoon English mustard
1 tablespoon balsamic vinegar	150ml (5fl oz) double cream
1 *bouquet garni*	

1. Preheat the oven to Gas Mark 4/180°C/350°F.

2. Cut the beef into large cubes, removing any gristle or fat. Heat the dripping in a flameproof casserole, add the beef and brown all over for about 4 minutes. Then remove the meat with a slotted spoon and set on one side.

3. Add the shallots and mushrooms and cook for 3 minutes. Return the meat to the casserole, sprinkle with the seasoned flour and cook for 2 minutes.

4. Add the sugar, vinegar, *bouquet garni*, thyme, beef stock and champagne, stirring for 4 minutes. Season with salt and pepper, and add the mustard. Cover with cooking foil and then a tight-fitting lid and cook in the centre of the oven for 3 hours.

5. Remove the lid and foil, and leave the casserole to stand for 5 minutes. Then stir, pour a large swirl of double cream around the top, and serve.

Beef Casserole with Bacon & Beef Rosti

SERVES 6–8

*D*ifferent and thoroughly yummy. For a more rustic taste, add crushed almonds or walnuts to the casserole and fry the rosti in beef dripping.

Just for the sun-dried tomato, olive oil and wild mushroom brigade, you can add a tablespoon of all three to the rosti should you wish to do so!

900g (2lb) rump steak (fat and gristle removed), diced
350g (12oz) rindless smoked streaky bacon, chopped
50g (2oz) flour, well seasoned
50g (2oz) beef dripping
2 onions, peeled and sliced
570ml (1 pint) Basic Beef Stock (p. 13)
150ml (5fl oz) stout
salt and freshly ground black pepper (to taste)
2 large potatoes, peeled and diced
100g (4oz) swede, peeled and diced

1 large carrot, peeled and diced
175g (6oz) button mushrooms, wiped and sliced
100g (4oz) fresh or frozen peas

For the rosti

25g (1oz) butter
2 tablespoons olive oil
450g (1lb) potatoes, peeled and coarsely grated
100g (4oz) grated onion
salt and freshly ground black pepper

1. Preheat the oven to Gas Mark 4/180°C/350°F.

2. Toss the meat and bacon in the seasoned flour. Heat the dripping in a large saucepan and fry the beef, bacon and onions for 5 minutes. Add the beef stock and stout, seasoning well with salt and pepper.

3. Bring to the boil and use a ladle to remove any scum floating on the surface. Add the rest of the casserole ingredients. Pour into an ovenproof casserole and cook slowly in the oven for 2 hours.

4. To make the rosti, remove about 175g (6oz) meat and the same amount of smoked bacon from the casserole. Allow it to cool and chop it very fine.

5. Heat the butter and olive oil in a large heavy-based frying pan. Mix all the rosti ingredients together, including the chopped meat, press them into the pan in an even layer and cook over a gentle heat for 10 minutes, shaking the pan to prevent the rosti sticking. Invert a plate over the pan and turn it over, so that the rosti falls onto the plate. Add a little more olive oil to the pan and slide the rosti back in. Cook for a further 12 minutes, cut into 8 wedges, and serve with the casserole.

Casserole of Steak, Peppers & Onions in Lime Sauce

SERVES 4

Try this casserole with my Cheese Scone topping (p. 174). About 30 minutes before the end of the cooking time, simply top with cheese scone pastry.

3 tablespoons cooking oil
4 × 225g (8oz) sirloin steaks, fat and
   gristle removed
50g (2oz) flour, seasoned
450g (1lb) (peeled weight) baby onions
   or shallots, sliced
175g (6oz) green and red peppers, de-
   seeded and thinly sliced

150ml (5fl oz) chicken stock
juice and zest of 2 limes
2 green chillies, chopped
2 tablespoons oyster sauce
1 teaspoon Worcester sauce
salt and freshly ground black pepper (to
   taste)

1. Preheat the oven to Gas Mark 5/190°C/375°F.

2. Heat the oil in a large frying pan. Coat the steaks in the seasoned flour and cook them for about 3 minutes on each side until brown.

3. Lift the steaks into a large deep casserole and sprinkle with the sliced baby onions or shallots.

4. Slowly fry the peppers in the steak juice. Add the chicken stock, lime juice and zest, and cook for a further 5 minutes.

5. Add the chillies, oyster sauce and Worcester sauce. Taste, then season with salt and pepper. Pour the sauce over the steak and onions.

6. Cover the casserole with a lid or cooking foil, place in the centre of the oven, cook for 70 minutes until the meat is very tender, and serve.

Beef, Bean & Beetroot Casserole

SERVES 6

Magnificent in winter – served with thick crusty bread and a mug of strong tea. Use tinned flageolet beans if you wish.

450g (1lb) flageolet beans, soaked overnight and drained
25g (1oz) butter
2 tablespoons olive oil
3 rindless smoked streaky bacon rashers, chopped
900g (2lb) stewing steak, trimmed and cut into 5cm (2 inch) cubes
1 tablespoon plain flour

275ml (10fl oz) red wine
275ml (10fl oz) Basic Beef Stock (p. 13)
salt and freshly ground black pepper (to taste)
14 shallots, peeled
2 tablespoons clear honey, warmed
225g (8oz) ready-cooked Red Velvet beetroot, diced

1. Preheat the oven to Gas Mark 3/170°C/325°F.

2. Cook the beans in salted boiling water for about 25 minutes and drain.

3. Heat the butter and olive oil in a flameproof casserole, add the bacon and steak, and cook for 5 minutes. Sprinkle with plain flour, add the red wine and beef stock, season and bring to the boil. Toss in the beans, cover tightly with a lid or cooking foil, and bake in the centre of the oven for 2 hours.

4. About 15 minutes before the end of the cooking time, remove the lid or cooking foil from the casserole. Place the shallots and honey in a frying pan and cook slowly for 5 minutes, then turn off the heat. Alternate the shallots and cooked beetroot around the top of the casserole and return to the oven for the last 15 minutes.

Sirloin of Beef with Port & Coriander

SERVES 4

*S*erve this with fresh pasta spirals and a glass of good claret.

3 tablespoons olive oil
25g (1oz) flour, seasoned and sifted
4 × 225g (8oz) sirloin steaks, fat and gristle removed
450g (1lb) button mushrooms, wiped and roughly chopped
275ml (10fl oz) chicken stock
6 tablespoons port

2 tablespoons chopped fresh coriander
a pinch of mace
1 tablespoon tomato purée
salt and freshly ground black pepper (to taste)
150ml (5fl oz) fromage frais
extra chopped fresh coriander

1. Preheat the oven to Gas Mark 3/170°C/325°F.

2. Heat the olive oil in a large frying pan. Coat the steaks in the seasoned and sifted flour and brown them all over, cooking for about 4 minutes. Lift them into a large deep casserole.

3. Slowly fry the mushrooms in the steak juices. Add the chicken stock, port, coriander, mace and tomato purée. Taste, then season with salt and pepper.

4. Pour the port sauce over the steak, cover the casserole with a lid or cooking foil, place in the centre of the oven and cook for 2 hours until the meat is very tender. Add the fromage frais, cook for a further 12 minutes, sprinkle with extra fresh coriander, and serve.

Beef Casserole with Young Turnips & Cider

SERVES 8

Alistair MacDougall, at Public Relations Intercommunications and Marketing (PRIAM to you and me), in Crowborough, East Sussex, gave this recipe 12 out of 10 and then asked me to make it again, so that he could take away 2 points!

3 tablespoons cooking oil
900g (2lb) rump steak (fat and gristle removed), diced
50g (2oz) flour, seasoned
450g (1lb) shallots, peeled
2 cloves garlic, crushed with a little olive oil
675g (1½lb) young white turnips, peeled and halved

1 tablespoon clear honey
275ml (10fl oz) Basic Beef Stock (p. 13)
2 tablespoons Worcester sauce
3 tablespoons French mustard
150ml (5fl oz) strong dry cider
salt and freshly ground black pepper (to taste)
a little plain flour (optional)

1. Preheat the oven to Gas Mark 4/180°C/350°F.

2. Heat the oil in a large frying pan. Coat the meat in the seasoned flour and brown it all over, cooking for about 6 minutes. Lift it into a large deep casserole.

3. Slowly fry the shallots, crushed garlic and turnips in the steak juices. Add the honey, beef stock, Worcester sauce, mustard and cider. Taste, then season with salt and pepper.

4. Pour the sauce over the steak, cover the casserole with a lid or cooking foil, place in the centre of the oven and cook for 2 hours until the meat is very tender. Thicken with a little flour if required, and serve.

Beef Bourguignonne

SERVES 6–8

This is commonly known as Beef in Red Wine and a good-quality wine should always be used for it. Deep-fry 8 large heart-shaped croûtons in beef dripping and use them as a garnish.

4 tablespoons sunflower oil	1 tablespoon plain flour
900g (2lb) chuck steak, cut into 2.5cm (1 inch) cubes	275ml (10fl oz) good-quality red wine
225g (8oz) baby button mushrooms, wiped	275ml (10fl oz) Basic Beef Stock (p. 13)
100g (4oz) rindless smoked bacon, diced	1 *bouquet garni* (1 bay leaf, a sprig of thyme, celery, parsley and sage tied
225g (8oz) shallots, peeled	with string)
2 cloves garlic, peeled and crushed	salt and freshly ground black pepper (to taste)

1. Heat the sunflower oil in a flameproof casserole and quickly fry the steak, browning it all over. Using a slotted spoon, remove the meat and set on one side.

2. Add the mushrooms, bacon, shallots and garlic to the fat in the casserole and cook for 4 minutes. Return the beef, sprinkle with flour, and cook for a further 2 minutes.

3. Meanwhile, preheat the oven to Gas Mark 2/150°C/300°F.

4. Add the wine and beef stock and stir until boiling. Add the *bouquet garni* and season well with salt and pepper. Cover and place in the centre of the oven for 3 hours. Remove the *bouquet garni* and serve.

Carbonnade of Beef

SERVES 8

This is a joint venture between the French and the Irish. It is a classic French dish but, without Guinness, a true Carbonnade cannot be made. Serve it with slices of French bread.

900g (2lb) rump steak (all fat removed), cut into 2.5cm (1 inch) cubes
salt and freshly ground black pepper (to taste)
2 tablespoons olive oil
2 tablespoons butter
450g (1lb) onions, peeled and sliced
225g (8oz) button mushrooms, wiped and sliced
1 tablespoon plain flour
275ml (10fl oz) Guinness

1. Season the beef with salt and pepper. Heat the olive oil in a frying pan and brown the steak all over, then transfer to a flameproof casserole.

2. Add the butter to the frying pan and sauté the onions, stirring constantly, until they are golden brown. Add the mushrooms and cook for a further 2 minutes. Sprinkle with the flour, stir well and add to the casserole. Add the Guinness and cook over a low heat for 2 hours.

3. Taste, season again if required, and serve.

Osso Buco Tom Bridge-Style

SERVES 6

Moving on to Italy, Osso Buco is very well known. The Italians use veal marrow bone simmered in a rich tomato sauce. Try my recipe using shin of beef and beef marrow, which should be savoured to the very last morsel. It makes an excellent main course, served with saffron rice or salad.

900g (2lb) shin of beef, cut into 5cm (2 inch) cubes
seasoned flour
2 tablespoons olive oil
25g (1oz) butter
3 tablespoons beef marrow
3 cloves garlic, peeled and finely chopped

1 large Spanish onion, peeled and finely chopped
570ml (1 pint) Basic Beef Stock (p. 13)
150ml (5fl oz) dry red wine
4 tablespoons tomato purée
1 tablespoon chopped fresh tarragon
salt and freshly ground black pepper (to taste)

1. Boil a pan of salted water, add the shin of beef, boil for 2 minutes and remove the beef. Discard the water.

2. Dredge the pieces of beef with the seasoned flour. Heat the olive oil and butter in the pot and brown the beef pieces, adding the beef marrow, garlic and onion. Pour over the beef stock and wine. Add the tomato purée, stir well, sprinkle with the tarragon, cover and simmer for 3 hours over a low heat.

3. Taste, season with salt and pepper, and serve.

Scottish Beef Sausage Pot with Scone Dumplings

SERVES 6

A true taste of Scotland. Add a wee dram of 'Afore ye go' if you must!

450g (1lb) beef sausages
450g (1lb) onions, peeled and sliced
3 tablespoons cooking oil
25g (1oz) butter
225g (8oz) button mushrooms, wiped
225g (8oz) potatoes, peeled and diced
100g (4oz) carrots, peeled and diced
100g (4oz) turnips, peeled and diced
1 red and 1 green pepper, de-seeded
   and chopped
8 tomatoes, chopped
225ml (8fl oz) Basic Beef Stock (p. 13)
3 tablespoons tomato purée
2 tablespoons paprika

1 teaspoon dried marjoram
150ml (5fl oz) beer
6 tablespoons soured cream
salt and freshly ground black pepper (to
   taste)

For the scone dumplings

100g (4oz) self-raising flour
50g (2oz) shredded beef suet
25g (1oz) butter, softened
1 teaspoon oatmeal
1 teaspoon snipped fresh chives
salt and freshly ground black pepper (to
   taste)

1. Slice the sausages into bite-size chunks. Fry the sausage with the onions in the cooking oil and butter without colouring for 3 minutes in a large flameproof casserole.

2. Add the mushrooms, potatoes, carrots, turnips, peppers and tomatoes and continue frying for a further 4 minutes. Pour in the stock and add the tomato purée, paprika, marjoram and beer. Bring to the boil and simmer over a low heat for 1 hour.

3. Meanwhile make the scone dumplings. Preheat the oven to Gas Mark 3/170°C/325°F.

4. Mix all the dumpling ingredients together in a bowl, and add enough water to make a soft dough. Turn out onto a floured surface and cut out the dumplings with a small scone cutter.

5. Season the casserole to taste. Place the dumplings around the top of the casserole and cook in the oven, uncovered, for a further 45 minutes. Spoon the soured cream into the centre and serve.

Spanish Hot Pot

SERVES 6

Memories of Porto Banus, when it was not full of posers... Serve with French bread. (Have you tasted Spanish bread?!)

2 tablespoons butter
2 tablespoons olive oil
450g (1lb) shallots, peeled and halved
900g (2lb) stewing beef, cut into 2.5cm
   (1 inch) cubes
seasoned flour
450g (1lb) tomatoes, finely chopped
3 cloves garlic, peeled and finely
   chopped
225g (8oz) button mushrooms, wiped
   and sliced

225g (8oz) smoked ham, finely chopped
275ml (10fl oz) Basic Beef Stock
   (p. 13)
275ml (10fl oz) red Spanish wine
4 tablespoons tomato purée
freshly ground black pepper (to taste)
1 teaspoon dried marjoram
1 teaspoon dried thyme
a little cornflour blended to a paste
   with water (optional)

1. Heat the butter and oil in a flameproof casserole, add the shallots and cook for a few minutes.

2. Dip the stewing steak into the seasoned flour and fry gently with the shallots for 10 minutes, sealing the beef thoroughly. Add the tomatoes and garlic, and cook for a further 5 minutes. Then add all the rest of the ingredients, except the cornflour paste, stirring them well, and cook slowly for 3 hours until tender.

3. Thicken with a little cornflour paste if needed, and serve.

Lombo de Boeuf

SERVES 6–8

This Portuguese dish is a winter warmer. It is supposed to be served with olive bread, dipped in olive oil.

900g (2lb) sirloin of beef, cut into 2.5cm (1 inch) cubes
seasoned flour
2 tablespoons olive oil
25g (1oz) butter
2 large onions, peeled and sliced
1 clove garlic, peeled and finely chopped
1 green chilli, very finely chopped
3 carrots, peeled and diced
2 celery stalks, washed and sliced

1 red, 1 green and 1 yellow pepper, de-seeded and sliced
1 × 400g (14oz) tin plum tomatoes, finely chopped or the same quantity of chopped fresh tomatoes
2 tablespoons tomato purée
150ml (5fl oz) rosé wine
150ml (5fl oz) Basic Beef Stock (p. 13)
1 teaspoon chopped fresh basil
salt and freshly ground black pepper (to taste)

1. Coat the beef in the seasoned flour.

2. Heat the olive oil and butter in a large flameproof casserole. When hot, cook the beef until it is a nice brown colour, turning it so that it is equally browned on all sides.

3. Add the onions, garlic and chilli, and cook for a further 5 minutes. Then add all the other ingredients, seasoning well. Simmer for 2 hours and serve.

Hutspot met Klapstuck (Hotchpotch)

SERVES 8

This is one of the great Dutch national dishes, though Hotchpotch is also cooked in England, France and Belgium, and is of very ancient origin. In the English version mutton is generally used, while in France beef and pork are the chief ingredients together with a variety of vegetables. In the Belgian version there is a mixture of different meats. But in Holland beef and chicken are always used.

450g (1lb) lean minced steak
450g (1lb) rough chuck steak, diced
450g (1lb) chicken meat and livers, diced
seasoned flour
25g (1oz) butter
2 tablespoons cooking oil
570ml (1 pint) Basic Beef Stock (p. 13)

275ml (10fl oz) white wine
450g (1lb) carrots, peeled and sliced
450g (1lb) potatoes, peeled and diced
225g (8oz) unripe Bramley apples, diced
1 large onion, peeled and sliced
salt and freshly ground black pepper (to taste)
1 teaspoon freshly grated nutmeg

1. Dredge the meats in the seasoned flour. Heat the butter and oil in a large flameproof casserole, and place the meat in the hot fat, cooking until browned.

2. Add the beef stock and wine, and cook for 10 minutes. Add all the other ingredients and simmer for 2 hours. The dish is ready when the stock and wine have completely evaporated.

3. Taste and adjust the seasoning, and serve.

Ragout of British Beef or Oxtail

SERVES 6

Ragouts are commonly known as casseroles. This is an excellent healthy, low-fat recipe I created for my mother's diet. Serve with sliced or jacket potatoes, low-fat buttered aspara-gus, baby sweetcorn and Red Velvet baby beetroot. You can choose whether to use stewing beef or fresh oxtails for this recipe. I adore oxtails and their flavour really makes the dish outstanding. Alternatively, you could try using half of each meat.

675g (1½lb) stewing steak (fat and gris-tle removed) or oxtail

sea salt and freshly ground black pepper (to taste)

2 tablespoons sunflower oil

2 medium-sized onions, peeled and thinly sliced

225g (8oz) baby button mushrooms, wiped and sliced

1 teaspoon chopped fresh basil

2 cloves garlic, peeled and crushed

1 tablespoon plain flour

570ml (1 pint) Basic Beef Stock (p. 13)

2 tablespoons tomato purée

350g (12oz) potatoes, peeled and diced

350g (12oz) cherry tomatoes, blanched and peeled

1. Preheat the oven to Gas Mark 2/150°C/300°F.

2. Cut the steak into 1cm (½ inch) × 7.5cm (3 inch) strips and season them well with salt and pepper. Heat the oil in a deep flameproof casserole and brown the meat. When it is brown, transfer it to a warm dish. If using oxtail, follow the same method as above but blanch the pieces in boiling water for 5 minutes first.

3. Fry the onions and mushrooms with the basil and garlic for 5 minutes. Add the flour and cook for 1 minute. Add the beef stock and simmer for 3 minutes. Return the meat to the casserole, cover with a lid and cook in the centre of the oven for 2 hours.

4. Add the tomato purée and stir in well. Add the potatoes and cherry tomatoes, season to taste, return to the oven for 1 hour, and serve.

Cliveden Fillet of Scotch Beef Poached in Madeira Sauce

with Creamed Celeriac Spiked with Grain Mustard

SERVES 4

Ron Maxfield, who gave me this recipe, is Head Chef at The Cliveden at Taplow in Berkshire and he is, without doubt, an avid supporter of British beef. Being a chef, the first version he sent me was about three pages long and almost impossible to follow, unless you shared his amazing talent. Left to simmer for almost six months, it has reduced down very nicely!

50g (2oz) butter
12 shallots, peeled and roughly chopped
570ml (1 pint) Madeira Sauce (p. 43)
275ml (10fl oz) chicken stock
salt and freshly ground black pepper (to taste)
275ml (10fl oz) peanut oil
350g (12oz) celeriac, peeled
150ml (5fl oz) single cream

3 tablespoons grain mustard
4 potatoes, peeled and grated
12 baby asparagus tips, trimmed
12 baby carrots, cleaned with green stalks left on
225g (8oz) baby broad beans
4 × 175g (6oz) beef fillets
4 courgette flowers

1. Heat the butter in a large saucepan and when hot add the shallots. Cook for 3 minutes, then add the Madeira Sauce and boil until the sauce is nearly evaporated.

2. Add the chicken stock and reduce again by two-thirds. Allow the sauce to cool slightly, pass through a fine muslin cloth and season with salt and pepper. Keep warm and place on one side.

3. To make the garnish, heat the peanut oil in a deep frying pan. Cut one third of the celeriac into thin discs about 2.5cm (1 inch) in diameter. Deep-fry in the peanut oil for 4 minutes and season. Grate the remainder of the celeriac, cook in the cream for 3 minutes, add the grain mustard and keep warm.

4. Season the grated potatoes, make them into 4 saucer shapes and fry in a little peanut oil until golden brown on both sides. Keep warm.

5. Steam the asparagus, carrots and broad beans.

6. Season the beef fillets and sear them on both sides in a hot pan.

7. Place the sauce in a large saucepan and reheat. Add the fillets and poach for 8 minutes, turning after 4 minutes.

8. To serve, place a potato 'saucer' in the centre of each plate, and spoon some creamed celeriac on top. Place a fillet of beef on top of the creamed celeriac and arrange the steamed vegetables around the beef fillets. Fill the courgette flowers with the deep-fried celeriac chips and place one on top of each fillet. Pour the sauce around the fillets and serve.

Poached Fillet of Beef with Horseradish & Brandy Sauce

SERVES 6

By now you will have realised that I love developing new recipes. Here's one I made earlier!

25g (1oz) butter
50g (2oz) leeks, washed and shredded
50g (2oz) carrot, peeled and diced
50g (2oz) celery, washed and diced
50g (2oz) shallots, peeled and sliced
570ml (1 pint) Basic Beef Stock (p. 13)
675g (1½lb) whole fillet of beef, trimmed

50ml (2fl oz) good-quality brandy
200ml (7fl oz) crème fraîche
2 tablespoons freshly grated horseradish
1 teaspoon clear honey, warmed
1 teaspoon chopped fresh parsley
salt and freshly ground black pepper (to taste)

1. Melt the butter in a large saucepan and add the leeks, carrot, celery and shallots. Cook for 3 minutes, add half the beef stock and cook for another 8 minutes.

2. Add the remaining beef stock, bring to the boil, add the beef and cook for 10 minutes. Remove the beef, slice thinly, place on a large hot serving dish and keep warm.

3. In another saucepan, boil the brandy until reduced by half, add the beef stock (strained through a fine sieve), and boil again until reduced by half.

4. Add the crème fraîche, grated horseradish and warm honey. Heat gently, and add the parsley, salt and pepper.

5. Pour a little of the Horseradish and Brandy Sauce around the beef and put the rest in a sauceboat. Serve with a vegetable patty made from the left-over cooked vegetables and some mashed potato.

Oxtail with Sausages

A dear friend and Euro-Toques colleague, Adrian Park, works for a company called Pubs Limited in Chester, creating the recipes for their food outlets. These are Adrian's three favourite braised recipes: Oxtail with Sausages, Minced Beef Parmentier and his Cold Spiced Beef Brisket (overleaf).

Oxtail with Sausages was a childhood favourite of Adrian's. His gran would make extra, add fresh field mushrooms and cover it with a suet crust to create a great pie.

Adrian says, 'For an extra special treat, add smoked Cumberland sausages from the Old Smokehouse at Brougham, Cumbria.' He serves this on a bed of creamed potatoes with a hint of garlic, and offers crusty brown bread to dip into the sauce.

2 oxtails (ask your butcher to chop them into pieces)	1 *bouquet garni*
50g (2oz) beef dripping	900g (2lb) Cumberland pork sausages
570ml (1 pint) Basic Beef Stock (p. 13)	salt and freshly ground black pepper (to taste)
150ml (5fl oz) dry white wine	

1. Blanch the oxtail pieces in boiling water for 5 minutes.

2. Heat the dripping in a large flameproof casserole, add the oxtail pieces and simmer for 15 minutes with the casserole lid on.

3. Add the beef stock, wine and *bouquet garni*, cover, and simmer for 3 hours.

4. Brown the Cumberland sausages in a separate pan. Skim the fat off the oxtail casserole, add the sausages, season to taste and braise gently over a low heat for a further hour.

Minced Beef Parmentier

SERVES 6

*U*se the Cold Spiced Beef Brisket (p. 106) or some left-over boiled or braised beef and
serve this with young broad beans in parsley sauce.

450g (1lb) creamy mashed potato, well
   seasoned
3 tablespoons cooking oil
2 large onions, peeled and finely
   chopped

4 beef tomatoes, peeled, de-seeded and
   chopped
900g (2lb) boiled or braised beef, finely
   minced and seasoned
75g (3oz) Gruyère cheese, grated

1. Preheat the oven to Gas Mark 6/200°C/400°F.

2. Spread half the mashed potato over the bottom of a shallow ovenproof dish.

3. Heat the oil in a large frying pan, add the onions and cook for 2 minutes. Add
the tomatoes, cook for a further 2 minutes, then add the seasoned beef. Blend thoroughly and spoon onto the potato base.

4. Cover with the remaining mashed potato, sprinkle with the Gruyère cheese and
bake in the centre of the oven for 25 minutes.

Cold Spiced Beef Brisket

SERVES 10–12

Eight days to complete! And only 20 minutes preparation! But well worth the effort... The method might sound extreme but I can assure you that it does work. This is an Irish recipe which can be served at any time of the year – for picnics, buffets or dinners – but it's especially good for supper with crusty bread, home-made pickles and a glass of good ale.

1.8kg (4lb) lean brisket of beef, boned
275g (10oz) cooking salt
1 carrot, peeled and chopped
1 leek, washed and chopped
1 celery stalk, washed and chopped
1 onion, peeled and sliced

For the spice mixture
4 shallots, peeled and finely diced

4 dried bay leaves, crumbled
1 teaspoon allspice
4 tablespoons brown sugar
1 teaspoon cloves, crushed
1 teaspoon powdered mace
1 teaspoon black peppercorns, crushed
2 teaspoons fresh thyme leaves

1. Wipe all the excess blood off the boned (not rolled) brisket with a clean dry cloth.

2. Place the meat in a suitable container. Take 225g (8oz) of the salt and rub it well into the meat, cover and place in the refrigerator for 24 hours.

3. Mix all the spice mixture ingredients and the remaining salt together in a bowl and remove the meat from the fridge. Rub the mixture into the brisket and repeat every day for 7 days, pouring off any liquid that seeps out of the joint.

4. On the seventh day, when all the spice mixture has been absorbed, carefully roll and tie the joint of beef and place it in a heavy-bottomed pan with a lid. Add enough cold water to just cover the beef, and add the carrot, leek, celery and onion.

5. Gently simmer for 5 hours, then remove the pan from the heat. Leave the brisket in the liquid to cool, lift out, place in a container, press down with a heavy weight and place in the fridge overnight.

Beef with Thyme, Orange & Red Wine

SERVES 8

You must think that I am having a love affair with Nell Gwyn. Well, you're right! I love oranges – and they're full of vitamin C. This is traditionally served with sauerkraut and Red Velvet baby beetroot.

25g (1oz) beef dripping
900g (2lb) stewing beef (fat and gristle removed), diced
100g (4 oz) rindless smoked streaky bacon, cubed
2 large onions, peeled and sliced
3 cloves garlic, peeled and crushed
450g (1lb) potatoes, peeled and diced

225g (8oz) swede, peeled and diced
juice and zest of 2 large oranges
6 tbsp Orange Curaçao
4 sprigs of fresh thyme
salt and ground black pepper (to taste)
150ml (5fl oz) Basic Beef Stock (p. 13)
275ml (10fl oz) good-quality red wine

1. Preheat the oven to Gas Mark 2/150°C/300°F.

2. Heat the dripping in a large flameproof casserole and fry the meat with the bacon until browned all over. Add the onions and garlic, and cook for 4 minutes. Add the rest of the ingredients and bring to the boil.

3. Cover, place in the centre of the oven to simmer for 4 hours, and serve.

AWT's Pickled Tongue

SERVES 4–6

*A*ntony Worrall Thompson's recipe also uses saltpetre (which is available with permission from a chemist), though it is not vital. Serve the tongue sliced thinly with pickles, grain mustard, new potato salad and Creamed Horseradish (p. 26).

75g (3oz) Maldon sea salt	a pinch of cayenne pepper
2 teaspoons freshly ground white pepper	2 tablespoons soft brown sugar
2 teaspoons ground ginger	zest of 2 oranges
½ teaspoon ground cloves	4 cloves garlic, peeled and finely
1 bay leaf, crumbled	chopped
a pinch of nutmeg	1 ox tongue, fat removed
a pinch of paprika	1 tablespoon saltpetre (optional)

1. Mix together the salt, spices, sugar, orange zest and garlic, and rub into the tongue. Dissolve the saltpetre (if using) in 150ml (5fl oz) warm water and pour over the tongue in a non-reactive container (e.g. a glass or china bowl).

2. Press the meat down with a heavy weight and refrigerate for 12 days, turning the meat every 2–3 days.

3. At the end of the marinating period, place the tongue in a large saucepan of cold water and bring to the boil. Discard the water when it reaches boiling point and repeat this process three times. Cover the tongue with cold water again and bring to the boil, reduce the heat and simmer gently for 2 hours or until the meat is tender. Allow to cool slightly, then remove the tongue to a cutting board and carefully peel off the skin.

4. Return the tongue to the cooking liquor to cool completely.

Below is an 1856 Hamburg recipe for pickling beef or tongue:

PICKLED TONGUE

✦

Ingredients: 6 quarts water; 9lb common salt; ¾lb coarse sugar, 6oz saltpetre.
Method: Boil all the ingredients together, skim clear. When cold put in the beef or tongues. Keep them well-covered with the liquor 8 or 9 days; they will then be fit for use but may be kept longer if wished. The liquor can be boiled and skimmed once a month, and used again and again, fresh being added to it when necessary.

Braised Steak & Onions in Whisky Sauce

SERVES 6

I often wonder whatever happened to the chefs I taught this recipe to while I was work-ing in Burns country (Ayrshire) – Alister McGovern, and Tony Smith, who I believe now works in Malta. The sauce in this recipe is thickened using thin slices of haggis, then strained before serving. I devised this for Burns Night in 1973 from an original 1840s recipe. You can replace the whisky with your favourite spirit or liqueur if you wish. Serve it with freshly cooked broccoli and great British chunky chips.

3 tablespoons cooking oil
4 × 225g (8oz) braising steaks, fat and
   gristle removed
50g (2oz) flour, seasoned
450g (1lb) (peeled weight) baby onions
   or shallots, sliced

175g (6oz) haggis, thinly sliced
150ml (5fl oz) Basic Beef Stock (p. 13)
100ml (4fl oz) whisky
1 teaspoon Worcester sauce
salt and freshly ground black pepper (to
   taste)

1. Preheat the oven to Gas Mark 2/150°C/300°F.

2. Heat the oil in a large frying pan. Coat the steaks in the seasoned flour and brown them on both sides, cooking for about 3 minutes each side.

3. Lift them into a large deep casserole and sprinkle with the sliced baby onions or shallots.

4. Slowly fry the haggis in the steak juices, breaking the slices up. Add the beef stock and whisky and cook for 10 minutes. Add the Worcester sauce, taste, then sea-son with salt and pepper.

5. Strain the sauce through a fine sieve over the steak and onions. Cover the casse-role with a lid or cooking foil, place in the centre of the oven, cook for 2 hours until the meat is very tender, and serve.

Braised Beef with Chestnuts & Beetroot

SERVES 6

This recipe from Nigel Smith makes a really good alternative for Christmas. The flavour of chestnuts and Red Velvet beetroot is so striking, garnished with shallots tossed in honey and served with baby roast potatoes.

450g (1lb) fresh chestnuts, with slits cut in their skins
25g (1oz) butter
2 tablespoons olive oil
3 rindless bacon rashers, chopped
900g (2lb) stewing steak, trimmed and cut into 5cm (2 inch) cubes
1 tablespoon plain flour

275ml (10fl oz) red wine
275ml (10fl oz) Basic Beef Stock (p. 13)
salt and freshly ground black pepper (to taste)
14 shallots, peeled
2 tablespoons clear honey, warmed
225g (8oz) ready-cooked Red Velvet beetroot

1. Preheat the oven to Gas Mark 3/170°C/325°F.

2. Cook the chestnuts in salted boiling water for about 5 minutes. Peel off the outer skins and set on one side.

3.. Heat the butter and olive oil in a flameproof casserole, add the bacon and steak, and cook for 5 minutes. Sprinkle with the plain flour, add the red wine and beef stock, season and bring to the boil. Toss in the chestnuts, cover tightly with a lid or cooking foil, and bake in the centre of the oven for 2 hours.

4. About 15 minutes before the end of the cooking time, remove the lid or foil from the casserole. Place the shallots and honey in a frying pan and cook slowly for 5 minutes. Turn off the heat under the pan and alternate shallots and cooked beetroot around the top of the casserole. Return to the oven, uncovered, for the last 15 minutes, and serve.

Braised Steak & Shallots in Wild Mushroom & Ginger Sauce

SERVES 6–8

A taste of the Orient. Use only fresh ginger for this recipe, not powdered. For added flavour, toss in some chopped spring onions, cinnamon stick and lemon grass. Serve with wild rice.

6 tablespoons sesame oil (see Chef's Tip, p. 87)

900g (2lb) braising steak (fat and gristle removed), diced

50g (2oz) flour, seasoned

450g (1lb) (peeled weight) shallots, sliced

450g (1lb) wild mushrooms, roughly chopped

275ml (10fl oz) Basic Beef Stock (p. 13)

2 tablespoons Worcester sauce

1 tablespoon clear honey

2 tablespoons grated fresh root ginger

salt and freshly ground black pepper (to taste)

150ml (5fl oz) plain yoghurt

1. Preheat the oven to Gas Mark 2/150°C/300°F.

2. Heat the oil in a large frying pan. Coat the meat in the seasoned flour and brown it all over, cooking it for about 5 minutes. Lift it into a large, deep ovenproof casserole.

3. Slowly fry the shallots and mushrooms in the steak juices. Add the beef stock, Worcester sauce, honey and fresh ginger. Taste, then season with salt and pepper.

4. Pour the sauce over the steak, cover the casserole with a lid or cooking foil, place in the centre of the oven and cook for 2 hours until the meat is very tender. Add the yoghurt, cook for a further 10 minutes, and serve.

Braised Silverside of Beef with Olives

SERVES 6–8

Not everyone likes olives, so you can replace them with baby pickled onions for a sour taste if you wish. Serve this with fresh pasta and garlic bread.

900g (2lb) silverside of beef, cut into 5cm (2 inch) cubes
25g (1oz) flour, seasoned
25g (1oz) beef dripping
2 onions, peeled and sliced
1 clove garlic, peeled and crushed
3 juniper berries, crushed
100g (4oz) pitted black olives

1 tablespoon brandy
a sprig of fresh thyme
1 sage leaf
275ml (10fl oz) Basic Beef Stock (p. 13)
salt and freshly ground black pepper (to taste)
1 large green pepper, de-seeded and sliced

1. Preheat the oven to Gas Mark 3/170°C/325°F.

2. Toss the meat in the seasoned flour. Heat the dripping in a flameproof casserole with a lid. Brown the floured beef in the dripping for 3 minutes. Add the onions and garlic and cook for a further 2 minutes.

3. Add the crushed juniper berries, black olives, brandy, thyme, sage leaf and beef stock, and cook for 6 minutes. Season with salt and pepper, place a piece of cooking foil over the casserole and then the lid, and cook in the centre of the oven for 2 hours.

4. About 30 minutes before the end of the cooking time, add the green pepper, blending it into the casserole, and return to the oven. After 30 minutes, remove the thyme and sage leaf, and serve.

Red Hot Beef Curry

SERVES 6

I am a great lover of curries, so I have included seven of my favourites in this section. The longer you keep them, the better they taste. Never overcook the meat when making a curry and always allow it to rest for 24 hours before you actually eat it.

You might look at the list of ingredients and think it would be cheaper and easier to buy a curry paste or sauce and throw the beef into it. No. The true art of cookery means putting time and patience into something that cannot be replaced by a jar or a packet.

900g (2lb) rump steak, cut into 2.5cm
  (1 inch) cubes
50g (2oz) flour, seasoned with salt,
  freshly ground black pepper and
  1 teaspoon paprika
1 onion, peeled and sliced
450g (1lb) shallots, peeled and chopped
1 red and 1 green pepper, de-seeded
  and chopped
2 tablespoons olive oil
25g (1oz) butter
1 tablespoon paprika

1 tablespoon Tabasco sauce
1 teaspoon of each of the following:
  grated fresh ginger, chilli powder,
  ground cardamom, crushed cloves,
  ground cinnamon, ground cumin,
  ground coriander
2 tablespoons tomato purée
275ml (10fl oz) Basic Beef Stock (p. 13)
150ml (5fl oz) claret
1 × 400g (14oz) tin chopped tomatoes
150ml (5fl oz) soured cream
a sprig of parsley

1. Toss the meat in the seasoned flour, generously.

2. In a flameproof casserole, fry the onion, shallots and peppers in the olive oil and butter for 3 minutes. Add the meat and cook for a further 4 minutes. Sprinkle with the paprika, Tabasco, ginger, chilli, cardamom, cloves, cinnamon, cumin and coriander, and let it rest for 4 hours.

3. Preheat the oven to Gas Mark 3/170°C/325°F.

4. Add the tomato purée, beef stock, claret and chopped tomatoes. Cover and cook in the centre of the oven for 3 hours.

5. Remove the casserole from the oven, and leave it to stand for 24 hours. Reheat, add the soured cream, garnish with the parsley, and serve.

Beef & Coconut Curry

SERVES 6–8

Serve this with garlic naan bread. For a special party, spoon it into coconut shells and serve with a selection of popadums and pickles.

900g (2lb) rump steak, cut into 2.5cm (1 inch) cubes

50g (2oz) flour, seasoned with salt, freshly ground black pepper and 1 teaspoon paprika

1 onion, peeled and sliced

450g (1lb) shallots, peeled and chopped

1 red and 1 green pepper, de-seeded and chopped

2 tablespoons olive oil

25g (1oz) butter

1 tablespoon paprika

1 tablespoon Tabasco sauce

1 teaspoon of each of the following: grated fresh ginger, chilli powder, ground cardamom, crushed cloves, ground cinnamon, ground cumin, ground coriander

5 tablespoons tinned coconut milk

8 tablespoons creamed coconut

1 tablespoon tomato purée

275ml (10fl oz) Basic Beef Stock (p. 13)

150ml (5fl oz) soured cream

1 tablespoon chopped fresh parsley

1. Toss the meat in the seasoned flour, generously.

2. In a flameproof casserole, fry the onion, shallots and peppers in the olive oil and butter for 3 minutes. Add the meat and cook for a further 4 minutes. Add the paprika, Tabasco, ginger, chilli, cardamom, cloves, cinnamon, cumin, coriander, coconut milk and creamed coconut and let it rest for 2 hours.

3. Preheat the oven to Gas Mark 3/170°C/325°F.

4. Add the tomato purée and beef stock, cover and cook in the centre of the oven for 3 hours.

5. Let it stand for 24 hours. Reheat, add the soured cream and serve hot, sprinkled with the chopped parsley.

Creamy Beef & Wild Mushroom Curry

SERVES 6–8

If you don't like wild mushrooms, use button or oyster mushrooms instead. Serve this with wild rice.

3 tablespoons cooking oil

900g (2lb) braising steak (fat and gristle removed), diced

50g (2oz) flour, seasoned

450g (1lb) wild mushrooms, roughly chopped

275ml (10fl oz) Basic Beef Stock (p. 13)

2 tablespoons Worcester sauce

10 tablespoons creamed coconut

1 tablespoon paprika

1 tablespoon Tabasco sauce

1 teaspoon of each of the following: grated fresh ginger, chilli powder, ground cardamom, crushed cloves, ground cinnamon, ground cumin, ground coriander

5 tablespoons tinned coconut milk

150ml (5fl oz) double cream

salt and freshly ground black pepper (to taste)

1. Preheat the oven to Gas Mark 2/150°C/300°F.

2. Heat the oil in a large frying pan. Coat the meat in the seasoned flour and brown it all over, cooking for about 6 minutes. Lift the meat into a large deep casserole.

3. Slowly fry the mushrooms in the steak juices. Add the beef stock, Worcester sauce and the rest of the ingredients, except the double cream. Season well with salt and pepper.

4. Pour the sauce over the steak, cover the casserole with a lid or cooking foil, place in the centre of the oven and cook for 2 hours until the meat is very tender. Add the double cream, cook for a further 10 minutes and serve.

Garlic Beef Curry with Apple & Sultanas

SERVES 6–8

You can also use pineapple, mango or pears in this recipe, and garnish it with some seedless grapes. Serve it with Patna rice, naan bread and mango chutney.

3 tablespoons cooking oil
900g (2lb) rump steak (fat and gristle removed), diced
50g (2oz) flour, seasoned
450g (1lb) shallots, peeled and roughly chopped
4 cloves garlic, peeled and crushed with a little olive oil
3 cooking apples, peeled, cored and diced

100g (4oz) sultanas
1 tablespoon clear honey
275ml (10fl oz) Basic Beef Stock (p. 13)
2 tablespoons Worcester sauce
3 tablespoons hot curry paste
salt and freshly ground black pepper (to taste)
150ml (5fl oz) soured cream

1. Preheat the oven to Gas Mark 4/180°C/350°F.

2. Heat the oil in a large frying pan. Coat the meat in the seasoned flour and brown it all over, cooking for about 6 minutes. Lift the meat into a large deep casserole.

3. Slowly fry the shallots, garlic, apples and sultanas in the steak juices. Add the honey, beef stock, Worcester sauce and curry paste. Taste, then season with salt and pepper.

4. Pour the sauce over the steak, cover the casserole with a lid or cooking foil, place in the centre of the oven and cook for 2 hours until the meat is very tender. Add the soured cream, cook for a further 15 minutes and serve.

Hot Beef Curry with Lime & Rosemary

SERVES 6–8

The flavours of the lime, chillies and potatoes, combined with the rosemary, give this curry a unique taste. Serve with a vegetable curry and rice or naan.

4 tablespoons groundnut oil

2 large onions, peeled and sliced

900g (2lb) rump steak (fat and gristle removed), diced

50g (2oz) flour, seasoned

4 cloves garlic, peeled and crushed with a little olive oil

4 tomatoes, chopped

juice and zest of 1 lime

2 green chillies, finely chopped

3 large potatoes, peeled and diced

1 teaspoon crushed fresh rosemary leaves

1 teaspoon garam masala

275ml (10fl oz) Basic Beef Stock (p. 13)

2 tablespoons Worcester sauce

3 tablespoons Tabasco sauce

salt and freshly ground black pepper (to taste)

a sprig of fresh rosemary

150g (5oz) fromage frais

1. Preheat the oven to Gas Mark 4/180°C/350°F.

2. Heat the oil in a large frying pan. Coat the onions and meat in the seasoned flour and brown all over, cooking for about 6 minutes. Lift them into a large deep casserole.

3. Slowly fry the garlic, tomatoes, lime juice, zest, chillies, potatoes, rosemary and garam masala in the steak juices. Add the beef stock, Worcester sauce and Tabasco. Taste, then season with salt and pepper, finally adding the sprig of rosemary.

4. Pour the sauce over the steak and onions, cover the casserole with a lid or cooking foil, place in the centre of the oven and cook for 2 hours until the meat is very tender. Remove the sprig of rosemary, add the fromage frais, cook for a further 10 minutes and serve.

Champagne & Beef Curry

SERVES 8

I have been a great curry fan ever since I met Pat Chapman. He is a real wizard when it comes to curries. He told me to experiment and not to follow trends … Try this with chapattis and naan bread.

4 tablespoons sunflower oil

3 onions, peeled and finely chopped

a 2.5cm (1 inch) piece fresh root ginger, peeled and grated

2 green chillies, finely chopped

4 tablespoons garlic, crushed with a little groundnut oil and salt

2 tablespoons ground coriander

1 teaspoon ground cumin

1 teaspoon ground cinnamon

1 teaspoon ground fenugreek

900g (2lb) best sirloin of beef, cubed

seasoned flour

4 tablespoons rose petal vinegar (p. 48)

150ml (5fl oz) guava juice

150ml (5fl oz) champagne (drink the rest while cooking!)

275ml (10fl oz) Rich Beef Stock (p. 14)

salt and freshly ground black pepper (to taste)

1 tablespoon garam masala

4 tablespoons natural yoghurt

3 tablespoons chopped fresh coriander

1. Heat the sunflower oil in a large pan. Add the onions, ginger, chillies, garlic, coriander, cumin, cinnamon and fenugreek, and cook for 2 minutes. Meanwhile, toss the meat in the seasoned flour, add to the pan, and brown for 5 minutes.

2. Add the vinegar, guava juice and champagne, and cook for 15 minutes over a low heat, stirring every 5 minutes. Add the beef stock, cover and simmer for 2 hours, stirring every 15 minutes.

3. Taste, season with salt and pepper, add the garam masala, and blend. Stir in the yoghurt and coriander, and serve.

OPPOSITE Barbecued Sirloin Steaks with Herb Butters – parsley (page 124), pink peppercorn (page 125) and lemon (page 124)

Persian Royal Beef Korma

SERVES 6–8

This recipe was taught to me by Ramon Kapoor who is not just a man of knowledge but the owner of one of the finest Indian restaurants in Europe, The Gaylord in Manchester. There, time stands still, curries are made using traditional methods, and his naan bread is to die for. Served with rice, naan and chapattis, this really is a beautiful recipe.

900g (2lb) rump steak, cut into 2.5cm (1 inch) cubes
275ml (10fl oz) double cream
½ teaspoon garam masala

For the korma paste
6 cloves garlic, peeled
a 2.5cm (1 inch) piece fresh root ginger, peeled and coarsely chopped
50g (2oz) blanched almonds
6 tablespoons Basic Beef Stock (p. 13)

1 teaspoon ground cardamom
4 cloves, crushed
1 teaspoon ground cinnamon
2 large onions, peeled and chopped
1 teaspoon coriander seeds
2 teaspoons ground cumin
a pinch of cayenne
salt and freshly ground black pepper (to taste)
6 tablespoons sunflower oil

1. Place all the ingredients for the korma paste in a blender or food processor and thoroughly blend together until you get a very smooth paste.

2. Coat the beef with the mixture, cover and place in the fridge for 6 hours.

3. Slowly simmer the meat in a large saucepan, adding a little more beef stock if required. Simmer for 35 minutes, add the cream and garam masala and simmer for a further 30 minutes. Allow the korma to stand for 10 minutes before serving.

OPPOSITE Mexican T-Bone Steak Supreme (page 135)

CHAPTER 4

Grilling and Barbecuing

✦

Grilling and barbecuing have a great deal in common. I like the flavour of bar-becued food, and I am sure these open-air cookery sessions bring out the macho male in every man – when he can be chef for a day! Marinades are really an essen-tial part of grilling and barbecuing so this section begins with a selection of mari-nades, sauces and herb butters.

The most popular barbecue food is beef, and sirloin is the most widely used cut. Always buy British beef – it is by far the best to use on a barbecue, especially for the 'boy scout' chefs. *Never* use frozen meat – always use fresh. And if you really have to use frozen meat, please make sure that it's properly thawed out beforehand. (Allow it to defrost for at least 8 hours at room temperature.)

When cooking meat, cut off any excess fat to prevent too much fat dripping into the grill or barbecue and causing it to flare up. If you are preparing a joint, always use a meat thermometer to ensure it is cooked properly (see p. 42).

To prevent steaks curling, cut them at 0.5cm (¼ inch) intervals into the fat edge. I also recommend that you turn the steaks frequently to keep the meat moist.

Porterhouse, a thick steak cut from the chump end of the sirloin and containing part of the fillet, is my own favourite piece of meat for the grill or barbecue. I like it to be about 2.5cm (1 inch) thick, well seasoned and cooked medium rare.

When using minced beef for barbecues, make sure that the meat is not a cheap cut. It should be lean, with the Meat and Livestock Commission's Minced Beef Quality Mark, or the British Meat Quality Standard for Beefburgers which are made in the UK, using only regular cuts from prime cattle less than 30 months old, and are offal-free.

Another popular cut of meat is T-bone, which is cut on the bone, from between the chump end and the wing rib. Rump is excellent for grilling and barbecuing; it should have 0.5cm (¼ inch) of fat on the outside edge which you must cut at 0.5cm (¼ inch) intervals to stop it curling.

And finally fillet, lean and boneless, that slightly more expensive cut: this should be cut into 225–275g (8–10oz) portions and always lightly grilled or pan-fried. If it is barbecued, it should be undercooked.

All meat should be put on the barbecue when the coals turn white-grey and the heat registers 180–200°C/350–400°F. When cooking steaks, sear them on both sides very quickly to hold in the juices and the flavour. Grill to the degree you like your steak. Always season well with sea salt and freshly ground black pepper. Cooking time for each side depends on the thickness of the steak.

Marinated steaks will not stick to the grill if you brush them lightly with oil on both sides before cooking.

Marinades, Sauces & Bastes

Marinades are vitally important – not only for flavour but also for tenderising the tougher and less expensive cuts of meat. The length of time required for marinating varies but you should always use china or glass bowls because of the acid content which could cause a reaction in a metal container.

There are three basic marinades for meat. Besides adding flavour, they prevent the meat getting too dry on the surface. All meats cook easier and taste better for being marinated. I am sure you have your favourite herbs, wine and fruits – do not be afraid to use them in your marinades whenever you like. That is the fun of barbecuing – you can experiment and create your own recipes. This section just offers a few guidelines and suggestions.

I marinate my meat for two days before using it. You might leave it for three days; it is quite safe to do so. But always keep it in a refrigerator and bring it out about 3 hours before cooking.

Forerib and Silverside Marinade

For a 1.3kg (3lb) forerib or silverside. Add crushed fennel seeds to this mixture for barbecued ribs of any kind, and add your favourite wine or herb.

225ml (8fl oz) red wine	½ tablespoon freshly ground black pepper
100ml (4fl oz) cooking oil	2 bay leaves
1 large onion, peeled and sliced	1 teaspoon pink peppercorns
2 cloves garlic, peeled and crushed	1 *bouquet garni*
½ tablespoon salt	1 teaspoon English mustard

1. Mix all the ingredients together in a glass or china bowl.

2. Place the meat in the marinade, making sure the meat is covered. Refrigerate for at least 24 hours, turning the meat every 6 hours.

Marinade for Carbonnade

Using a 1.3kg (3lb) rump, diced or sliced, this would serve 8–10 people.

570ml (1 pint) red wine
275ml (10fl oz) cider
225g (8oz) onions, peeled and sliced
225g (8oz) carrots, peeled and sliced
100g (4oz) celery stalks, washed and
    sliced
50g (2oz) parsley stalks, washed and
    chopped

1 tablespoon black peppercorns
a sprig of thyme
2 bay leaves
4 tablespoons garlic vinegar (available
    from supermarkets)
1 teaspoon salt

1. Mix all the ingredients together in a very large glass or earthenware bowl.

2. Pour over the beef and leave to marinate for 5 hours at least, turning occasionally. Leave it for 24–48 hours, if you can, for perfect results.

Fillet and Sirloin of Beef Marinade

This marinade will cover 6–8 × 275g (10oz) sirloin or fillet steaks.

225ml (8fl oz) red wine
100ml (4fl oz) cooking oil
1 small onion, peeled and sliced
1 bay leaf

½ teaspoon salt
1 tablespoon white peppercorns
1 clove garlic, peeled and crushed
1 teaspoon five spice powder

1. Mix all the ingredients together in a glass or china bowl, then marinate the meat for at least 12 hours, turning from time to time.

2. Add your favourite wine, herb and fruit if you wish.

Sirloins with Lemon & Chive Marinade Sauce

SERVES 6

This recipe makes use of the marinade to create a delicious tangy sauce. Serve with minted Jersey Royal potatoes.

6 × 250g (9oz) sirloin steaks, trimmed

For the marinade
225ml (8fl oz) white wine
4 tablespoons cooking oil
1 onion, peeled and sliced
1 carrot, peeled and sliced
1 celery stalk, washed and sliced
1 bay leaf
1 teaspoon white peppercorns
3 tablespoons fresh lemon juice

1 teaspoon fresh lime juice
1 tablespoon snipped fresh chives

For the sauce
1 tablespoon cornflour, blended with
  3 tablespoons milk
150ml (5fl oz) double cream
zest of 1 lemon
1 lemon, sliced
1 tablespoon snipped fresh chives

1. Mix all the marinade ingredients together in a glass or china bowl, and place the sirloin steaks in the marinade for at least 4 hours. Then grill the steaks for 4 minutes on either side.

2. Meanwhile, sieve the marinade into a saucepan and boil rapidly for 4 minutes. Add the cornflour paste, cream and lemon zest, and boil slowly for 2 minutes.

3. Pour the sauce over the steaks, garnish with slices of lemon and snipped chives, and serve.

Barbecued Sirloin Steaks with Herb Butter

Steaks and herb butters are a beautiful combination as well as being simple and quick to make. Here are a few tips and suggestions for making your own herb butters. Steaks in foil are excellent with herb butters, because they marinate while cooking. Serving herb butter from small butter dishes is popular at the moment. Herb butters can also be spread onto French sticks, wrapped in foil, placed on the grill for 5 minutes and served hot or cold.

It is best to use a 225g (8oz) pack of butter. After you have prepared it, shape it into a large sausage, wrap it in greaseproof paper or cooking foil and refrigerate until required. This amount of butter can be used on 8 x 275g (10oz) sirloin, fillet or rump steaks.

To make the following butters, place 225g (8oz) softened unsalted butter in a large bowl and beat in the ingredients listed:

Almond Butter: 100g (4oz) ground almonds, 1 teaspoon lemon juice, salt and pepper

Garlic Butter: 4 large garlic coves, peeled and crushed with a little salt and pepper

Mustard Butter: 2 tablespoons of your favourite mustard (paste or dried)

Herb Butter: 2 tablespoons of your favourite chopped fresh herb, 1 tablespoon lemon juice, salt and pepper

Lemon Butter: juice and zest of 1 lemon

Beurre Noir (or Black Butter Sauce): 2 tablespoons chopped fresh parsley, 3 tablespoons capers and 3 tablespoons white wine vinegar

Parsley Butter: 2 tablespoons finely chopped fresh parsley, 1 teaspoon lemon juice, salt and pepper

Lobster or Shrimp Butter: 3 tablespoons lobster tail or shrimps, finely chopped and pounded with the butter, 1 teaspoon anchovy paste, a little lemon juice and cayenne pepper

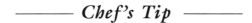

——— Chef's Tip ———

For a spiced butter, simply add 1 tablespoon of your favourite spice, e.g. curry powder, Tabasco sauce, or chilli powder. This is also one of the easiest ways of flavouring your steaks in foil.

The Pink Peppercorn Steak

SERVES 8

*S*erve this with new potatoes and a salad.

225g (8oz) unsalted butter, softened	1 teaspoon virgin olive oil
100g (4oz) pink peppercorns	1 teaspoon celery salt
1 teaspoon lemon juice	freshly ground black pepper (to taste)
1 teaspoon balsamic vinegar	8 × 225g (8oz) sirloin steaks, trimmed

1. Place the softened butter, peppercorns, lemon juice, vinegar, olive oil, celery salt and freshly ground black pepper in a bowl. Blend the ingredients thoroughly.

2. Season the steaks and barbecue them to your taste. Coat each steak with 25g (1oz) butter and serve immediately.

Creole Noisettes of English Beef H.R.H.

SERVES 10

*O*ne of H.R.H. Prince Andrew's favourite meats is beef, and I cooked several beef dishes for him while I was Executive Chef at Wembley Stadium and Wembley Arena. I was taught this recipe in San Francisco and cooked it several times while I was in Ireland and at Wembley for Prince Andrew during the World Badminton Championships. So this English beef recipe really has travelled the world! Serve with English mustard and a crisp salad of exotic leaves.

10 × 175g (6oz) noisettes of fillet of beef	50ml (2fl oz) dark soy sauce
	4 cloves garlic, peeled and crushed
For the marinade	3 tablespoons concentrated orange juice
50ml (2fl oz) vegetable oil	salt and freshly ground black pepper (to taste)
150ml (5fl oz) dry sherry	
6 teaspoons demerara sugar	a pinch of fennel seed

1. Put all the marinade ingredients in a glass or china bowl, mixing them thoroughly. Place the noisettes of beef in the marinade, covering all the meat, and let it stand for 6 hours at room temperature.

2. Place the noisettes on the barbecue and cook to your liking on each side, basting them with the marinade.

Beefburgers from Around the World

Anyone who loves beef will enjoy a really good-quality beefburger, yet several well-known so-called hamburger restaurants do not sell a 100% per cent beefburger. An exception to the rule are the Starvin Marvin diners, as I know the butcher and the very high quality of meat he supplies to this chain.

I have heard numerous stories about the beefburger and that it was introduced to England from America in the 1950s when the Wimpy Bar boom started. Being a food historian, it is my job to put my neck on the line!

The hamburger originated, without doubt, in Europe. Indeed, it gets its name from the German city of Hamburg. An early hamburger recipe was sent to me by my favourite British lady cook, Veronica Shaw, who is the proprietor of Veronica's Restaurant and Shaw Food Catering Services. Veronica, like me, enjoys researching recipes from earlier centuries, and serves her customers traditional British food, using only the freshest ingredients, in her delightful restaurant in London.

The recipe Veronica sent me was by Hannah Woolley, who wrote *The Accomplish'd Lady's Delight* (printed in London by B. Harris and sold at his shop at the Stationer's Arms in Swithins Rents by the Royal Exchange in 1675). In her letter, Veronica says, 'Is this our earliest hamburger recipe? Maybe it was taken to the States.' My feeling is that it was taken from Germany around 1650, translated into English and used in Great Britain from around 1670.

One of the greatest authorities on hamburgers was James Beard who I had the pleasure of meeting several years ago in the USA. He wrote several very well-known cookery books and he recalled that the first hamburger with a bun was served with a topping of fried onions during a world fair around 1911. One of the first hamburger shops to start a chain was Yaw's in Portland, Oregon. The boom in America started in the 1920s when a hamburger was first cooked to order and served on a toasted bun, with butter, relish, onion, tomato, sliced dill pickle, lettuce with a layer of mayonnaise on top and tomato ketchup on the base, at a cost of 12 cents or 6 English pennies.

Now a truly universal food, this book would not be complete without a section on this famous entrée, with recipes from Veronica Shaw, Antony Worrall Thompson, Colin Capon, Paul Reed and my collection from over the years.

Just a small request here: *please* use baguettes, naan bread or pitta bread instead of those boring buns with bird seed on top … or go one step further and use my recipe for Cheesy Burger Baps (*opposite*).

Tom's Cheesy Burger Baps

Should you want to use these baps for sausages, simply shape into a sausage (or finger roll) shape. If you are a lover of garlic baps, add 3 cloves of crushed garlic when mixing the dry ingredients.

575g (1¼lb) strong white flour
25g (1oz) dried milk powder
½ teaspoon salt
½ teaspoon sugar
25g (1oz) white shortening (vegetable fat)

225g (8oz) Cheddar cheese, grated
25g (1oz) fresh yeast
1 egg, beaten with 1 tablespoon milk
1 tablespoon poppy seeds

1. Sift the flour, milk powder and salt together into a large clean glass or china bowl. Add the sugar, shortening and cheese, blending them together thoroughly.

2. Dissolve the yeast with 350ml (12fl oz) warm water. Add this to the flour ingredients and mix them well for 4 minutes.

3. Cover the dough with a warm damp cloth and place in a very warm area for 50 minutes.

4. Lightly grease 3 baking trays. Divide the mixture into 12–14 small balls, or 8 large balls for larger baps. Place them at least 7.5cm (3 inches) apart on the trays and, with the heel of your hand, gently push into a burger bun shape. Cover again with warm damp cloths and place in a warm area for a further 40 minutes.

5. Preheat the oven to Gas Mark 7/220°C/425°F.

6. Remove the cloths carefully, glaze the tops with the egg and milk, sprinkle with poppy seeds, and bake in the centre of the oven for 30 minutes. Remove the baps from the oven and let them rest for at least 10 minutes before serving.

HANNAH WOOLLEY'S BURGER RECIPE

◆

Take sives [chives], parsley, thyme, marjoram & Roast 3 or 4 eggs hard and a quantity of mutton suet, Chop fine altogether & season it with cloves, mace, ginger, sugar and cinnamon and a little salt. Then fry them with a little sweet butter.

Hannah Woolley, from *The Accomplish'd Lady's Delight* (London, 1675)

Veronica's Seventeenth-Century Beefburgers

SERVES 4

Veronica Shaw (who runs Veronica's Restaurant, Hereford Road, London) adapted this recipe from Hannah Woolley's original version. Serve them with my Cheesy Burger Baps (p. 127).

450g (1lb) lean organic minced beef
4 tablespoons chopped fresh mixed herbs (e.g. chives, parsley, marjoram and thyme)
4 hard-boiled free-range eggs, shelled and chopped
1 tablespoon chopped capers
2 tablespoons chopped marinated anchovy fillets
1 teaspoon ground ginger
½ teaspoon ground nutmeg
1 teaspoon brown sugar
1 teaspoon ground cinnamon
¼ teaspoon ground cloves
sea salt and freshly ground black pepper (to taste)
1 egg, beaten
2 tablespoons olive oil

1. Put all the ingredients, except the olive oil, in a large bowl and blend them thoroughly.

2. Let the mixture stand at room temperature for 3 hours, then shape into 4 × 100g (4oz) burgers.

3. Heat the oil in a frying pan and fry for 6 minutes on each side, or barbecue for the same time.

AWT's Spiced Mediterranean Burgers

SERVES 8

Anthony Worrall Thompson is well known for his vast knowledge of Mediterranean cuisine and he never does anything by halves. Try these minced beef and lamb burgers served in split hot pitta bread or small baguette rolls.

8 small baguette rolls or pitta breads

For the burgers
450g (1lb) finely minced beef
450g (1lb) finely minced lamb
½ onion, peeled and finely grated
1 teaspoon finely chopped garlic
1 tablespoon extra virgin olive oil
2 tablespoons chopped flat leaf parsley
1 tablespoon chopped fresh coriander
1 teaspoon dried oregano
½ teaspoon ground cinnamon

½ teaspoon ground cumin
1 teaspoon chilli sauce
½ teaspoon freshly ground black pepper

For the garnish
8 shallots, peeled and thinly sliced,
  mixed with chopped flat leaf parsley
4 beef tomatoes, thinly sliced
a few whole fresh coriander leaves
150ml (5fl oz) plain Greek yoghurt (*not*
  ordinary yoghurt)

1. Preheat the barbecue or grill.

2. Place the burger ingredients in a large bowl and blend the mixture with your hands, being careful not to overwork it.

3. Form the mixture into 8 long oval sausage shapes, about 2.5cm (1 inch) thick.

4. Chargrill, grill or fry the burgers for about 5 minutes on each side for rare, or to your taste.

5. Split the rolls or pitta breads without completely cutting through. Remove some of the bread from the centre of the rolls. Place the burgers in the rolls or pitta bread and garnish with the shallots, flat leaf parsley, tomatoes, coriander and Greek yoghurt.

Tom's Ultimate Whopper Burgers

SERVES 4–6

A whopping double beef and pork burger with everything on it, served with jacket pota-
toes. The importance of the peppermill is quite obvious when biting into a home-made burger.

2 large onions, peeled and sliced
a little oil
4–6 large Cheesy Burger Baps (p. 127)

For the burgers
560g (1¼lb) minced beef fillet
560g (1¼lb) minced pork
3 large onions, peeled and finely
   chopped
100g (4oz) fresh breadcrumbs
2 tablespoons chopped fresh coriander

2 tablespoons Worcester sauce
salt and freshly ground black pepper (to
   taste)

For the filling
4 slices Lancashire cheese
4 tablespoons English mustard
4 tablespoons mayonnaise
shredded lettuce
2 beef tomatoes, sliced
4 tablespoons chopped fresh coriander

1. Put the minced beef and pork, chopped onions, breadcrumbs, coriander and
Worcester sauce in a large bowl and mix well. Season well with salt and pepper, and
shape into 8–12 burgers.

2. Grill the burgers until they are cooked – about 6 minutes on each side. Fry the
sliced onions in a little oil, split the baps and toast them gently on the barbecue.

3. Place the bottom half of each bap on a serving plate. Place some cooked onion
on the bottom, followed by a burger, a slice of cheese, some English mustard, another
burger, mayonnaise, shredded lettuce, tomato and coriander, and top with the top
half of the cheesy bap.

Basic American Beefburgers

SERVES 4

This is a typical American burger mix and can be used as the basis for any burger.

1 small onion, peeled and chopped
a little butter
450g (1lb) good quality British minced
   beef

2 egg yolks
1 teaspoon salt and freshly ground black
   pepper (mixed)
3 tablespoons fine breadcrumbs

1. Fry the onion in a little butter until soft. Put the meat and onion in a bowl with the rest of the ingredients and blend them together thoroughly.

2. Shape into 4 burgers, and fry, grill or barbecue for about 5 minutes on each side.

To make the following beefburgers, use the Basic American Beefburger recipe and method, and add the ingredients listed:

Portuguese: 50g (2oz) tomato purée, 1 teaspoon Tabasco sauce, 1 tablespoon chopped fresh parsley

Swedish: 1 tablespoon tarragon vinegar, 4 tablespoons double cream, 2 tablespoons finely chopped capers, 2 finely chopped small pickled beetroot, salt and pepper

Italian: 1 finely chopped large clove garlic, 1 tablespoon Worcester sauce, 6 drops Tabasco sauce, 1 teaspoon dried oregano, salt and pepper

Spanish: 1 crushed clove garlic, 1 tablespoon tomato purée, 2 tablespoons chopped wild mushrooms, a pinch of nutmeg, 1 teaspoon crushed black peppercorns, a pinch of mixed herbs

Irish: 2 peeled and grated potatoes, 2 tablespoons finely chopped fresh parsley, 2 tablespoons Guinness, a drop of Worcester sauce

English Fillet Beefburgers

SERVES 4

This is my idea of a perfect burger. It is essential to season the meat well with salt and freshly ground black pepper. Serve with my Cheesy Burger Baps (p. 127) flavoured with garlic.

8 spring onions, washed, trimmed and finely chopped
1 Bramley cooking apple, peeled, cored and finely chopped
2 tablespoons sunflower oil
450g (1lb) minced beef fillet
75g (3oz) breadcrumbs

1 teaspoon crushed fresh rosemary leaves
1 tablespoon chopped fresh coriander
1 tablespoon tomato purée
salt and freshly ground black pepper (to taste)

1. Fry the spring onions and cooking apple in the oil for 3 minutes.

2. Remove from the heat, allow to cool, put in a bowl with all the remaining ingredients and mix thoroughly.

3. Shape into 4 burgers and grill on the barbecue for 6 minutes on each side.

San Francisco Garlic Burgers

SERVES 4

This is one of my favourite burgers and the one I always make when I have friends to a barby. It's also excellent for pan-frying. Sprinkle the burgers with freshly ground black pepper, and serve with garlic mayonnaise, crisp lettuce and tomato in my Cheesy Burger Baps (p. 127).

4 spring onions, washed, trimmed and finely chopped
100g (4oz) tomato purée
1 tablespoon Worcester sauce
1 clove garlic, peeled and crushed
1 tablespoon brown sugar
3 drops Tabasco sauce

½ teaspoon garlic salt
½ teaspoon lemon juice
a pinch of crushed fennel seed
1 tablespoon chopped fresh coriander
450g (1lb) rough minced sirloin or fillet steak

1. Put all the ingredients, except the minced steak, in a saucepan. Bring to the boil, stirring all the time, and simmer for 5 minutes. Remove from the heat and allow to cool.

2. Add 6 tablespoons of the sauce mixture to the minced steak and blend thoroughly.

3. Shape into 4 burgers and grill on the barbecue for 5 minutes on each side, basting with the remaining sauce.

Macbeth's Aberdeen Angus Beef Special

SERVES 6–8

This will add a classy touch to any barbecue – a bit pricey but worth every pound, shilling and penny. Use only the finest Aberdeen Angus beef and serve it with garlic bread.
For Mike Gibson – enjoy!

900g (2lb) fillet of Macbeth's Aberdeen Angus beef	salt and freshly ground black pepper (to taste)
100g (4oz) any rough pâté	50g (2oz) butter, melted
2 tablespoons chopped fresh chives	150ml (5fl oz) brandy

1. Slice the beef fillet down the centre and plate the pâté and chives along the centre. Fold the fillet over to ensure that the filling does not come out.

2. Place the fillet on a large piece of greased cooking foil, season well with salt and pepper. Pour over the butter and half the brandy, wrap the fillet and seal it very securely in the foil. Cook over the barbecue for 12 minutes.

3. Remove the foil, reserving the juices. Place the fillet on the barbecue and grill until cooked, basting with the juices and finally finishing the basting with the remaining brandy. Carefully slice and serve.

Chateaubriand in Garlic Butter

SERVES 2

Chateaubriand is a thick, diagonally cut steak from the centre of the tenderloin, and your butcher will be only too pleased to cut it for you – it's one of the most expensive cuts of beef. It should always be served rare.

2 cloves garlic, peeled and very finely chopped

100g (4oz) fresh unsalted English butter, softened

2 × 560g (1¼lb) Chateaubriand steaks

salt and freshly ground black pepper (to taste)

1. Mix the finely chopped garlic with the butter and rub half of it into the steak. Season with plenty of freshly ground black pepper and a little salt.

2. Place the steaks on an oiled, preheated grill. Cook and seal on both sides, then baste slowly with the garlic butter until cooked to your liking.

Fillet of Beef with German Mustard & Asbach Brandy

SERVES 4–6

Asbach is a leading make of brandy in Germany and it is ideal for a marinade. It has a very oaky flavour which is excellent for barbecues. Serve this with baked jacket potatoes, and a selection of salads. Paul Heathcote of Simply Heathcotes restaurant serves an excellent chargrilled fillet of beef with a thyme and English mustard crust and an ale sauce. Perhaps that was my inspiration for this recipe.

2 tablespoons German mustard

4 tablespoons cooking oil

1 tot of Asbach brandy

salt and freshly ground black pepper (to taste)

4–6 × 225g (8oz) fillets of beef

6 rashers smoked bacon

6 large beef tomatoes

1. Blend together the mustard, oil, brandy and salt and pepper in a bowl. Add the fillets of beef and leave to marinate for 1 hour.

2. Lift out the fillets, cover again with the marinade and grill to your liking, basting and turning for the last 2 minutes.

3. Grill the bacon and tomatoes and serve with the remaining marinade. Not forgetting some more Asbach!

Mexican T-Bone Steak Supreme

The Tabasco gives the T-bone a real bite – a great start to a barby. The marinade makes enough for one T-bone steak. Increase the quantities according to the number of steaks you want to barbecue. And you can use the same mixture to marinate any other meats that you wish to give this unique spicy flavour.
Serve with a salad of mixed sliced peppers and baked jacket potatoes.

1 × 350g (12oz) T-bone steak per
    person

For the marinade
1 tablespoon tomato purée
2 tablespoons Tabasco sauce
1 teaspoon chilli powder

1 tablespoon American mustard
a pinch of dried basil
2 teaspoons mushroom ketchup
half a glass of port
salt and freshly ground black pepper (to
    taste)

1. Mix all the marinade ingredients in a bowl and then brush the T-bone steaks on both sides with the mixture. Let them stand for 2 hours, then brush them again.

2. Put them on the grill and seal them. Keep brushing them with the mixture until they are cooked to your taste.

OPPOSITE PAGE 134 Sirloins with Lemon and Chive Marinade Sauce (page 123)

OPPOSITE Ribs of Beef in Fennel Sauce (pages 138–9)

Peppered Steaks

SERVES 4

*T*his is a recipe I devised for a bacardi barbecue party at Peter and Lynn Wilkinson's. There are barbecues and barbecues – then someone invented the word Wilkinson and I have never been the same since! Their barby is built of brick and stainless steel. It's massive, with a double grill and a chimney so tall it would make steeplejack Fred Dibnah go dizzy. It's a chef's dream. And Peter and I must hold the world record for cooking at a barbecue – we started at 12 o'clock lunchtime and finished at 2.30am, 14 hours and 30 minutes later! Peter is a real cannibal. He loves his steaks rare and I mean rare! They barely touch the barbecue and then they are served. This recipe is better when they are cooked medium. Serve with hot, crusty garlic bread. Enjoy.

4 × 225g (8oz) sirloin steaks	salt (to taste)
2 tablespoons olive oil	50g (2oz) butter
1 clove garlic, peeled and crushed	1 teaspoon crushed thyme leaves
1 tablespoon English mustard	1 teaspoon Tabasco sauce
4 tablespoons dry British sherry	1 teaspoon clear honey, warmed
2 tablespoons black peppercorns, crushed	1 teaspoon whole black peppercorns
	150ml (5fl oz) double cream

1. Trim any excess fat or gristle off the steaks. Brush them all over with half the oil. Mix the garlic, mustard and half the sherry into a paste. Add the crushed peppercorns and salt and spread the mixture onto the meat on both sides. Leave them to marinate for 2 hours.

2. Place a little oil on the grill bars and cook the steaks for 2 minutes to seal them. Place them on the warm area of the barbecue, or gently shallow fry on a gas ring.

3. Heat the butter, remaining oil and thyme in a small frying pan and cook the steaks in the mixture for 2 minutes on each side.

4. Return to the barbecue and cook to your liking. Add the remaining sherry, the Tabasco, honey, whole black peppercorns and cream to the pan and let the sauce simmer until your steaks are ready. Serve with the steaks.

Los Angeles Steaks with Grilled Aubergine

SERVES 6

The Americans have a great deal to learn from the Brits and we have a great deal to learn from them when it comes to barbecues. They really do know how to throw one. These T-bone steaks must be marinated for at least 24 hours before use.

6 × 350g (12oz) T-bone steaks
3 large aubergines, thinly sliced

For the marinade
salt and freshly ground black pepper
8 cloves garlic, peeled and chopped

4 tablespoons lemon juice
200ml (7fl oz) extra virgin olive oil
4 tablespoons chopped fresh basil
2 tablespoons chopped fresh coriander

1. Place all the marinade ingredients in a large plastic tray and mix thoroughly.

2. Completely coat each T-bone with the marinade, then place the sliced aubergines in the marinade, ensuring that each slice is coated. Leave them on the bottom of the tray, place the T-bones on top, cover with cling film, and refrigerate for 24 hours.

3. Barbecue the steaks to your liking, barbecue the aubergines and serve them together.

Grilled Sirloin with Green Salad

SERVES 4

I also think that the best things in life are simple and a lightly grilled or pan-fried sirloin in a little seasoned olive oil can be very enjoyable, especially when served with a glass of claret.

4 × 225g (8oz) sirloin steaks, trimmed
3 tablespoons olive oil
salt and freshly ground black pepper (to
    taste)

For the green salad
450g (1lb) mixed spinach, watercress,
    radicchio and cos lettuce

50g (2oz) cooked green beans
1 green pepper, de-seeded and thinly
    sliced
juice of 1 lime
2 tablespoons olive oil
salt and freshly ground black pepper (to
    taste)

1. Coat the steaks with oil, season them well, and grill them to your liking.

2. Meanwhile, clean and trim the salad leaves, toss them in a bowl with the rest of the ingredients, and serve with the steak.

Ribs of Beef in Fennel Sauce

SERVES 8

This is excellent served with rice and peppers. Make sure you use very meaty ribs – your butcher will cut them if you ask.

900g (2lb) meaty beef ribs

For the marinade
150ml (5fl oz) olive oil
2 teaspoons lemon juice
1 tablespoon white wine vinegar

1 large onion, peeled and chopped
1 teaspoon fennel seeds, crushed
salt and freshly ground black pepper (to
    taste)
2 tablespoons port

1. Mix all the marinade ingredients together in a bowl and leave the mixture to stand for 2 hours.

2. Add the ribs, completely cover them with the marinade, and chill for a further 3 hours. Barbecue the ribs for about 5 minutes on each side.

3. Pour the marinade into a saucepan, bring it to the boil, reduce and simmer for 10 minutes. Strain through a non-metallic sieve and serve with the barbecued beef ribs.

Ribs of Scottish Beef with Garlic Sauce

SERVES 8

You don't have to use garlic. Try coriander or finely chopped chillies, or a combination of all three. Try serving these ribs with warm bread to dip into the sauce. Have a sprig of fresh parsley at hand to get rid of the smell of garlic from your breath afterwards.

1.8kg (4lb) Aberdeen Angus ribs, cut
  into 7.5cm (3 inch) lengths

For the marinade
3 tablespoons crushed garlic
100ml (4fl oz) soy sauce
100ml (4fl oz) sweet cider
4 tablespoons finely chopped spring
  onions

1 teaspoon fennel seeds, crushed
1 tablespoon tomato purée
2 tablespoons clear honey
freshly ground black pepper
1 tablespoon cornflour, mixed with
  2 tablespoons dry sherry
5 tablespoons soured cream or plain
  yoghurt

1. Combine all the marinade ingredients, except the cornflour paste and soured cream or yoghurt, in a non-metallic container. Add the ribs, mix well and let them marinate for 24 hours.

2. Remove the ribs from the marinade, place the ribs on the barbecue and cook for 5 minutes on each side.

3. Pour the marinade into a saucepan, bring to the boil and simmer for 4 minutes. Add the cornflour paste and soured cream, and simmer for a further 3 minutes to make a thick creamy Garlic Sauce to serve with the ribs.

Rump Steaks with Pear Rings

SERVES 6

The combination of flavours in this recipe – from the mustard, bacon, brown sugar and pears – is astonishing. Barbecues are really about experimentation, so add a few of your own touches like a favourite herb or pineapple rings instead of pear. Garnish the steaks with mango or kiwi fruit. Enjoy yourself!

6 × 275g (10oz) rump steaks, trimmed	50g (2oz) soft brown sugar
salt and freshly ground black pepper (to taste)	12 large rashers rindless smoked streaky bacon
6 tablespoons English or Dijon mustard	a little sweet cider
6 cored slices of fresh pear	

1. Season the steaks well and barbecue them for 3 minutes on each side. Remove them and allow them to cool.

2. Coat them with mustard, top each steak with a ring of pear, and sprinkle with some soft brown sugar. Wrap each steak in a couple of rashers of bacon, season again and put back on the barbecue pear-side down. Barbecue for 3 minutes on each side, sprinkling with a little sweet cider during the cooking process.

Sirloin Steaks in Foil

SERVES 4

These steaks are sure to keep the sun shining down on you! Serve them with baked potatoes. You can also try using different herb butters (p. 124).

4 × 225g (8oz) sirloin steaks	4 tablespoons chopped fresh parsley and chives
100g (4oz) unsalted butter	4 sprigs of fresh parsley
4 tablespoons lemon juice	a little soured cream
4 tablespoons lime juice	snipped fresh chives
freshly ground black pepper (to taste)	

1. Place each steak on an individual piece of buttered cooking foil, enough to completely seal. Add 25g (1oz) butter, 1 tablespoon lemon juice, 1 tablespoon lime juice, some pepper and 1 tablespoon chopped parsley and chives.

2. Wrap the steaks in the foil, sealing them completely. Then place them in the fridge for 3 hours.

3. Bake the steaks in the foil on the barbecue for 25 minutes until tender.

4. Carefully open the foil, place the steaks on individual plates, pour over the juices, and serve with a sprig of fresh parsley, garnished with a little soured cream and freshly snipped chives.

Devilled Steaks

SERVES 8

I created this recipe in Brittany several years ago at a family barbecue. My father-in-law, Jim Fitzpatrick, who this book is dedicated to, declared them 'after a lace [taste] of Irish [whiskey]'. Wonderful!

8 × 175–200g (6–7oz) rump steaks

For the marinade
8 teaspoons French mustard
2 cloves garlic, peeled, crushed and blended with a little oil

1 teaspoon paprika
4 tablespoons demerara sugar
2 teaspoons dry vermouth
a pinch of crushed fresh rosemary leaves

1. Mix all the marinade ingredients together in a glass or china bowl, brush onto the steaks, and refrigerate for 4 hours.

2. Grill or barbecue for at least 5 minutes on each side, basting with the mixture.

TTB's Barbecued Pepper Ribs

SERVES 6

I never use my full name which is Thomas Talbot-Bridge. Maybe it's because my dad named me after a car! I find it embarrassing, but whenever I am asked what the other T stands for, I always say 'Tabasco'. Use the best, meatiest ribs you can get your hands on for this recipe. They take 24 hours to marinate, but what a bite ... Try the Mexican Red Hot Pepper Sauce (below) if you're even bolder! Serve them with rice and a tomato salad.

1.3kg (3lb) meaty beef ribs
a little cornflour

For the marinade
2 tablespoons honey
3 cloves garlic, peeled and finely
   chopped
3 tablespoons balsamic vinegar

2 teaspoons English mustard
4 tablespoons black peppercorns,
   crushed
2 tablespoons Worcester sauce
2 tablespoons Tabasco sauce
salt (to taste)

1. Place all the marinade ingredients in a deep ceramic dish, toss the ribs in and refrigerate for 24 hours, turning the ribs every 6 hours.

2. Remove the ribs from the marinade and barbecue until cooked.

3. Place the marinade in a saucepan and heat. Thicken with a little cornflour and pour over the ribs. Let the sauce coat the ribs for 15 minutes, then quickly barbecue again until brown and sizzling.

TTB's Mexican Red Hot Pepper Sauce

SERVES 6

Use the same amount of ribs (1.3kg/3lb) for this, ensuring they are meaty. This sauce should make the summer even warmer!

2 tablespoons clear honey
4 garlic cloves, peeled and finely
   chopped
4 shallots, peeled and finely chopped
3 tablespoons balsamic vinegar
4 tablespoons tomato ketchup

5 tablespoons black peppercorns,
   crushed
2 tablespoons Worcester sauce
2 teaspoons chopped fresh red chillies
4 tablespoons Tabasco sauce
salt (to taste)

1. Place all the ingredients in a deep ceramic dish, toss the ribs in and refrigerate for 24 hours, turning the ribs every 6 hours.

2. Remove the ribs from the marinade and barbecue until cooked.

3. Place the marinade in a saucepan and heat. Thicken with a little cornflour and pour over the ribs. Let the sauce coat the ribs for 15 minutes then quickly barbecue again until reddish-brown and sizzling.

Spanish Beef Kebabs

SERVES 8

Spit and skewer cookery sometimes involves long periods of marinating, so it is worth planning your barbecue ahead of time. And if the great British weather changes, the kebabs can always be cooked on a domestic grill.

Metal skewers get very hot, making it easy to burn yourself. For this reason, I tend to use wooden or bamboo skewers. These need to be soaked in water for 15 minutes beforehand to avoid catching fire.

900g (2lb) sirloin steak	225g (8oz) button mushrooms, wiped
2 large apples, cored	Fillet and Sirloin of Beef Marinade
1 red and 1 green pepper, de-seeded	(p. 122)
225g (8oz) shallots, peeled	

1. Cut all the above ingredients into bite-sized pieces, place in the beef marinade and refrigerate overnight.

2.. Drain the ingredients, reserving the marinade. Then thread all the ingredients onto 8 large bamboo skewers (pre-soaked in water for 15 minutes), placing a piece of steak after each mushroom, onion, pepper and piece of apple.

3. Place on the barbecue and cook for about 4 minutes on each side until tender, brushing with the marinade.

Sirloin & Pineapple Kebabs

SERVES 6

Try using fresh pineapple if you can. The tinned I find too sweet and it does not taste anything like fresh pineapple. You can also try this recipe using pieces of melon or mango. Serve the kebabs with pitta bread.

900g (2lb) sirloin of beef, cut into small
   pieces
1 small pineapple, peeled and cubed
20 shallots, peeled and blanched
2 red peppers, de-seeded and cut into
   chunks
100g (4oz) button mushrooms

For the marinade
1 tablespoon lemon juice
1 tablespoon walnut oil
1 tablespoon white wine vinegar
2 cloves garlic, peeled and crushed
100ml (4fl oz) soured cream
salt and freshly ground black pepper (to
   taste)

1. Mix all the marinade ingredients together.

2. Mix the meat and other ingredients with the marinade in a bowl and chill for at least 3 hours.

3. Remove the beef, pineapple and vegetables from the marinade and alternate them onto bamboo skewers (pre-soaked in water for 15 minutes). Grill them on the barbecue for 15 minutes, turning and basting with the marinade every 5 minutes.

Surf & Turf Kebabs

SERVES 8

This is based on one of my favourite recipes, combining the flavours of fillet steak and king prawns. Place the kebabs on a shallot or spring onion salad and serve with chunks of garlic bread.

900g (2lb) fillet of beef, cut into 2.5cm
   (1 inch) cubes
450g (1lb) uncooked king prawns, shells
   removed
26 scallops, shells removed
26 oysters, shells removed

4 tablespoons oyster sauce
4 tablespoons fresh lime juice
50g (2oz) clarified butter
1 tablespoon sherry vinegar
3 tablespoons sesame oil
freshly ground black pepper (to taste)

1. Place all the ingredients in a large bowl and leave them in the fridge to marinate for 24 hours.

2. Soak 8 wooden or bamboo skewers in water for at least 15 minutes.

3. Place a piece of fillet, king prawn, scallop and oyster on each skewer, finishing with a piece of fillet steak.

4. Barbecue for 3–4 minutes, basting with the marinade and seasoning again with black pepper before you serve the kebabs.

Italian Meat Ball Kebabs Filled with Mozzarella

SERVES 4

It does not have to be Mozzarella – you can use any stringy cheese. I like to use Cheddar when I cannot get hold of Mozzarella. Serve with fresh pasta and tomato sauce from the Meat Balls on p. 31.

600g (1lb 5oz) minced fillet of beef
100g (4oz) dried breadcrumbs, soaked
    in a little red wine
100g (4oz) onion, peeled and finely
    chopped
2 tablespoons finely chopped fresh pars-
    ley
2 tablespoons finely chopped fresh basil

50g (2oz) grated Parmesan cheese
2 eggs
100g (4oz) smoked ham, chopped
salt and freshly ground black pepper (to
    taste)
225g (8oz) Mozzarella, cut into small
    cubes
a bunch of fresh basil leaves

1. Place the meat in a bowl with the breadcrumbs, onion, parsley, basil, grated Parmesan, eggs and smoked ham. Season well with salt and pepper, and mix well.

2. Divide the mixture into little balls, place them on a moistened surface or board and flatten them out with the heel of your hand. Place a cube of Mozzarella on each one, and wrap the meat around the cheese to enclose it. Shape into a little meat ball.

3. Thread the meat balls onto metal skewers with a basil leaf between each meat ball. Gently grill them for about 6 minutes, turning frequently.

Beef Fillet Kebabs with English Mustard

SERVES 4

A sprinkling of fresh coriander at the end of the cooking process gives these kebabs a lovely aroma.

450g (1lb) beef fillet, cut into bite-size cubes

20 cherry tomatoes

100g (4oz) button mushrooms, wiped

100g (4oz) tinned pineapple chunks, drained and syrup reserved

1 green pepper, de-seeded and cut into bite-size pieces

4 tablespoons English mustard

2 tablespoons chopped fresh coriander

1. Thread the above items onto bamboo skewers (pre-soaked in water for 15 minutes), then brush them with the English mustard.

2. Place them on a grill and cook for 12 minutes, turning and basting with a little more mustard blended with the syrup from the pineapple chunks.

3. Sprinkle with the fresh coriander and serve.

Rump Steak Kebabs with Barbecue Salsa

SERVES 4

It's the Barbecue Salsa that gives these kebabs their great taste.

450g (1lb) rump steak, cut into 2.5cm (1 inch) cubes

12 button mushrooms, wiped

12 shallots, peeled

2 large apples, cored and cut into bite-size pieces

Fillet and Sirloin of Beef Marinade (p. 122)

Barbecue Salsa (p. 147)

1. Alternately thread the meat, mushrooms, shallots and apples onto bamboo skewers (pre-soaked in water for 15 minutes). Marinate overnight in the kebab marinade.

2. Barbecue for 15 minutes, turning frequently. Serve with Barbecue Salsa.

Barbecue Salsa

SERVES 4

This sauce must be smooth, with a bite. It can be used with most dishes in this book.

4 tablespoons olive oil
2 red peppers, de-seeded and thinly
    sliced
4 cloves garlic, peeled and crushed
2 dried red chillies, chopped
1 onion, peeled and chopped
350g (12oz) fresh plum tomatoes,
    peeled and chopped

2 tablespoons tomato purée
1 teaspoon brown sugar
1 teaspoon fennel seeds, crushed
1 teaspoon Tabasco sauce
salt and freshly ground black pepper (to
    taste)

1. Heat the oil and fry the peppers, garlic, chillies and onion. Add the rest of the ingredients and cook gently for 30 minutes. Season with a little salt and pepper.

2. Allow the mixture to cool, then put it through a blender or food processor. Pour into a serving dish and serve with the kebabs.

Sirloin of Beef Spit Roast

SERVES 6

This is a very simple dish. Should you not have a spit then you can always cut the beef into bite-size pieces, thread them onto kebab skewers and barbecue them instead.

Garlic oil is available from specialist food shops. Or you can make your own by leaving a bulb of garlic in 570ml (1 pint) of any oil for 8 days.

900g (2lb) sirloin of beef (boned and
    rolled)
1.2 litres (2 pints) Portuguese wine
3 cloves garlic, peeled

salt and freshly ground black pepper (to
    taste)
garlic oil

1. Place the sirloin of beef in a deep dish with the wine and the cloves of garlic. Season with salt and pepper, and refrigerate for 6 hours, turning the meat frequently.

2. Remove the loin and pass the spit through it, making sure the spit is evenly balanced or it will not turn. Secure the spit with the screws. Let the spit turn slowly and cook for 1 hour, basting all the time with the marinade and garlic oil.

Beef on Skewers with Pears & Whisky

SERVES 6

This is one of my party pieces, which usually gives the conversation that little extra boost!

450g (1lb) fillet of beef, cut into 2.5cm (1 inch) cubes
2 large pears, peeled, cored and cut into 2.5cm (1 inch) cubes
12 shallots, peeled and halved
150ml (5fl oz) whisky

2 cloves garlic, peeled and crushed
2 tablespoons olive oil
salt and freshly ground black pepper
1 tablespoon soy sauce
1 tablespoon clear honey, warmed
1 teaspoon freshly grated nutmeg

1. Toss the beef and pears into a large clean bowl, with the rest of the ingredients. Leave to marinate for 4 hours, turning every 30 minutes.

2. Thread the beef, pears and shallots alternately onto 6 metal skewers.

3. Grill for 2 minutes on each side on a preheated grill.

Beef Teriyaki

SERVES 4

This requires a 24-hour marinade. You can use any good cut of beef, trimmed of fat.

900g (2lb) sirloin of beef, cut into 5cm (2 inch) × 10cm (4 inch) pieces

For the Teriyaki Sauce
200ml (7fl oz) sweet sherry
200ml (7fl oz) soy sauce

1 tablespoon chopped fresh ginger
4 cloves garlic, peeled and finely chopped
2 tablespoons soft brown sugar
3 tablespoons chopped fresh coriander

1. Make up the Teriyaki Sauce in a large glass bowl and place the sirloin pieces in the bowl. Blend them thoroughly and refrigerate for 24 hours.

2. About two hours before barbecuing, remove the meat from the fridge and let it rest at room temperature.

3. Thread the chunks onto bamboo skewers (pre-soaked in water for 15 minutes) and cook to your liking.

Beef & Tiger Prawn Teriyaki

SERVES 4–6

This requires a 24-hour marinade. The combination of fish and beef may surprise you, but I can assure it is a winning one.

450g (1lb) sirloin of beef, cut into 5cm (2 inch) × 10cm (4 inch) pieces, fat and gristle removed

450g (1lb) Tiger prawns, shells removed
1 quantity Teriyaki Sauce (p. 148)

1. Make up the Teriyaki Sauce in a large glass bowl and place the beef pieces and tiger prawns in the bowl. Blend them thoroughly and refrigerate for 24 hours.

2. About two hours before barbecuing, remove them from the fridge and let them rest at room temperature.

3. Thread them alternately onto bamboo skewers (pre-soaked in water for 15 minutes) and barbecue or grill for 2 minutes on each side.

Beef & Lobster Tail Teriyaki

SERVES 4–6

This also requires a 24-hour marinade.

450g (1lb) sirloin of beef, cut into 5cm
(2 inch) × 10cm (4 inch) pieces, fat
and gristle removed

450g (1lb) sliced lobster tail
450g (1lb) shallots, peeled
1 quantity Teriyaki Sauce (p. 148)

1. Make up the Teriyaki Sauce in a large glass bowl and place the beef pieces and lobster tail in the bowl. Blend them thoroughly and refrigerate for 24 hours.

2. About two hours before barbecuing, remove the meat from the fridge and let it rest at room temperature.

3. Thread the beef and lobster tail alternately onto bamboo skewers (pre-soaked in water for 15 minutes) and barbecue or grill for 2–3 minutes on each side.

Beef & Chicken Teriyaki

SERVES 4–6

Chicken and beef have been used as a combination in several of my recipes. This one only requires a 12-hour marinade.

450g (1lb) sirloin of beef, cut into 5cm
(2 inch) × 10cm (4 inch) pieces, fat
and gristle removed
450g (1lb) chicken breast, cut into 5cm

(2 inch) × 10cm (4 inch) pieces, skin
removed
1 quantity Teriyaki Sauce (p. 148)

1. Make up the Teriyaki Sauce in a large glass bowl and place the beef and chicken pieces in the bowl. Blend them thoroughly and refrigerate for 12 hours.

2. About two hours before barbecuing, remove the meat from the fridge and let it rest at room temperature.

3. Thread the beef and chicken alternately onto bamboo skewers (pre-soaked in water for 15 minutes) and barbecue or grill for 2–3 minutes on each side.

Beef Satay

SERVES 4–6

These South-East Asian dishes are becoming more popular at barbecues, partly because they are often finger foods, making them easy to eat while you enjoy a conversation. Ensure that the bamboo skewers have been soaked in cold water before threading the meat onto them (in order to prevent them catching fire). These only need to marinate for 3 hours but the longer you leave them the more flavour you will get. Serve with a crisp salad.

675g (1½lb) sirloin of beef, cut into
    2.5cm (1 inch) cubes

For the Satay Sauce
150ml (5fl oz) soy sauce
100ml (4fl oz) olive oil
100ml (4fl oz) fresh lime juice

4 shallots, peeled and finely chopped
3 cloves garlic, peeled and crushed
1 teaspoon freshly ground black pepper
1 teaspoon chilli powder
1 tablespoon curry paste or powder
3 tablespoons clear honey, warmed

1. Mix all the sauce ingredients together in a large glass bowl. Add the cubes of beef, blend them thoroughly in the satay mixture and set on one side for 3 hours.

2. Thread 3–4 cubes of beef onto each bamboo skewer (pre-soaked in water for 15 minutes) and barbecue to your taste.

3.. Pour the marinade into a saucepan, heat gently and pour into a bowl so that your guests can dip their beef satay into the sauce.

Korean Beef Satay

SERVES 6

Should any of your guests be allergic to peanuts, please do not use this recipe.

675g (1½lb) sirloin of beef, cut into
    2.5cm (1 inch) cubes

For the Satay Sauce
150ml (5fl oz) soy sauce
100ml (4fl oz) peanut oil
10ml (4fl oz) fresh lime juice
4 shallots, peeled and finely chopped

3 cloves garlic, peeled and crushed
1 teaspoon freshly ground black pepper
1 teaspoon chilli powder
4 tablespoons peanuts, completely
    crushed
3 tablespoons clear honey, warmed

1. Mix all the sauce ingredients together in a large glass bowl. Add the cubes of beef, blend them thoroughly in the satay mixture and set on one side for 3 hours.

2. Thread 3–4 cubes of beef onto each bamboo skewer (pre-soaked in water for 15 minutes) and barbecue to your taste.

3. Pour the marinade into a saucepan, heat gently, and pour into a bowl so that your guests can dip their beef satay into the sauce.

Indian Fillet Steak with Corn & Rice Fritters

SERVES 4

This is one of my favourite dinner party dishes. Served with rice, salad and all the Indian trimmings, it is well worth the time and effort.

100g (4oz) sweetcorn niblets	***For the fritter batter***
100g (4oz) cooked rice	100g (4oz) plain flour
4 × 225g (8oz) fillet steaks	a pinch of salt
2 tablespoons mild curry paste	2 eggs
salt and freshly ground black pepper (to taste)	275ml (10fl oz) milk
	1 tablespoon sunflower oil
oil for deep-frying	

1. To make the fritters, sift the flour and salt into a bowl. Make a well in the centre, place a whole egg and 1 egg yolk in the well and mix with a wooden spoon. Gradually add the milk and oil, then let the batter rest for 40 minutes.

2. Whisk the egg white until stiff and fold into the batter.

3. When you are ready to serve the steak, add the sweetcorn and rice to the batter, blending the mixture. Tablespoon out little balls into hot oil and cook until golden brown.

4. Lightly coat the fillet steaks with the curry paste, season and grill to your liking, and serve with the corn and rice fritters.

Barbecued American Beef and Boston Baked Beans

SERVES 8

*T*his is, without doubt, the most famous of all bean dishes. It developed as a natural combination of what the New England soil provided and what was originally made with maple syrup or maple sugar. This ingredient was replaced by molasses when the shipping industry began to flourish.

Beef and beans used to be an American Saturday night ritual, served with brown bread. They were reheated on the Sabbath, when cooking (along with other activities) came to a halt.

Since the original recipe, which I have recreated below, came into being, several other ingredients have crept into the dish – like onions or an onion stuck with cloves, a bay leaf and sweet herbs.

900g (2lb) haricot or cannellini beans
1 tablespoon salt
225g (8oz) salt pork or pickled pork, skin scored
900g (2lb) rump steak, diced

4 tablespoons maple syrup
1 teaspoon dry mustard powder
salt and freshly ground black pepper (to taste)

1. Soak the beans overnight in hot water twice the depth of the beans.

2. Drain, and renew the water. Add the salt and bring to the boil. Boil for 10 minutes.

3. Transfer the beans to an ovenproof casserole and push in the piece of scored salt pork. Add the rest of the ingredients.

4. Preheat the oven to Gas Mark 2/150°C/300°F and bake for 3 hours.

5. Simmer on the barbecue for 1 hour, remove the pork, stir and serve.

CHAPTER 5

Pan Frying

✦

Pan frying is every chef's favourite technique, because the flair and expertise really come to the fore. The best cuts to use are fillet, sirloin and rump and make sure you have a very good peppermill – it's essential. You also need a very strong, heavy-based frying pan. I use Circulon non-stick heavy-based pans, which are very hard-wearing. I have had the same frying pan and wok for the last three years and I use them daily. They are not very costly and they are in stock at Makro, the House of Fraser and most catering outlets. Chefs use Black ironware and Battle Brand which are made in Birmingham. They are stainless steel-lined with a copper base.

Always try to season your steaks well when pan frying. And remember that safety comes first. Keep the handle of the pan away from you and any heat source, and keep a dry cloth/oven cloth close at hand should the handle get too hot.

Bridge Tournedos with Red Velvet Sauce

SERVES 4

I *created this recipe using my favourite fashionable vegetable, Red Velvet beetroot, which I feel is one of the most underrated vegetables being used in the British household today. This dish is made in three easy stages.*

4 tablespoons olive oil
salt and freshly ground black pepper (to taste)
4 × 175g (6oz) fillets of beef, trimmed
225g (8oz) wild mushrooms, cleaned and trimmed
2 lamb's kidneys, skinned, halved, cores removed, and thinly sliced
2 shallots, peeled and sliced

225g (8oz) ready-cooked Red Velvet beetroot, diced
100g (4oz) raspberries, crushed
1 tablespoon plain flour
150ml (5fl oz) Basic Beef Stock (p. 13)
50ml (2fl oz) red wine
50ml (2fl oz) cooking oil
450g (1lb) potatoes, peeled and sliced
150ml (5fl oz) single cream
a few fresh chives

1. Heat the olive oil in a deep frying pan. Season the steaks and cook them all over for 3 minutes on each side. Place on a warm serving plate in a warm oven until required.

2. Add the mushrooms to the pan, fry gently for 2 minutes and place them on the dish with the steaks. Fry the kidneys for 3 minutes, then keep warm with the steaks and mushrooms.

3. Using the same pan, add the shallots, beetroot and raspberries to the juices, and cook for 4 minutes. Sprinkle with the flour, add the beef stock and wine and season. Boil for about 12 minutes until reduced by half. Meanwhile, heat the cooking oil and fry the potatoes until they are crisp.

4. When the sauce is reduced, add half the cream, cook for 1 minute, and pour the sauce through a fine sieve or muslin.

5. Looking at the photograph of the finished dish, make a small circle with the fried potatoes, and place the fillet to one side of the potato. Garnish with the kidney and mushrooms, surround with the beetroot sauce, swirl a little cream around the plate and garnish with fresh chives.

Tournedos Rossini

SERVES 4

I think this recipe is attributed to the French. It is music to the Italians and mouth-watering to the rest of the European Community. Of course it's named after the famous composer.

Use foie gras *pâté if you can afford it, but it's not essential.*

4 × 225g (8oz) tournedos (*filet mignon*)	1 tablespoon cooking oil
salt and freshly ground black pepper (to taste)	half a glass of Marsala
	150ml (5fl oz) Basic Beef Stock (p. 13)
4 thick slices white bread	150ml (5fl oz) Espagnole Sauce (opposite)
75g (3oz) butter	4 slices pâté

1. Trim the steaks and season them well. Place them on the grill or in a greased frying pan and cook them to your liking.

2. Trim the slices of bread into rounds. Melt 50g (2oz) butter in another pan with the oil and fry the croûtons until they are golden brown. Place them on a serving dish with a serviette to drain off the excess butter.

3. Add the Marsala to the pan you used for the croûtons. Bring it to the boil, then add the stock and the Espagnole Sauce. Bring to the boil, then let it simmer for 4 minutes until it thickens. Season with salt and pepper.

4. It will now be time to check the steaks or turn them over. Remove them from the pan when cooked and keep them warm. Add the remaining butter to the pan and fry the pâté slices for 1 minute on each side.

5. To serve, place each tournedos on a croûton, top with a pâté slice, pour over a little sauce and serve the rest in a sauceboat.

Espagnole Sauce

SERVES 6

This is without doubt one of the classic French sauces, and it is very important to both English and French chefs, for it is the foundation for brown sauce. When it comes to this sauce, England and France agree that no short cuts or errors are allowed.

25g (1oz) butter
25g (1oz) flour
1 tablespoon tomato purée
1 litre (1¾ pints) Basic Beef Stock (p. 13), boiling
2 tablespoons wine vinegar
a little oil or butter
100g (4oz) rindless smoked bacon, finely diced
100g (4oz) carrot, peeled and finely diced

100g (4oz) onion, peeled and finely diced
50g (2oz) celery, washed and finely diced
50g (2oz) leeks, washed and finely diced
50g (2oz) fresh fennel, washed and finely diced
a sprig of thyme
1 small bay leaf
salt and freshly ground black pepper (to taste)

1. Heat the butter in a heavy-based saucepan and stir in the flour to make a roux, taking care not to let the mixture burn.

2. Add the tomato purée to the roux, then slowly add the boiling brown stock and the vinegar.

3. In a separate saucepan heat the oil or butter and cook the bacon and vegetables until they are a light golden colour.

4. Drain the vegetables. add them to the sauce with the herbs and seasoning, and simmer slowly for at least 4 hours.

5. Skim with a ladle, strain through a fine sieve into a clean saucepan, and heat up when ready to serve.

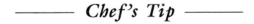

Chef's Tip

For a simple Pepper Sauce for a Steak au poivre, add 1 tablespoon green peppercorns, some freshly ground black pepper and 2 tablespoons double cream to 150ml (5fl oz) Espagnole Sauce.

Tournedos a la Béarnaise

SERVES 6–8

A dream to make and a dream to taste. All in all, dreamy … Serve it with my Waldorf Summer Beef Salad (p. 39) minus the chunks of beef.

1.3kg (3lb) fillet of beef, cut into 5cm
(2 inch) slices
salt and freshly ground black pepper (to
taste)
25g (1oz) beef dripping

8–12 rounds of bread the same size and
shape as the fillets
1 quantity Béarnaise Sauce (below)
chopped fresh parsley

1. Season the steaks, heat the dripping in a large frying pan and cook the steaks to your liking. Place them on a warm serving plate and keep warm.

2. Fry the rounds of bread in the dripping until they are crisp on both sides. Place them on a large hot serving plate, place a tournedos on each round of bread, pour over a little of the Béarnaise Sauce, sprinkle with chopped parsley and serve.

Béarnaise Sauce

MAKES approx 250ml (9fl oz)

4 tablespoons good-quality white wine,
e.g. Chardonnay
6 tablespoons tarragon vinegar
25g (1oz) shallots, peeled and finely
chopped
1 tablespoon chopped fresh tarragon,
plus a little extra to finish

1 teaspoon chopped fresh chervil, plus a
little extra to finish
salt and coarsely ground black pepper
(to taste)
3 egg yolks, lightly beaten
200ml (7fl oz) clarified butter, melted
a pinch of cayenne pepper

1. Put the wine, vinegar, shallots, tarragon, chervil, salt and pepper in a saucepan over a high heat and boil until reduced by two-thirds.

2. Remove the pan from the heat and allow to cool slightly.

3. Put the sauce in the top of a double boiler over gently simmering water, or in a heatproof bowl that will fit over a pan with plenty of room underneath. Put some warm water in the pan, then place the bowl in the pan, making sure the bottom does not touch the water. Whisk in the egg yolks and continue whisking for about 12 minutes until the sauce is thick and creamy. Remove the sauce from the heat and slowly whisk in the clarified butter.

4. Pass the sauce through a fine non-metallic sieve. Add a little more finely chopped fresh tarragon and chervil and season with a dash of cayenne. Pour the sauce into a sauceboat, ready for the fillet steaks.

Steak Diane

SERVES 4

There are several versions of this recipe. Some cooks add cream, yoghurt or crème fraîche, but we can create healthier dishes by omitting rich cream and butter and replacing dripping with a healthy cooking oil. The Health Education Authority are now looking to British chefs to create healthier dishes so this one's for Karen Peploe from me and AWT! Serve it with a crisp salad and a glass of claret.

450g (1lb) fillet steak	4 tablespoons Basic Beef Stock (p. 13)
4 tablespoons pure corn oil	1 tablespoon chopped fresh parsley
8 shallots, peeled and sliced	3 tablespoons good-quality brandy,
juice and zest of 1 lemon	warmed
Worcester sauce	

1. Cut the fillet into 4 even pieces, cover them with cling film and beat them flat with a wooden meat mallet or a rolling pin.

2. Heat the oil in a large frying pan and fry the steaks for 2 minutes on each side. Add the shallots and cook for a further 3 minutes.

3. Sprinkle with the lemon juice and zest and add the Worcester sauce and beef stock. Cook for 2 minutes and sprinkle with the parsley. Finally, add the warm brandy, flame the steaks, cook until the flame goes out, and serve.

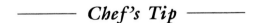

Chef's Tip

As long as you warm the brandy gently, it is quite safe to flame it.

Julian Groom's Steak Waldorf with a Pear & Blue Cheese Salad

SERVES 6

It takes about two days to prepare this dish and about an hour to chew over its brilliance, once you've eaten it. The world-renowned Waldorf Meridien Hotel, famous for its tea dances, recently celebrated its 87th birthday, although Julian does not look all that old!

6 × 225g (8oz) fillet steaks
4 tablespoons olive oil
salt and freshly ground black pepper (to taste)
6 shallots, peeled and sliced
1 clove garlic, peeled and crushed
2 tablespoons chopped fresh tarragon
1 tablespoon English mustard
1 tablespoon plain flour
150ml (5fl oz) Basic Beef Stock (p. 13)
1 apple, cored and finely diced
1 tablespoon chopped walnuts

2 tablespoons double cream

For the salad

225g (8oz) boiled rice, well drained and chilled
2 large dessert pears, cored and diced
150g (5oz) blue cheese, diced
1 red pepper, de-seeded and diced
salt and freshly ground black pepper (to taste)
1 tablespoon chopped fresh coriander
1 tablespoon sesame oil

Enjoy.

1. Trim the fillet steaks, removing any fat. Put the olive oil, salt, pepper, sliced shallots, garlic, tarragon and English mustard in a deep bowl and mix thoroughly.

2. Place the beef fillets in the marinade, completely cover with cling film, and refrigerate for 48 hours.

3. Using a large, deep non-stick frying pan, quickly seal and fry the steaks for 3 minutes on each side, reserving the marinade. Remove the steaks from the pan and place on a warm serving dish.

4. Add the marinade to the pan, bring it to the boil and sprinkle with the flour. Add the beef stock, diced apple and walnuts, and let the sauce simmer gently for 5 minutes. Place the steaks back in the sauce, add the cream and cook for 2 more minutes.

5. Blend the salad ingredients together, then place a little salad on each plate with a steak and some of the Waldorf Sauce.

Milanese Risotto with Sirloin of Beef

SERVES 4

*T*his famous dish is perhaps the best-known of all Italian risottos, although there are many others. I have adapted the recipe to take in the flavour of sirloin steak.

100g (4oz) butter
50g (2oz) beef marrow, chopped
675g (1½lb) sirloin of beef, diced
1 large onion, peeled and chopped
450g (1lb) Italian rice (preferably
  Arborio)

570ml (1 pint) Basic Beef Stock (p. 13),
  boiling
150ml (5fl oz) white wine
1 teaspoon saffron strands, crumbled
salt and freshly ground black pepper
50g (2oz) grated Parmesan cheese

1. Put half the butter and all the beef marrow in a deep frying pan. When hot, add the steak and chopped onion and cook until golden brown, then add the rice and stir well, cooking for 15 minutes.

2. Add the boiling stock, the white wine, saffron, salt and pepper, and mix well. Simmer gently for 20 minutes, stirring occasionally.

3. Let the risotto settle and, just before serving, add a little more stock and simmer for a further 10 minutes. Sprinkle with the grated Parmesan cheese, melt the remaining butter and pour over, and serve.

Thai Stir-Fried Beef with Vegetables

SERVES 4

I created this recipe for Euro-Toque member, Thassiseuth Phouthavong, of the famous Blue Elephant on Fulham Broadway, London.

3 tablespoons sesame oil (see Chef's
  Tip, p. 87)
350g (12oz) beef fillet, thinly sliced
salt and freshly ground black pepper
8 shallots, peeled and sliced
2 cloves garlic, peeled and finely
  chopped
a 2.5cm (1 inch) piece fresh root
  ginger, peeled and grated

1 green chilli, finely chopped
1 red and 1 green pepper, de-seeded
  and thinly sliced
3 courgettes, washed and thinly sliced
2 tablespoons ground almonds
1 teaspoon ground cinnamon
1 tablespoon oyster sauce
50g (2oz) creamed coconut, grated

1. Heat the sesame oil in a wok, season the beef fillet with salt and ground pepper, add the beef to the wok and stir-fry for 3 minutes.

2. Add the shallots, garlic, ginger and chilli, and cook for 2 minutes. Add the peppers and courgettes, and cook for 1 minute.

3. Finally add the ground almonds, cinnamon, oyster sauce and creamed coconut. Stir-fry for 1 minute and serve immediately.

Chinese Egg Noodles with Beef

SERVES 4

There are Chinese restaurants and then there's the Yang Sing, an establishment where the food is conducted like a symphony. Harry Yeung is a chef with noodles of talent, and this is one of the dishes that will stir-fry you into submission at his Manchester emporium.

275g (10oz) Chinese egg noodles	100g (4oz) button mushrooms, wiped and thinly sliced
3 tablespoons walnut oil	
2.5cm (1 inch) piece fresh root ginger, peeled and cut into thin strips	350g (12oz) fillet steak, thinly sliced and seasoned
5 spring onions, washed and finely shredded	1 tablespoon cornflour, mixed with 5 tablespoons dry sherry and 3 tablespoons soy sauce
2 cloves garlic, peeled and finely chopped	1 teaspoon soft brown sugar
1 red pepper, de-seeded and thinly sliced	225g (8oz) bean sprouts
	1 tablespoon sesame oil

1. Boil 2.3 litres (4 pints) water in a large saucepan. Cook the noodles according to the instructions on the packet. Drain them and set aside.

2. Heat the walnut oil in a wok until it is hot. Stir in the ginger, spring onions and garlic, and stir-fry for 45 seconds. Add the red pepper, mushrooms and fillet steak. Stir-fry for 4 minutes.

3. Pour over the cornflour mixture and sprinkle with brown sugar. Stir-fry for a further 2 minutes, then add the bean sprouts, drained noodles and sesame oil. Stir and toss for 1 minute, then serve.

Salt & Peppered Fillet Steak

SERVES 4

*A*nother classic from chef Harry Yeung of the Yang Sing. *During an evening meal with* *John Warmisham, Harry presented this dish, and his* Beef with Peppers and Blackbean Sauce *(p. 165). It was a very worthwhile visit to this temple of food in Manchester.* *Perasa seasoning is available from Chinese supermarkets.*

450g (1lb) best-quality British steak, diced

a little cooking oil

100g (4oz) shredded iceberg lettuce

For the marinade

1 carrot, peeled and diced

1 celery stalk, diced

a bunch of coriander, leaves and stems separated

2 cloves garlic, peeled and roughly chopped

a generous pinch of the following dry ingredients: garlic powder, onion powder, chilli powder, custard powder, self-raising flour, cornflour, salt, sugar, Perasa seasoning and freshly ground white pepper

1 hot red chilli

25g (1oz) coriander stems

25g (1oz) spring onion, washed

salt and freshly ground white pepper (to taste)

1. Place the carrot, celery, coriander leaves and garlic cloves in a blender or food processor. Lay the steak in a clean bowl and cover with the carrot mixture and the dry marinade. Stir well and leave for 2 hours.

2. Meanwhile, finely chop the coriander stems, chilli and spring onion.

3. Add the beef to a lightly oiled wok or deep frying pan and fry for 3–4 minutes, until the beef is crisp on the outside. Add the chopped coriander stems, chilli and spring onion.

4. Season with salt and freshly ground white pepper and serve on a bed of finely chopped iceberg lettuce.

Beef Jambalaya with Prawns & Smoked Oysters

SERVES 6

Many years ago, in my home town of Bolton, Lancashire, I opened the very first Creole restaurant and this recipe was the most popular dish on the menu. If you do not like seafood, replace it with the same weight of raw chicken and thinly sliced ham. Add them when you add the rice, and cook for a further 20 minutes. Smoked oysters can now be bought in tins from most major supermarkets or ask your fishmonger.

25g (1oz) beef dripping

2 onions, peeled and chopped

225g (8oz) spicy smoked sausage, thinly sliced

450g (1lb) sirloin steak, cut into thin strips and fat removed

1 tablespoon seasoned flour

4 tomatoes, skinned, de-seeded and chopped

200g (7oz) uncooked rice

2 cloves garlic, peeled and crushed

450ml (15fl oz) Basic Beef Stock (p. 13)

1 tablespoon tomato purée

1 teaspoon cayenne pepper

a pinch of each of the following: rosemary, thyme, paprika, crushed fennel seeds, basil, oregano and saffron

juice and zest of 1 lime

1 large green and 1 red pepper, deseeded and thinly sliced

100g (4oz) mushrooms, wiped and sliced

450g (1lb) king prawns, peeled

12 smoked oysters and their juice

sea salt and freshly ground black pepper (to taste)

a large bunch of fresh parsley, washed and chopped

1 lime, sliced

1. Heat the dripping in a very large, deep frying pan with a tight-fitting lid or a very large saucepan. Fry the onions, smoked sausage and steak for 5 minutes, then sprinkle with the seasoned flour.

2. Add the tomatoes and rice and simmer for 5 minutes. Add the rest of the ingredients up to the sliced red and green peppers. Simmer for 12 minutes, then add the rest of the ingredients except the parsley and sliced lime, blending them thoroughly.

3. Place the lid on the pan and cook for a further 5 minutes, until the rice is completely cooked but not mushy. Place the Jambalaya in a warm serving dish, sprinkle with fresh parsley, garnish with slices of lime, and serve.

Topside of Beef with Peppers & Blackbean Sauce

SERVES 4

Topside is a really tasty cut of beef and, presented properly with blackbean sauce in the Chinese style, as cooked by Harry Yeung of the Yang Sing restaurant, Manchester, it is very good value for money. Serve it with freshly cooked noodles.

400g (14oz) topside of best British beef
a pinch of salt
a pinch of cornflour
2 tablespoons vegetable oil
1 teaspoon crushed garlic
1 tablespoon blackbean sauce
175g (6oz) green pepper, cut into strips
50g (2oz) red pepper, cut into strips
50g (2oz) hot red chillies, finely
  chopped
75g (3oz) mushrooms, wiped and sliced
1 onion, peeled and chopped

50g (2oz) spring onion, washed and
  chopped

For the seasoning

½ teaspoon salt
½ teaspoon sugar
3 tablespoons chicken stock
1 tablespoon dark soy sauce
2 tablespoons Basic Beef Stock (p. 13)
2 tablespoons rice wine
1 teaspoon cornflour, blended with a
  little rice wine

1. Slice the beef into thin strips, place them in a clean bowl, add a pinch of salt and cornflour, and cover with water. Leave to stand for 40 minutes.

2. Heat half the oil in a wok or deep frying pan and stir-fry the beef for 2 minutes. Transfer the beef to a warm serving dish and clean the wok or pan.

3. Reheat the wok or pan using the remaining oil. Add the garlic, blackbean sauce, green and red peppers, chillies, mushrooms, onion and spring onion in that order. Stir-fry for 2 minutes, then add the beef.

4. Add the seasoning ingredients. Fry for 3 minutes, thicken with a little more cornflour if required, and serve.

TTB's Home-Made Sausages

SERVES 6–8

Today sausage machines can be bought at most kitchenware stores and the butcher will also give you the sausage skins. I think the flavour of home-made is always better, and your guests appreciate it if you have taken the time and effort. If you have a large piping bag with a wide nozzle, simply put the skins onto the end of the nozzle and squeeze the sausage mixture into them. These sausages are perfect for a good fry up or great British breakfast. Or serve them with mashed potato and Onion Gravy (p. 44) for a comforting supper dish.

900g (2lb) very lean sirloin or fillet of beef, roughly minced (your butcher will do this for you)
350g (12oz) shredded beef suet
1 large onion, peeled and very finely chopped

225g (8oz) fresh white breadcrumbs, very fine
1 teaspoon of each of the following: salt, freshly ground black pepper, dried sage and parsley
25g (1oz) cooking oil or dripping

1. Mix all the ingredients, except the cooking oil or dripping, together in a large bowl.

2. Put the sausage meat into the skins, either with a machine or with a wide nozzle and a piping bag. Knot one end of the skin and slowly pipe the mixture in. When it is full, draw the skin away from the nozzle, knot the end and twist it at intervals of about 10cm (4 inches) to make the sausages.

3. Put the sausages in the fridge for at least 6 hours to allow the mixture to blend properly.

4. Heat the oil or dripping in a large frying pan. Prick the sausages with a fork in three different places and gently fry them, cooking them for about 6 minutes, until golden brown all over.

OPPOSITE Lasagne (page 33)

OPPOSITE PAGE 167 Spaghetti with Italian Sauce (page 34)

Beef Tails with Fried Vegetables and a Very Interesting Sauce

SERVES 6

John Benson Smith is a chef with a wonderful imagination, whose talent is well known. Try this more than interesting recipe from his repertoire. Beef fillet tails are the end of a beef fillet. They must be marinated in red wine and olive oil overnight and the sultanas soaked in brandy overnight.

Serve by displaying on a large plate. Don't forget the side order of mashed potatoes made with milk and the addition of a good-quality olive oil and freshly ground black pepper...

12 × 100g (4oz) beef fillet tails, marinated overnight in 200ml (7fl oz) red wine and 50ml (2fl oz) olive oil
175g (6oz) butter
100g (4oz) shallots, peeled and finely chopped
25g (1oz) caster sugar
75ml (3fl oz) sherry vinegar
1 tablespoon English mustard
15 black peppercorns, crushed under a pan
275ml (10fl oz) Red Wine Sauce (p. 73)
salt (to taste)

175g (6oz) sultanas, soaked in 50ml (2fl oz) brandy overnight
75g (3oz) mangetout, blanched and cut into strips
75g (3oz) fine green beans, blanched and cut into strips
12 small broccoli florets, blanched
12 small cauliflower florets, blanched
2 medium carrots, peeled, cut into flower shapes and blanched
175g (6oz) seasoned cornflour
cooking oil for deep-frying
75g (3oz) toasted almonds
a sprig of fresh parsley, chopped

1. Heat a non-stick pan. Add the beef fillet tails (having previously removed most of the marinade). Sear each side of the beef to the required cooking stage and remove from the pan, ready to serve.

2. Melt 150g (5oz) butter in another non-stick pan. Chuck in the shallots and cook (without letting them colour). Then add the caster sugar, sherry vinegar, English mustard and black peppercorns. Boil until reduced to a very small amount, then add the red wine sauce and simmer. The finished sauce needs to be re-seasoned and the taste should be fine-tuned just before serving. Finally, whisk in the remaining butter and add the brandy-soaked sultanas.

3. Dust the vegetables with the seasoned cornflour. Heat the oil in a deep fryer and fry the vegetables until they are crispy and golden brown. Turn them out onto kitchen paper, pat dry to remove any excess fat and sprinkle with a little salt.

4. Use the deep-fried vegetables as a bed to sit the beef tails upon. Coat with a serving of the sauce and crown with a sprinkling of almonds and chopped parsley.

Highland Beef Fillet

SERVES 4

*B*ob Gledhill, *of the* Caterer and Hotelkeeper, *very kindly advertised the fact that I was looking for beef recipes for my book, and this is one of the special ones I received. Stephen Rowe, the Head Chef at The Brewery Conference and Banqueting Centre, London, created this dish for a British-themed dinner for the 'Réunion des Gastronomes' at The Brewery. Thanks Steve…*

4 large Savoy cabbage leaves
50g (2oz) cooked lentils
50g (2oz) cooked mashed carrot
salt and freshly ground black pepper (to taste)
a little oil
4 × 150g (5oz) fillet steaks
4 rashers rindless streaky bacon
75ml (3fl oz) Basic Beef Stock (p. 13)
25g (1oz) beef dripping

75g (3oz) shallots, peeled and finely chopped
1 tablespoon seasoned flour
75ml (3fl oz) red wine
4 slices black pudding

For the garnish
12 roast cocotte (barrel) potatoes
12 boiled cocotte (barrel) carrots
a sprig of fresh thyme

1. Blanch the cabbage leaves in slightly salted boiling water for 1 minute. Remove and drop the leaves into ice cold water (to retain the colour), then dry them well on absorbent kitchen paper or a clean towel.

2. Place the lentils and carrots in a mixing bowl and season with salt and pepper. Blend the mixture together.

3. Place a tablespoon of the mixture in the centre of a cabbage leaf, roll the cabbage leaf over into a ball shape enclosing the stuffing. Trim off any excess cabbage. Put the cabbage parcels join-side down on a lightly oiled tray, cover with cling film and refrigerate.

4. Preheat the oven to Gas Mark 2/150°C/300°F.

5. Wrap each steak in bacon and tie with butcher's string. Remove the cling film from the cabbage parcels, sprinkle with a little beef stock and reheat in the oven for 10 minutes.

6. Meanwhile, heat the beef dripping, sealing the steaks on both sides for 4 minutes. Arrange the steaks on a warm serving dish and place in the oven with the cabbage parcels.

7. Add the shallots to the beef dripping and cook for 2 minutes. Add the flour and red wine and reduce for 5 minutes. Add the beef stock and boil until reduced by half.

8. Grill the black pudding on both sides and place in the centre of a large serving dish. Place the steaks on the black pudding, and garnish with the cabbage parcels, cocotte potatoes, cocotte carrots and the sprig of fresh thyme.

Stroganoff with Sliced Roast Potatoes & Mangetout

SERVES 6

It's great when chefs, cooks and friends from all over Great Britain back their own country's produce. One of my mates is Deborah Holden at La Bouffe in Castle Street, Liverpool. Every bit of produce she uses is the freshest you can get and she prides herself on the quality of her ingredients, not just in her restaurant but in her outside catering assignments where her chefs create some of the finest buffets. This is Deb's signature dish ... try it!

900g (2lb) rump steak, cut into 1cm
    (½ inch) thick slices
freshly ground black pepper (to taste)
freshly grated nutmeg (to taste)
50g (2oz) best British butter
8 shallots, peeled and sliced
225g (8oz) button mushrooms, wiped
    and sliced

salt (to taste)
2 tablespoons Basic Beef Stock (p. 13)
275ml (10fl oz) soured cream
450g (1lb) potatoes, sliced and roasted
    in beef dripping
225g (8oz) mangetout, blanched

1. Flatten the steak slices with a wooden mallet or rolling pin and season them well with freshly ground black pepper and nutmeg.

2. Heat the butter in a large frying pan and cook the shallots for 4 minutes. Add the beef and cook for a further 5 minutes. Add the mushrooms and cook for 2 minutes.

3. Season with salt and a little more nutmeg, add the beef stock and soured cream, cook for 1 minute, and serve with the sliced roast potatoes and blanched mangetout.

CHAPTER 6

Pies, Puddings and Terrines

✦

I have developed pastry products for several very well-known food companies and, without a shadow of a doubt, my favourite subject is Ye Olde Englishe Pyes ...

This chapter is dedicated to my very own private club, the Pie Society, of which there are only *three* members – myself, Peter Vickers and Hubert Lowry. Together, we *are* the Pie Society. On the last Friday of every month we meet at my cottage to indulge in pie-making with a difference. I will select what pie we are going to make for our individual families, and our wives will select a rare malt whisky (label and top removed). While the pie is cooking, we have to try and guess what whisky we are drinking! The end result is that a great day is had by all. The wives go shopping, Pete and Hubert get free cookery lessons and we enjoy our favourite pastime – whisky tasting.

So, to start my Pie Society section, I feel it is essential to know how to make good pastry to complement the best of British beef. My very dear friend Brian Sack, who I have known for a lora, lora years, is an expert on pastry. Brian and Francis Coulson, who established the famous Sharrow Bay Country House Hotel in Cumbria, are known to thousands of foodies around the world.

During the filming of my video, *A Taste of Sharrow*, Brian and I sat down to a scrummy lunch of steak and kidney pie created by Francis, Johnnie Martin and Colin Akrigg, the chefs at The Sharrow Bay, and Brian and I talked at great length on the making of the perfect pie – the texture of the pastry, the moistness of the filling and the richness of the gravy. Francis is now retired from the kitchens at Sharrow Bay but very active when making a suet pastry that melts in your mouth, said Brian. So what is the secret? Read on...

'Warm hands make a warm heart but not really good pastry.' My mum, 1960s

---

Shortcrust Pastry

MAKES about 450g (1lb)

*G*ood *pastry should be light in texture. It is important that you always weigh the ingredients accurately and keep all the ingredients, utensils and your hands as cool as possible.*

350g (12oz) plain flour, sifted	75g (3oz) good-quality lard
½ teaspoon salt	extra sifted flour
75g (3oz) butter	

1. Sift the flour and salt into a clean bowl, then gently rub in the butter and lard until the mixture resembles fine breadcrumbs.

2. Add enough cold water to make a stiff dough. Press the dough together with your fingertips. Sprinkle with a little sifted flour, then roll the pastry out on a lightly floured surface, and use. Or refrigerate until ready to use.

Puff Pastry

MAKES 450g (1lb)

*W*hen *making puff pastry, it is worth making a large batch and freezing half of it, because it is a long and time-consuming job. It will keep in the freezer for up to three months.*

225g (8oz) plain flour, sifted	½ teaspoon lemon juice
¼ teaspoon salt	extra flour
225g (8oz) butter	

1. Sift the flour and salt into a clean mixing bowl. Gently rub in 50g (2oz) of the butter. Add the lemon juice and a little cold water to make a smooth dough.

2. Shape the remaining butter into a rectangle on a sheet of greaseproof paper.

3. Carefully roll out the dough on a lightly floured surface to make a strip a little wider than the butter and twice the length. Place the butter on half of the pastry and gently fold over the other half, pressing the edges with the floured rolling pin. Leave the pastry in a cool place for 20 minutes to let the butter harden.

[continues…]

4. Roll out the pastry on a lightly floured surface. Fold the bottom third up and the top third down, pressing the edges together with the rolling pin. Then turn the pastry so the folded edges are on the left and right of you. Roll and fold again, cover and leave in a cool place for 15 minutes. Repeat this process of folding and rolling out six times. The pastry is now ready to use.

Hot Water Pastry

MAKES 450g (1lb)

This is your typical pork pie pastry and was used to make hand-raised pies in the Victorian era. (Melton Mowbray pork pies originated with Mrs Beeton.) Care and patience is required for this pastry.

150g (5oz) lard
350g (12oz) plain flour, seasoned with ½ teaspoon salt
1 large egg yolk

1. Put the lard in a saucepan with 200ml (7fl oz) hot water and heat gently until the lard has melted.

2. Bring to the boil, remove from the heat and beat in the seasoned flour to form a soft dough. Beat the egg yolk into the dough, cover the dough with a damp cloth and leave to rest in a warm place for 15 minutes. Do not allow the dough to cool.

3. Roll out the pastry and pat two-thirds of it into the base and sides of the pie tin. Distribute it evenly to leave space for the pie filling. Use the remaining pastry for the lid.

Francis Coulson's Suet Pastry

MAKES about 450g (1lb)

Whenever I hear the name Francis Coulson my heart smiles. He taught me several light-hearted movements in the delicate area of pastry. I was a complete flop with his scones, but made up for it with my Beef Wellington! Francis and Brian Sack are legends in their own right and the MBE awarded to them by HM The Queen was more than justified. Like Catherine Cookson and chefs around the globe, I wait with anticipation for their book on Sharrow Bay.

Suet should be fresh if at all possible and your butcher will sell you suet at any time. It should be grated on a cheese grater and seasoned with a little salt before use.

275g (10oz) self-raising flour, sifted
50g (2oz) butter, softened
75g (3oz) freshly shredded beef suet
salt and freshly ground black pepper (to taste)

1 egg (large), beaten
extra flour

1. Place the sifted flour, butter and suet in a bowl, and season with a little salt and pepper. Rub together with your fingertips until the mixture resembles fine bread-crumbs.

2. Mix the egg with 1 tablespoon water, make a well in the centre of the flour mixture and pour in the egg. Mix together until a soft paste forms. Turn the mixture out onto a floured work surface and knead into a soft but fairly firm dough.

Herb Suet Pastry (Method 1)

MAKES about 450g (1lb)

I use herb suet when making a beef steak pudding using the richer cuts of meat. See Fillet of Beef in Herb Suet Pastry (p. 179).

225g (8oz) self-raising flour, sifted
1 tablespoon chopped fresh coriander
75g (3oz) butter, softened
50g (2oz) freshly shredded beef suet

salt and freshly ground black pepper (to taste)
1 egg (size 3), beaten
extra flour

1. Place the sifted flour, coriander, butter and suet in a bowl, and season with a little salt and pepper. Rub together with your fingertips until the mixture resembles fine breadcrumbs.

2. Mix the egg with 1 tablespoon water, make a well in the centre of the flour mixture and pour in the egg. Mix together until a soft paste forms. Turn the mixture out onto a floured work surface and knead into a soft but fairly firm dough.

Cheese Scone Pastry

MAKES about 450g (1lb)

This is a very original recipe from my mother's old cookery book. Dedicated to Gill Owen, and to my very own commis chef Mark Owen at Granada Television, the finest television presenter in the North, here is another of my trade secrets!

225g (8oz) self-raising flour, sifted
50g (2oz) butter, softened
50g (2oz) lard
salt and freshly ground black pepper (to
   taste)

50g (2oz) English Cheddar, grated
2 tablespoons finely chopped shallots
50ml (2fl oz) yoghurt, blended with
   6 tablespoons water
extra flour

1. Place the sifted flour, butter and lard in a bowl, and season with a little salt and pepper. Rub together with your fingertips until the mixture resembles fine breadcrumbs. Add the grated cheese and shallots.

2. Make a well in the centre and pour in the yoghurt mixture. Mix together until a soft paste forms. Turn the mixture out onto a floured work surface and knead into a soft but fairly firm dough.

TTB's Beef Wellington with Lancashire Cheese & Mustard

SERVES 6–8

I created this recipe for a dinner party and Pie Society meeting. It was Susan Vickers' birthday and we decided to come up with something completely different. The addition of Lancashire cheese and mustard really made it very tasty. The Beef Wellington was served with a Madeira Sauce (p. 43). For a traditional Beef Wellington, omit the cheese and mustard.

900g (2lb) fillet or sirloin of beef
salt and freshly ground black pepper (to taste)
75g (3oz) butter
2 onions, peeled and finely chopped
275g (10oz) button mushrooms or wild mushrooms, roughly chopped

900g (2lb) Puff Pastry (p. 171)
225g (8oz) chicken liver pâté
225g (8oz) creamy Lancashire cheese, crumbled
4 tablespoons English mustard
1 egg, lightly beaten

1. With a sharp knife, trim the fat from the beef. Season the meat well with salt and pepper.

2. Melt the butter in a large frying pan and add the beef. Seal the meat all over, cooking for at least 10 minutes. Remove the meat from the pan, placing it on one side.

3. Add a little more butter to the same pan and add the chopped onion and mushrooms, cooking until all the moisture has evaporated. Allow them to cool.

4. Preheat the oven to Gas Mark 6/200°C/400°F.

5. Roll out the pastry into a large rectangle and place on a greased baking sheet. Spread the onion and mushroom mixture over the centre of the pastry, and place the beef on top. Top the fillet with a layer of pâté, then cheese and mustard. Brush the edges of the pastry with the beaten egg, fold and seal, pressing the edges together to seal the pastry. Make some flowers and leaves from the left-over pastry to decorate the Beef Wellington and brush it completely with the beaten egg.

6. Bake in the centre of the oven for 20 minutes, then lower the temperature to Gas Mark 4/180°C/350°F for a further 15 minutes until golden brown.

Individual Beef Wellingtons

SERVES 8

I have used this style of Beef Wellington for small parties. Serve with gravy or Madeira Sauce (pp. 42–4), if you like.

900g (2lb) fillet of beef, cut into 8 × 100g (4oz) portions
salt and freshly ground black pepper (to taste)
75g (3oz) butter
2 onions, peeled and finely chopped

275g (10oz) button mushrooms or wild mushrooms, roughly chopped
900g (2lb) Puff Pastry (p. 171)
225g (8oz) chicken liver pâté
1 egg, lightly beaten

1. With a sharp knife, trim the fat from the beef fillets. Season the meat well with salt and pepper.

2. Melt the butter in a large frying pan and add the beef. Seal each fillet all over, cooking for at least 3 minutes on each side. Remove the fillets from the pan, placing them on one side.

3. Add a little more butter to the same pan and add the chopped onion and mushrooms, cooking until all the moisture has evaporated. Allow them to cool.

4. Preheat the oven to Gas Mark 6/200°C/400°F.

5. Roll out the pastry into a large square, cut out 8 × 15cm (6 inch) squares and place on greased baking sheets. Spread equal amounts of onion and mushroom mixture over the centre of each pastry square, place a piece of beef fillet on the mixture, and top each fillet with a layer of pâté. Brush the edges of the pastry with the beaten egg, fold and seal, pressing the edges together to seal the pastry. Make some flowers and leaves from the left-over pastry to decorate the Beef Wellingtons, and brush them completely with the beaten egg.

6. Bake in the centre of the oven for 15 minutes, then lower the temperature to Gas Mark 4/180°C/350°F for a further 10 minutes until golden brown.

Beef Roly Poly with Herb Suet Pastry

SERVES 4

This is an old wartime recipe from the 1940s when my dad was up to his neck in muck and bullets, so he says! Serve it with Onion Gravy (p. 44) and new potatoes.

We thank thee Lord, for this poor meit,
If mooar we had, mooar we'd eit;
But since eaur fortunes have bin so bad,
We'll thank the Lord for what we'n had.

'The Grace of an Old Lady in the Workhouse', Bolton, Lancashire, 1896

25g (1oz) beef dripping
450g (1lb) roughly minced beef
225g (8oz) sirloin (fat removed), diced
2 large onions, peeled and sliced
2 carrots, peeled and diced
a pinch of fresh rosemary
salt and freshly ground black pepper (to taste)
25g (1oz) plain flour
275ml (10fl oz) Basic Beef Stock (p. 13)
2 tablespoons port
1 tablespoon Worcester sauce

1 tablespoon tomato purée
100g (4oz) garden peas

For the herb suet pastry (Method 2)

450g (1lb) self-raising flour, sifted
¼ teaspoon salt
225g (8oz) freshly shredded beef suet
1 teaspoon *fines herbes*
150ml (5fl oz) cold Basic Beef Stock (p. 13)

1. Preheat the oven to Gas Mark 6/200°C/400°F.

2. Melt the dripping in a large saucepan and fry the minced and diced beef for 10 minutes. Add the onions, carrots and rosemary, fry for a further 5 minutes, and season with salt and pepper.

3. Add the flour and cook for a further 2 minutes. Very slowly add the stock and port. Finally add the Worcester sauce and tomato purée and cook for a further 25 minutes, stirring every 4 minutes. Blend in the peas and allow the mixture to cool.

4. To make the suet pastry, sift the flour and salt into a bowl. Add the beef suet and *fines herbes* and just enough beef stock to make a scone-like dough.

5. Let the pastry stand for 10 minutes, then roll it out into a large rectangle. Spread the surface with the beef mixture. Roll up the pastry and fold the sides underneath. Wrap it carefully in greased greaseproof paper and then in a muslin cloth.

6. Steam in a steamer for 2 hours or place the roly poly on a grill rack in a large roasting tin half-filled with water. Cover with cooking foil and bake in the oven at Gas Mark 6/200°C/400°F for 45 minutes, then at Gas Mark 4/180°C/350°F for 45 minutes.

Brian Sack's Traditional Steak & Kidney Pudding or Pie

SERVES 6

*E*veryone's favourite and the most popular pudding and pie around Great Britain, not only in households but in many hotels and restaurants – nowhere more so than the renowned Sharrow Bay Country House Hotel in Ullswater. Yet the list of ingredients is surprisingly simple.

I know of one chef who has more grease on his hair than his apron and he actually puts carrots into his steak pie. Please do not try this at home!

Do not use cheap cuts of meat – it takes the best rump steak and lamb's kidney to achieve the perfect pie. I have given two methods using suet and puff pastry – the choice is yours.

Serve with the gravy in a sauceboat, fresh carrots and swede mashed with a little butter and nutmeg, garnished with roast potatoes.

'Never decry the word Gravy' *Francis Coulson MBE*

560g (1¼lb) rump steak	275ml (10fl oz) Basic Beef Stock (p. 13)
175g (6oz) lamb's kidneys	salt and freshly ground black pepper (to taste)
25g (1oz) seasoned flour with a generous pinch of curry powder	about 350g (12oz) Suet Pastry (p. 173) or Puff Pastry (p. 171)
25g (1oz) butter	1 quantity 'Real' Gravy (pp. 42–43)
1 large onion, peeled and chopped	

1. Trim the gristle and fat off the steak and cut into 2.5cm (1 inch) cubes. Remove the fat and skin from the kidneys, core them, and dice quite small. Toss the steak and kidney into the seasoned flour with a hint of curry powder.

2. Melt the butter in a large frying pan and quickly seal the meat all over. Add the chopped onion and cook for 4 minutes. Add the beef stock, season and simmer for a further 45 minutes.

3. While the beef is simmering, line a large well-greased pudding basin with the suet pastry, leaving enough pastry to make a lid. (If using puff pastry, just make a lid.)

4. Put the steak and kidney into the basin and top with a pastry lid, damping the edges with water to make it stick. Make a small hole in the centre of the lid and pour in just enough stock to keep the meat moist. If you are using suet pastry, cover the basin with buttered tin foil or greaseproof paper. Stand the basin in a large saucepan with enough water to come halfway up the sides of the basin. Bring the water to the boil and steam for 2 hours, making sure you top up the water as necessary.

5. If using puff pastry, preheat the oven to Gas Mark 7/220°C/425°F and bake in the centre of the oven for 35–40 minutes until golden brown.

Fillet of Beef in Herb Suet Pastry

SERVES 8–10

The method is the same as for Beef Roly Poly (p. 177). Serve with a Green Salad (p. 138) and jacket potatoes. Enjoy!

1.3kg (3lb) piece of beef fillet, trimmed and flattened out
900g (2lb) Herb Suet Pastry Method 1 (p. 173)
salt and freshly ground black pepper (to taste)

100g (4oz) butter, softened
100g (4oz) button mushrooms, wiped and very finely chopped
175g (6oz) leaf spinach, blanched
2 tablespoons French mustard
1 tablespoon lemon juice

1. Ensure the fillet is completely flattened by covering it with cling film and flattening it with a steak mallet or rolling pin.

2. Let the pastry stand for 10 minutes, then roll it out into a large rectangle. Spread the surface with the flattened fillet of beef, and season it well with salt and pepper. Spread the butter over the beef, then cover the top with mushrooms, spinach and mustard blended with the lemon juice. Season again and roll the suet up, like a roly poly (Swiss roll) and fold the sides underneath. Wrap it carefully in well-greased greaseproof paper and then in a muslin cloth.

3. Steam in a steamer for 2 hours. Or place the fillet of beef on a grill rack in a large roasting tin half-filled with water. Cover with cooking foil and bake in the oven at Gas Mark 4/180°C/350°F for 90 minutes.

4. Remove from the oven, slice and serve.

Beef & Pork Pie

SERVES 6

The combination of flavours in this recipe will turn the heads of everyone tasting it.

900g (2lb) roughly minced beef
450g (1lb) roughly minced pork
50g (2oz) peeled and finely chopped onion
275ml (10fl oz) dry white wine
2 tablespoons brandy
½ teaspoon dried sage
1 tablespoon Dijon mustard
1 Bramley apple, peeled and coarsely grated
salt and freshly ground black pepper (to taste)
675g (1½lb) Shortcrust Pastry (p. 171)

1 egg, beaten with a little milk
150ml (5fl oz) pork stock
1 teaspoon powdered aspic

For the stuffing

50g (2oz) freshly minced Bramley apple
150ml (5fl oz) Basic Beef Stock (p. 13)
225g (8oz) black pudding (skin removed), mashed
75g (3oz) brown breadcrumbs, toasted
2 teaspoons chopped fresh basil
1 teaspoon chopped fresh coriander
50g (2oz) freshly minced onion

1. Preheat the oven to Gas Mark 6/200°C/400°F.

2. Mix the minced beef and pork with the onion, half the wine, the brandy, sage, mustard and grated apple, season well and set on one side.

3. To make the stuffing, put the minced apple and the beef stock in a saucepan and heat together until darkened. Blend in the mashed black pudding, and then the remaining stuffing ingredients.

4. Line the bottom of a pie mould with pastry. Put in a layer of the meat mixture and then the stuffing mixture, alternating until you have three layers of beef and pork and two of stuffing.

5. Roll out the remaining pastry, making a lid to fit the pie. Make a hole in the centre of the pie lid. Decorate with pastry leaves and brush with egg glaze.

6. Bake for 35 minutes. Reduce the oven temperature to Gas Mark 2/150°C/300°F and continue to bake for a further 45 minutes.

7. Remove the pie from the oven and allow it to cool. Warm the pork stock with the remaining white wine, mix with the powdered aspic, and pour the aspic mixture through the hole in the pie lid. When the aspic has set, wrap the pie in cling film and leave it in the fridge to mature for two days.

Beef 'n' Onion Pie

SERVES 4

This is the biggest-selling pie in central Scotland and the most requested pie whenever I do my Pie Society cookery demonstrations.

275g (10oz) Shortcrust Pastry (p. 171)
25g (1oz) butter
2 large onions, peeled and chopped
275g (10oz) cooked minced beef
100g (4oz) potatoes, cooked and diced

2 eggs, beaten with a little cream
a pinch of cayenne pepper
salt (to taste)
1 egg, beaten with a little milk

1. Preheat the oven to Gas Mark 7/220°C/425°F.

2. Roll out the pastry on a floured surface using two-thirds for the pie base and the rest for the lid. Grease a 1.2 litre (2 pint) pie dish and line with the pastry.

3. Melt the butter in a saucepan and gently fry the onions for about 4 minutes, until they are transparent, then allow them to cool. Put the onions in a large bowl with the rest of the ingredients, except the egg, and mix thoroughly.

4. Place the mixture in the lined pie dish and top with the pastry lid. Glaze with the beaten egg and bake in the oven for 30 minutes until golden brown.

Mrs Beeton's Boiled Beef & Carrot Pie

SERVES 4

A Cockney pie dating back to the early nineteenth century, when dripping and bully beef were the main ingredients. This one's for Graham Cornish and Peter Castell, at the Mrs Beeton Pie Company in Cornwall, who are doing their best to recreate the pies of yester-year.

275g (10oz) Shortcrust Pastry (p. 171)
25g (1oz) butter
1 large onion, peeled and chopped
400g (14oz) boiled beef, minced
175g (6oz) carrots, cooked and diced
150ml (5fl oz) Onion Gravy (p. 44)

a pinch of freshly grated nutmeg
a pinch of cayenne pepper
a pinch of thyme
salt (to taste)
1 egg, beaten with a little milk

1. Preheat the oven to Gas Mark 7/220°C/425°F.

2. Roll out the pastry on a floured surface using two-thirds for the base and the rest for the lid. Grease a 1.2 litre (2 pint) pie dish and line with the pastry.

3. Melt the butter in a saucepan and gently fry the onion for about 4 minutes, until it is transparent, then allow to cool. Put the onion in a large bowl with the rest of the ingredients, except the egg, and mix thoroughly.

4. Place the mixture in the lined pie dish and top with the pastry lid. Glaze with the beaten egg and bake in the oven for 30 minutes until golden brown.

Mark Owen's 'Trade Secret' Christmas Pie

SERVES 10

An alternative to the normal veal and ham, this really gives the pie an extra Christmas flavour that will have your guests talking! In January, February and March 1997 I was involved with Granada Television's Trade Secrets, *a well-known television programme with a television presenter who has become a close friend too. Mark Owen is a great lover of football and a Liverpool lad. We did several television interviews together for Granada Television's* Main Ingredient *a few years ago. He loves cookery and eats everything I make … To go back to trade secrets, what do you think is the secret ingredient that gives this pie its perfect flavour? Yes, you are right, the original mincemeat recipe on page 76! Serve with pickles and a red cabbage salad.*

450g (1lb) minced beef
450g (1lb) minced veal
150g (5oz) York ham, minced
1 tablespoon chopped fresh parsley
175g (6oz) Mincemeat (p. 76)
4 tablespoons cranberry jelly
grated rind of 1 lemon
2 onions, peeled and finely chopped
salt and freshly ground black pepper

3 tablespoons powdered aspic
275ml (10fl oz) clear apple juice,
    warmed

For the pastry
300g (10oz) lard
700g (1½lb) plain flour, seasoned with
    1 teaspoon salt
2 large egg yolks

1. Preheat the oven to Gas Mark 4/180°C/350°F.

2. Put the beef, veal, ham, parsley, mincemeat, cranberry jelly, lemon rind and onions in a large mixing bowl. Add 1 teaspoon salt and some freshly ground black pepper, mix well and place on one side.

3. To make the pastry, put the lard in a large saucepan with 400ml (14fl oz) hot water and heat gently until the lard has melted. Bring to the boil, remove from the heat and beat in the seasoned flour to form a soft dough. Beat the egg yolk into the dough, cover with a damp cloth and leave to rest in a warm place for 15 minutes. (Do not allow the dough to cool.)

4. Roll out the pastry and pat two-thirds of it into the base and sides of a 2 kilo (4½lb) loaf tin, distributing it evenly to leave space for the pie filling.

5. Place the meat mixture inside and make a lid with the remaining pastry. Cover the pie and seal the edges, using any pastry trimmings to decorate the top. Make a large hole in the centre of the pie lid. Bake for 90 minutes and allow to cool for 3 hours.

6. Make up the aspic jelly with the apple juice, cool for 10 minutes, then pour the aspic through the hole in the top of the pie. Chill the pie for 2–3 hours, then remove from the tin. Slice with a warm carving knife and serve.

After Christmas Beef & Turkey Pie

SERVES 6

A real after-Christmas treat, this was very popular during the Easter weekend and is often served at picnics and summer fêtes. When eating indoors, it's good with buttered broccoli and minted new potatoes.

25g (1oz) butter	450g (1lb) turkey meat, cut into strips
2 carrots, peeled and diced	2 tablespoons double cream
10 baby onions, peeled	salt and freshly ground black pepper (to
75g (3oz) ham, shredded	taste)
25g (1oz) plain wholemeal flour	1 teaspoon chopped fresh tarragon or
450ml (15fl oz) milk	your favourite herb
450g (1lb) cooked beef, shredded	275g (10oz) Puff Pastry (p. 171)

1. Preheat the oven to Gas Mark 6/200°C/400°F.

2. Melt the butter in a saucepan and lightly fry the carrots, onions and ham for 5 minutes. Blend in the flour and cook for 1 minute. Slowly add the milk, stirring continuously until the sauce thickens and becomes smooth, then simmer for 3 minutes.

3. Add the beef, turkey and cream, and season with salt and pepper. Should you wish to, at this stage you can sprinkle over your favourite chopped fresh herb. I like to use fresh tarragon to give it that sweet smell, when you cut into the pie.

4. Pour the mixture into a 1.2 litre (2 pint) pie dish and roll out the puff pastry to form a lid. Seal well, brushing the top with a little milk.

5. Bake for 25–30 minutes until golden brown, and serve.

Beef, Leek & Horseradish Pie

SERVES 6

My Pie Society committee pronounced this recipe quite sane, sensible, savoury and satisfying to the palate, but what do they know!

Serve this sumptuous pie with baked parsnips and creamed potatoes to soak up the very creamy sauce.

50g (2oz) butter	450g (1lb) beef, cooked and diced
2 leeks, washed and very finely sliced	25g (1oz) grated horseradish
8 shallots, peeled and sliced	salt and freshly ground black pepper (to taste)
100g (4oz) button mushrooms, wiped	
25g (1oz) plain flour	175g (6oz) Shortcrust Pastry (p. 171)
275ml (10fl oz) milk, warmed	100g (4oz) Puff Pastry (p. 171)
150ml (5fl oz) double cream	1 egg, beaten with a little milk

1. Preheat the oven to Gas Mark 6/200°C/400°F.

2. Melt the butter in a large saucepan and gently fry the leeks, shallots and button mushrooms for about 10 minutes, stirring occasionally with a wooden spoon.

3. Add the flour and cook for a further 2 minutes. Gradually add the warm milk and cream, stirring continuously until the sauce becomes thick and creamy. Simmer for 2 minutes.

4. Add the beef and grated horseradish to the sauce, seasoning well with salt and pepper, and allow the mixture to cool.

5. Roll out the shortcrust pastry and use it to line the base and sides of a greased 1.2 litre (2 pint) ovenproof pie dish. Pour in the meat and vegetable mixture, top with puff pastry, glaze with the egg, and bake in the centre of the oven for 30 minutes.

Beef & Guinness Pie

SERVES 6

To make this in the form of the original recipe created by Hubert Lowry, the well-known Northern Irish chef, the beef should be soaked in the Guinness for 24 hours and seasoned with salt and pepper. The beef is then dried slightly and tossed in the flour before cooking. Just before the puff pastry lid is placed on the pie, 100g (4oz) sliced black pudding is placed on top of the beef.

50g (2oz) butter
675g (1½lb) good-quality stewing beef
   (fat and gristle removed), cut into
   2.5cm (1 inch) cubes
10 shallots, peeled and sliced
100g (4oz) button mushrooms, wiped
25g (1oz) plain flour

275ml (10fl oz) Rich Beef Stock (p. 14)
150ml (5fl oz) Guinness
salt and freshly ground black pepper (to
   taste)
175g (6oz) Shortcrust Pastry (p. 171)
100g (4oz) Puff Pastry (p. 171)
1 egg, beaten with a little milk

1. Preheat the oven to Gas Mark 6/200°C/400°F.

2. Melt the butter in a large saucepan and fry the beef for 5 minutes. Add the shallots and button mushrooms and cook for about 10 minutes, stirring occasionally with a wooden spoon.

3. Add the flour and cook for a further 2 minutes. Gradually add the beef stock and Guinness, stirring continuously until the sauce thickens slightly. Simmer for 90 minutes. Season well with salt and pepper and allow the mixture to cool a little.

4. Roll out the shortcrust pastry and use it to line the base and sides of a greased 1.2 litre (2 pint) ovenproof pie dish. Pour in the meat mixture, top with puff pastry, glaze with the egg, and bake in the centre of the oven for 30 minutes.

Beef & Apricot Pie

SERVES 6

You can use your favourite cut of meat for this recipe. I recommend a juicy piece of rib, minced and seasoned. You could also try using a different fruit — mango, guava or even gooseberries. If you wish, you can use the same ingredients to make little individual pies — great for fun parties and those not-too-serious evenings when your friends turn up unexpectedly. Harrods wanted me to make these for their food hall but I didn't have the time! There aren't enough hours in the day!

1 quantity Hot Water Pastry (p. 172)
1 egg, beaten with a little milk
3 tablespoons powdered aspic
275ml (10fl oz) clear apple juice,
  warmed

For the filling
450g (1lb) lean minced beef
225g (8oz) minced bacon

225g (8oz) chopped apricots
1 teaspoon finely chopped fresh sage
a pinch of dried or fresh mixed herbs
1 onion, peeled and finely chopped
4 tablespoons oatmeal
2 tablespoons brandy

1. Preheat the oven to Gas Mark 4/180°C/350°F.

2. Combine all the filling ingredients in a large mixing bowl and set on one side.

3. Roll out the pastry, pat two-thirds of it into the base and sides of a 1.4 litre (2¼ pint) loaf tin, greased and lined with greaseproof paper. Distribute it evenly to leave space for the filling. Place in the filling. Make a lid with the remaining pastry, cover the pie and seal the edges, using any pastry trimmings to decorate the top. Glaze with the beaten egg. Make a large hole in the centre of the lid. Bake for 90 minutes and allow to cool for 3 hours.

4. Make up the aspic jelly with the warm apple juice, cool for 10 minutes, then pour the aspic through the hole in the top of the pie. Chill the pie for 2–3 hours, then remove from the tin, slice with a warm carving knife, and serve.

Fillet of Beef & Shallot Pie

SERVES 4–6

You don't have to use puff pastry for this recipe. Try it with Shortcrust (p. 171) or Cheese Scone Pastry (p. 174), or even steamed with Francis Coulson's Suet Pastry (p. 173). Either way this really is a treat for beef lovers.

25g (1oz) butter
1 tablespoon cooking oil
450g (1lb) fillet of beef, roughly minced
salt and freshly ground black pepper (to taste)
6 rashers rindless streaky bacon, finely chopped
12 shallots, peeled and sliced
1 small carrot, peeled and diced
75ml (3fl oz) red wine
150ml (5fl oz) Basic Beef Stock (p. 13)

2 tablespoons double cream
2 tablespoons cranberry jelly
275g (10oz) Puff Pastry (p. 171)
2 tablespoons chopped fresh parsley
a little milk

For the garnish
2 slices white bread, cut into quarters
3 tablespoons olive oil
25g (1oz) butter

1. Preheat the oven to Gas Mark 6/200°C/400°F.

2. Melt the butter with the cooking oil in a large saucepan. Add the minced beef, seal all over, and season with salt and pepper. Simmer for 3 minutes, and add the bacon, shallots and carrot, stirring briskly for a further 3 minutes. Add the wine and beef stock, bring to the boil and simmer for 25 minutes over a low heat, reducing the stock by at least one-third.

3. Allow the beef and sauce to cool slightly and blend in the double cream and cranberry jelly.

4. Roll out the puff pastry and use about two-thirds of it to line the base and sides of a lightly greased 1.2 litre (2 pint) pie dish. Add the filling mixture, sprinkle with the chopped parsley and use the remaining puff pastry to make a lid. Brush the top with a little milk and bake in the centre of the oven for 25 minutes.

5. To make the garnish, fry the bread in the oil and butter and place around the pie when it is ready to be served.

Beef & Game Pie

SERVES 6–8

*T*oday you can buy the complete range of game meat from The Hart of England Deer Company in Warwickshire. It's also available from supermarkets and your local butcher who will stock it fresh and frozen.

Traditionally Beef and Game Pie should be made with a puff pastry crust but I use my very own shortcrust pastry specially made for this recipe.

50g (2oz) butter

50g (2oz) dripping or lard

450g (1lb) sirloin steak (fat and gristle removed), cut into 2.5cm (1 inch) cubes

675g (1½lb) mixed game meat, consisting of 225g (8oz) haunch of venison, rabbit and pheasant (gristle and all fat removed), diced

225g (8oz) button mushrooms, wiped

225g (8oz) shallots, peeled

2 cloves garlic, peeled and chopped

3 tablespoons seasoned plain flour

275ml (10fl oz) claret

275ml (10fl oz) Rich Beef Stock (p. 14)

1 onion, peeled and chopped

8 juniper berries

a pinch of allspice

a pinch of marjoram

1 teaspoon salt

freshly ground black pepper (to taste)

For the pastry

175g (6oz) plain flour

50g (2oz) shredded beef suet

a pinch of salt

freshly ground black pepper (to taste)

75g (3oz) unsalted butter, softened

1 egg yolk, blended with 4 tablespoons cold water

a little milk

1. Put the fat into a very large saucepan and heat gently. Add the beef and game and cook for 7 minutes, extracting the juices and browning the meat.

2. Add the mushrooms, shallots and garlic, cooking for a further 5 minutes. Sprinkle with the flour and cook for 3 minutes. Slowly add the wine and beef stock. Add the rest of the filling ingredients, take off the heat and allow to stand for 6 hours.

3. Meanwhile make up the pastry. Sift the flour into a mixing bowl, and add the suet, salt and pepper. Blend in the butter lightly with your fingertips. When the mixture resembles fine breadcrumbs, add the water and egg, binding into a stiff dough. Knead the dough lightly for 4 minutes, then cover and leave in a warm place until required.

4. Bring the beef and game mixture to the boil and simmer, reducing the stock by half and cooking for at least 25 minutes.

5. Place the beef and game mixture in a 1.2 litre (2 pint) pie dish. Roll out the pastry and cover the pie dish, sealing all round. Brush with a little milk and bake in the centre of the oven for 50 minutes at Gas Mark 4/180°C/350°F.

Traditional Cottage Pie

SERVES 4–6

I have several versions of this recipe which is very good for someone who is convalescing and who cannot digest food properly. This traditional cottage pie is not topped with cheese but you can also follow the original method of using left-over meat, finely chopped, left over from the Sunday joint – just like my mum used to make.

25g (1oz) beef dripping
450g (1lb) roughly minced beef or left-over finely chopped meat
2 large onions, peeled and finely diced
2 carrots, peeled and finely diced
a pinch of fresh rosemary
salt and freshly ground black pepper (to taste)
25g (1oz) plain flour

275ml (10fl oz) Basic Beef Stock (p. 13)
1 tablespoon Worcester sauce
1 tablespoon tomato purée
100g (4oz) garden peas
560g (1¼lb) potatoes, peeled, boiled and mashed
100g (4oz) carrots, peeled, chopped, boiled and puréed
25g (1oz) butter, softened

1. Preheat the oven to Gas Mark 5/190°C/375°F.

2. Melt the dripping in a large saucepan and fry the beef for 10 minutes. Add the onions, carrots and rosemary, fry for a further 5 minutes, and season with salt and pepper.

3. Add the flour and cook for a further 2 minutes. Very slowly add the stock. Finally, add the Worcester sauce and tomato purée and cook for a further 25 minutes, stirring every 4 minutes. Blend in the peas and allow the mixture to cool.

4. Blend the mashed potato and carrot together with a knob of butter and season with salt and pepper.

5. Place the filling mixture in a deep pie dish and cover with the warm mashed potato and carrot, using a fork to spread it evenly. Dot with the softened butter and bake in the centre of the oven for 30 minutes.

TTB's Cottage Pie with Lancashire Cheese & Potato Topping

SERVES 4–6

This recipe is a very enjoyable, far more robust supper recipe, served with crusty bread.

25g (1oz) beef dripping
450g (1lb) roughly minced beef
225g (8oz) sirloin of beef (fat removed), diced
2 large onions, peeled and sliced
2 carrots, peeled and diced
a pinch of fresh rosemary
salt and freshly ground black pepper (to taste)
25g (1oz) plain flour
275ml (10fl oz) Basic Beef Stock (p. 13)

2 tablespoons port
1 tablespoon Worcester sauce
1 tablespoon tomato purée
100g (4oz) garden peas
675g (1½lb) potatoes, peeled, boiled, seasoned and mashed with a knob of butter
25g (1oz) butter, softened
100g (4oz) Lancashire cheese, crumbled

1. Preheat the oven to Gas Mark 5/190°C/375°F.

2. Melt the dripping in a large saucepan and fry the beef for 10 minutes. Add the onions, carrots and rosemary, fry for a further 5 minutes, and season with salt and pepper.

3. Add the flour and cook for a further 2 minutes. Very slowly add the stock and port. Finally, add the Worcester sauce and tomato purée and cook for a further 25 minutes, stirring every 4 minutes. Blend in the peas and allow the mixture to cool.

4. Place the mixture in a deep pie dish and cover with the warm mashed potato, using a fork to spread it evenly. Dot with the softened butter and sprinkle with the crumbled Lancashire cheese and bake in the centre of the oven for 30 minutes.

Cottage Pie with Leek & Potato Topping

SERVES 4–6

This is the Welsh version presented by master chef Paul Reed who lives in Rossett but carries out his labours of love at the Chester Grosvenor Hotel.

25g (1oz) beef dripping
450g (1lb) roughly minced beef
225g (8oz) sirloin of beef (fat removed), diced
2 large onions, peeled and sliced
2 carrots, peeled and diced
a pinch of fresh rosemary
salt and freshly ground black pepper (to taste)
25g (1oz) plain flour
275ml (10fl oz) Basic Beef Stock (p. 13)

2 tablespoons port
1 tablespoon Worcester sauce
1 tablespoon tomato purée
100g (4oz) garden peas
675g (1½lb) potatoes, peeled, boiled, seasoned and mashed with a knob of butter
25g (1oz) butter, softened
225g (8oz) leeks, washed and shredded
50g (2oz) Lancashire cheese, crumbled

1. Preheat the oven to Gas Mark 6/200°C/400°F.

2. Melt the dripping in a large saucepan and fry the beef for 10 minutes. Add the onions, carrots and rosemary, fry for a further 5 minutes, and season with salt and pepper.

3. Add the flour and cook for a further 2 minutes. Very slowly add the stock and port. Finally, add the Worcester sauce and tomato purée and cook for a further 25 minutes, stirring every 4 minutes. Blend in the peas and allow the mixture to cool.

4. Place the mixture in a deep pie dish and cover with warm mashed potato, using a fork to spread it evenly. Sprinkle with the softened butter, leeks and crumbled Lancashire cheese and bake in the centre of the oven for 25 minutes.

Pigeon & Beefsteak Pie

SERVES 6

Mrs Agnes B. Marshall wrote her 5 shilling cookery book in 1886. I started to read it page by page when I was a young commis chef and I still think that, even by today's standards, Mrs Marshall's is one of the finest books on British food ever written. Some of her recipes we could not possibly reproduce nowadays (like her Beef and Lark Pie), but her Rumpsteak with Oysters and this classic from the 1860s can be, so I have modernised them just for you.

Should you not be able to get hold of pigeon, try using quail, grouse or pheasant meat. Most supermarkets, Makro and other outlets will have frozen pigeons. Simply defrost and cut all the meat away from the bones, using the bones to add to your beef stock.

25g (1oz) beef dripping
350g (12oz) pigeon meat, cut into chunks
450g (1lb) rump steak, cut into chunks
225g (8oz) button mushrooms, wiped
1 bay leaf
a sprig of thyme
1 teaspoon chopped fresh parsley
10 shallots, peeled and sliced

salt and freshly ground black pepper (to taste)
1 tablespoon plain flour
200ml (7fl oz) Basic Beef Stock (p. 13)
150ml (5fl oz) red wine
3 hard-boiled eggs, halved
275g (10oz) Puff Pastry (p. 171)
1 egg, beaten with a little milk

1. Heat the dripping in a large saucepan and brown the meat, cooking all over for about 4 minutes. Add the mushrooms, bay leaf, thyme, parsley and shallots and cook for a further 3 minutes, seasoning with salt and pepper.

2. Sprinkle the meat with the flour and cook for 3 more minutes. Add the beef stock and red wine and simmer gently for 1 hour.

3. Carefully discard the bay leaf and thyme. With a slotted spoon, remove the meat and mushrooms from the saucepan and place in a deep pie dish with the hard-boiled eggs.

4. Boil the stock left in the saucepan until reduced by half. Meanwhile, preheat the oven to Gas Mark 4/180°C/350°F and roll out the puff pastry to make a lid to fit the pie dish.

5. Pour the beef stock onto the meat, top with the pastry, generously wash the top of the pastry with the egg and bake in the centre of the oven for 40 minutes.

Ruth Pinch's Beefsteak Pudding

SERVES 6

Ruth Pinch is a character in Charles Dickens' famous novel Martin Chuzzlewit. *She used 175g (6oz) butter for the crust of her pudding instead of suet, and moistened the flour into a paste with the well-beaten yolks of 4 eggs, mixed with a little water (an extravagant young woman, that!). Otherwise the ingredients and directions for making are the same as those in Eliza Acton's recipe written 122 years ago. Again, this wonderful food historian, chef and author TTB has adapted it for modern cooks!*

a little butter
1 quantity Suet Pastry (p. 173)
25g (1oz) beef dripping
675g (1½lb) rump steak, cut into chunks
1 large onion, peeled and finely chopped
25g (1oz) plain flour

450ml (15fl oz) Basic Beef Stock (p. 13)
salt and freshly ground black pepper (to taste)
1 tablespoon chopped fresh parsley
1 teaspoon lemon juice
12 oysters and their juice or 1 small tin smoked oysters

1. Line a large 1.3kg (3lb) pudding basin with buttered greaseproof paper and then the suet pastry, leaving a piece for the lid.

2. Fill a steamer with water, or half-fill a large saucepan to hold the pudding basin.

3. Heat the dripping in a large saucepan and fry the steak for 4 minutes. Add the onion and cook for a further 2 minutes. Sprinkle with the flour, cook for 3 minutes, add the beef stock, seasoning and parsley and simmer for 1 hour.

4. Remove from the heat, add the lemon juice and oysters, stir and fill the lined basin with the meat, oysters and stock.

5. Roll out the remaining suet lid and cover the pudding filling, press and secure the edges with a little water. Cover the pudding with a double piece of greaseproof paper, tied down with string, leaving room for the pastry to expand. Place in the steamer or saucepan of boiling water with a tightly closed lid and steam for 3 hours, taking great care to keep topping up with boiling water.

6. Let the pudding stand for 10 minutes before serving. Pour any left-over beef stock into a sauceboat and serve with the pudding.

Cornish Pasties

MAKES 4–6 pasties

The Cornish pasty is one of the few forms of English cookery that conserves all the value of the food. It contains meat, turnip and onion, with the pastry joined at the side – the ultimate portable lunch for the working men of Cornwall. It is very important to dice the meat and vegetables very small – about 1cm (½ inch) square.

A 1922 recipe from St Ives uses 100g (4oz) calves' liver, finely chopped and blended with the steak.

Nowadays, Ginsters of Callington, Cornwall, produce world-famous genuine Cornish pasties and supply them to shops the length and breadth of Britain.

'There is no love sincerer than the love of food' *Bernard Shaw, 1878*

Pastry rolled out like a plate,
Piled with turmut, tates and mate,
Doubled up, and baked like fate,
That's a Cornish pasty.

Cornish saying

25g (1oz) beef dripping
350g (12oz) rump steak, diced
4 potatoes, peeled and diced
1 large onion, peeled and chopped
1 large carrot, peeled and diced
100g (4oz) turnip, peeled and diced

salt and freshly ground black pepper (to taste)
1 tablespoon chopped fresh parsley
450g (1lb) Shortcrust Pastry (p. 171)
1 egg, beaten with a little milk

1. Preheat the oven to Gas Mark 7/220°C/425°F.

2. Heat the dripping in a large saucepan, add the meat and vegetables and cook for 8 minutes, stirring all the time with a wooden spoon. Season the mixture well, add the parsley, and allow it to cool completely.

3. Roll out the pastry to about 0.5cm (¼ inch) thick and cut out 4–6 × 15cm (6 inch) rounds. Put equal amounts of the mixture in the centre of each round. Dampen the edge of the rounds with the beaten egg, and fold each round over to make a half-moon shape. Turn the edges round to make small turns (horns), pinching and crimping the edges to seal the pasty completely. Glaze with the beaten egg and place the pasties on a greased baking sheet.

4. Bake in the centre of the oven (lowering the heat after 10 minutes to Gas Mark 4/180°C/350°F) for 30 minutes.

Forfar Bridies

This is very similar to the Cornish pasty except that it is more of a steak pasty than a Cornish. It was invented by Mr Jolly, a baker in Forfar, in the 1870s. Why bridies? Because they are a simple meal that a young bride could add to her book of recipes. The ingredients and method are exactly the same as for Cornish pasties (p. 195) but omit the potato, carrot and turnip and add a generous pinch of dried English mustard to the seasoning.

Beef & Leek Pasties

MAKES 6–8 pasties

A taste of Wales here. The Irish version of this recipe uses diced potatoes with strong onions in place of leeks. When they could not afford beef or chicken the miners often used sausage meat.

450g (1lb) sirloin of beef, roughly chopped	225g (8oz) potatoes, peeled, boiled and diced
50g (2oz) butter	salt and freshly ground black pepper (to taste)
4 leeks, washed and finely chopped	
2 sprigs of fresh parsley	450g (1lb) Shortcrust Pastry (p. 171)
3 tablespoons redcurrant jelly	1 egg, beaten with a little milk

1. Put the meat in a frying pan with the butter, leeks and parsley. Cover and cook for 25 minutes, stirring every 5 minutes. Add the jelly and potatoes, seasoning well, and allow to cool.

2. Roll out the pastry to 0.5cm (¼ inch) in thickness and cut out 6–8 × 15cm (6 inch) rounds. Place the meat mixture in the centre of each round, dampen the edges of each round and fold over to make a half-moon shape, pinching and crimping the edges. Glaze with the beaten egg, and put the pasties on a greased baking sheet.

3. Bake at Gas Mark 4/180°C/350°F for 35 minutes.

Beef, Mushroom & Potato Pasties

MAKES 8 pasties

Real West country pasties served at picnics in Victorian Britain.

450g (1lb) sirloin of beef, roughly minced

225g (8oz) mushrooms, wiped and sliced

1 onion, peeled and finely chopped

2 sprigs of fresh parsley, chopped

25g (1oz) butter

1 tablespoon cooking oil

225g (8oz) potatoes, peeled, boiled and diced

salt and freshly ground black pepper (to taste)

450g (1lb) Shortcrust Pastry (p. 171)

1 egg, beaten with a little milk

1. Put the meat into a large shallow frying pan with the mushrooms and onion, parsley, butter and cooking oil, cover and cook for 35 minutes.

2. Add the potatoes, seasoning well, and cook for a further 5 minutes. Allow the mixture to rest for 15 minutes.

3. Roll out the pastry to 0.5cm (¼ inch) in thickness and cut out 8 × 15cm (6 inch) rounds. Strain the mixture and place an equal amount in the centre of each round. Dampen the edges of each round and fold them over to make a half-moon shape, pinching and crimping the edges. Glaze with the beaten egg and put the pasties on a greased baking sheet.

4. Bake at Gas Mark 4/180°C/350°F for 35 minutes.

Tatie Pasties

MAKES about 8 pasties

A traditional northern recipe, that dates back to the early nineteenth century. We have had an Olde Pastie Shoppe in Bolton for nearly two hundred years and it is still going strong. Young Mrs Beeton would have died for one of these!

25g (1oz) beef dripping
675g (1½lb) roughly minced beef
900g (2lb) potatoes, peeled and diced
150g (5oz) carrots, peeled and diced
225g (8oz) onion, peeled and sliced
1 tablespoon chopped fresh mixed herbs
25g (1oz) plain flour

100g (4oz) garden peas
275ml (10fl oz) Basic Beef Stock (p. 13)
salt and freshly ground black pepper (to taste)
900g (2lb) Shortcrust Pastry (p. 171)
1 egg, beaten with a little milk

1. Melt the dripping in a large saucepan and fry the beef and diced potatoes for 15 minutes. Add the rest of the filling ingredients, cover and cook for 25 minutes, stirring every 5 minutes. Season well and allow to cool.

2. Roll out the pastry to 0.5cm (¼ inch) in thickness and cut out 8–10 × 15cm (6 inch) rounds. Place an equal amount of meat mixture in the centre of each round, dampen the edges of each round and fold over to make a half-moon shape, pinching and crimping the edges. Glaze with the beaten egg and put the pasties on greased baking sheets.

3. Bake at Gas Mark 4/180°C/350°F for 35 minutes.

OPPOSITE Individual Beef Wellington (pages 175–6)

Lancashire Pasties

SERVES 6

These pasties contain all the popular meats and food from the North and this should by now be a recognised recipe.

25g (1oz) beef dripping
350g (12oz) rump steak, minced
175g (6oz) black pudding (skin removed), diced
4 potatoes, peeled and diced
1 large onion, peeled and chopped
1 large carrot, peeled and diced

salt and freshly ground black pepper (to taste)
1 tablespoon chopped fresh parsley
450g (1lb) Puff Pastry (p. 171)
100g (4oz) Lancashire cheese, crumbled
1 egg, beaten with a little milk

1. Preheat the oven to Gas Mark 7/220°C/425°F.

2. Heat the dripping in a large saucepan, add the steak, black pudding and vegetables and cook for 15 minutes, stirring all the time with a wooden spoon. Season the mixture well, add the parsley and allow it to cool completely.

3. Roll out the pastry to about 0.5cm (¼ inch) thick and cut out 6 × 15cm (6 inch) rounds. Put equal amounts of the mixture in the centre of each round, and sprinkle with equal amounts of cheese. Dampen the edges of the rounds with beaten egg, and fold each round over to make a half-moon shape. Turn the edges round to make small turns (horns), pinching and crimping the edges to seal the pasty completely. Glaze with the beaten egg and place the pasties on a greased baking sheet.

4. Bake in the centre of the oven for 25–30 minutes.

OPPOSITE Cliveden Fillet of Scotch Beef Poached in Madeira Sauce (pages 102–3)

Tatie Pie with Cheese Scone Topping

SERVES 6–8

This is one of those recipes that I had passed onto me by my dad (Nobby). He was an ex-soldier so he loved home-cooked food! And he had his own very special way of cooking. If you could put a spoon in his Tatie pie mixture and it fell over it was not thick enough! That's a dad for ya.

Serve this with hot buttered broccoli and minted peas.

25g (1oz) beef dripping
675g (1½lb) roughly minced beef
900g (2lb) potatoes, peeled and diced
150g (5oz) carrots, peeled and diced
225g (8oz) onions, peeled and sliced
1 tablespoon chopped fresh mixed herbs
25g (1oz) plain flour

100g (4oz) marrowfat peas
275ml (10fl oz) Basic Beef Stock (p. 13)
salt and freshly ground black pepper (to taste)
225g (8oz) black pudding (skin removed), diced
1 quantity Cheese Scone Pastry (p. 174)

1. Preheat the oven to Gas Mark 6/200°C/400°F.

2. Heat the dripping in a large saucepan until it is quite hot, add the mince and very quickly seal and brown it for 5 minutes. Add the potatoes, carrots, onions and mixed herbs, cooking for 4 minutes. Sprinkle with the flour, stir, add the peas and beef stock, bring to the boil and simmer for 35 minutes. Season with salt and pepper.

3. Put the mixture into a 1.2 litre (2 pint) pie dish and scatter the diced black pudding over the top (this helps to thicken the sauce in the filling during the cooking process).

4. Roll out the cheese scone pastry enough to cover the pie dish. Mark out 6–8 slices on the pastry, cover the pie dish with cooking foil or greased greaseproof paper and bake in the centre of the oven for 30–45 minutes.

Beef Steak & Ale Pudding

SERVES 6

Every chippy in Britain used to make their own version of steak pudding served with lashings of thick gravy. There is no finer taste than that of Guinness, steak and kidney in a suet pastry case. Developing this recipe for Ann and Pat Gallagher, whose menu includes only the best of British food, was time-consuming but worth all the hours taken to make this their signature dish. It's well worth visiting Ann at Gallaghers Restaurant, Little Scotland, Blackrod, near Bolton, Lancashire, or Pat at the new Gallaghers Oyster Bar in Bolton.

450g (1lb) Suet Pastry (p. 173)
a little flour
1 teaspoon softened butter
450g (1lb) rump of beef (trimmed weight) cut into 2.5cm (1 inch) cubes
225g (8oz) ox kidneys (trimmed weight), diced
1 large onion, peeled and finely chopped

1 tablespoon plain flour
salt and freshly ground black pepper (to taste)
1 tablespoon Worcester sauce
1 tablespoon mushroom ketchup
5 tablespoons Guinness
275ml (10fl oz) Basic Beef Stock (p. 13)
a little milk

1. Roll out the pastry on a floured board, cutting off one-third and keeping it on one side to top the pudding. Use the teaspoon of butter to grease a 1.8 litre (3 pint) pudding basin and line it with two-thirds of the suet pastry, pressing it in to cover the basin completely and slightly overlap the edge of the basin.

2. Place the beef, kidney and onion in a bowl, sprinkle with the flour, and season with salt and pepper. Add the rest of the ingredients, except the milk, and blend thoroughly. Place the meat mixture in the pastry-lined pudding basin. Moisten the edge of the pastry with a little milk and place the remaining third of the pastry on top of the pudding, pressing and sealing the circular edges together and trimming off any excess pastry. Cover the basin with generously greased greaseproof paper and tie it tightly with string.

3. Place the pudding in a large pan with enough boiling water to come two-thirds of the way up the sides of the basin. Bring to the boil for 15 minutes, then reduce the heat and steam gently for 4 hours.

4. Remove the greaseproof paper. Place a large serving plate on top of the pudding. Then, holding the pudding and plate, reverse the pudding onto the plate and serve.

Beef & Chestnut Pudding

SERVES 4

Christmas is coming and the beef is getting fat. Yes, the flavour of chestnuts brings warm and festive cheer …

450g (1lb) Suet Pastry (p. 173)	2 tablespoons chopped fresh parsley
a little flour	a pinch of freshly grated nutmeg
1 teaspoon softened butter	225g (8oz) peeled pre-cooked chestnuts
450g (1lb) chuck steak, diced	3 tablespoons brandy
225g (8oz) rindless streaky bacon, diced	1 teaspoon clear honey, warmed
1 onion, peeled and finely chopped	275ml (10fl oz) chicken stock
1 tablespoon plain flour	a little milk
salt and freshly ground black pepper (to taste)	

1. Roll out the pastry on a floured board, cutting off one-third and keeping it on one side to top the pudding. Use the teaspoon of butter to grease a 1.8 litre (3 pint) pudding basin and line it with two-thirds of the suet pastry, pressing it in to cover the basin completely and slightly overlap the edge of the basin.

2. Place the beef, bacon and onion in a bowl and sprinkle with the flour, and season with salt and pepper. Add the rest of the ingredients, except the milk, and blend thoroughly. Place the meat mixture in the pastry-lined pudding basin. Moisten the edge of the pastry with a little milk and place the remaining third of the pastry on top of the pudding, pressing and sealing the circular edges together and trimming off any excess pastry. Cover the basin with generously greased greaseproof paper and tie it tightly with string.

3. Place the pudding in a large pan with enough boiling water to come two-thirds of the way up the sides of the basin. Bring to the boil for 15 minutes, then reduce the heat and steam gently for 4 hours.

4. Remove the greaseproof paper. Place a large serving plate on top of the pudding. Then, holding the pudding and plate, reverse the pudding onto the plate and serve.

Smoked Bacon, Beef & Oyster Pudding

SERVES 4–6

Now served at Gallaghers Oyster Bar in Bolton, this classical recipe dates back to William Kitchiner the Regency eccentric.

450g (1lb) Suet Pastry (p. 173)
a little flour
1 teaspoon softened butter
450g (1lb) rindless smoked back bacon, diced
450g (1lb) chuck steak, diced
1 onion, peeled and finely chopped
1 tablespoon plain flour
salt and freshly ground black pepper (to taste)

225g (8oz) minced pork
2 tablespoons chopped fresh parsley
a pinch of freshly grated nutmeg
12 oysters and their juice
1 teaspoon clear honey, warmed
200ml (7fl oz) Basic Beef Stock (p. 13)
a little milk

1. Roll out the pastry on a floured board, cutting off one-third and keeping it on one side to top the pudding. Use the teaspoon of butter to grease a 1.8 litre (3 pint) pudding basin and line it with two-thirds of the suet pastry, pressing it in to cover the basin completely and slightly overlap the edge of the basin.

2. Place the smoked bacon, beef and onion in a bowl and sprinkle with flour, seasoning with salt and pepper. Add the rest of the ingredients, except the milk, and blend thoroughly. Place the meat mixture in the pastry-lined pudding basin. Moisten the edge of the pastry with a little milk and place the remaining third of the pastry on top of the pudding, pressing and sealing the circular edges together and trimming off any excess pastry. Cover the basin with generously greased greaseproof paper and tie it tightly with string.

3. Place the pudding in a large pan with enough boiling water to come two-thirds of the way up the sides of the basin. Bring to the boil for 15 minutes, then reduce the heat and steam gently for 4 hours.

4. Remove the greaseproof paper. Place a large serving plate on top of the pudding. Then, holding the pudding and plate, reverse the pudding onto the plate and serve.

Beef & Game Pudding

SERVES 4

If you are bored with turkey at Christmas this makes an excellent change.

450g (1lb) Suet Pastry (p. 173)	1 tablespoon plain flour
a little flour	salt and freshly ground black pepper (to taste)
1 teaspoon softened butter	1 tablespoon Worcester sauce
450g (1lb) rump of beef (trimmed weight), cut into 2.5cm (1 inch) cubes	1 tablespoon mushroom ketchup
225g (8oz) your favourite game meat, diced	150ml (5fl oz) red wine
	150ml (5fl oz) Basic Beef Stock (p. 13)
1 large onion, peeled and finely chopped	1 teaspoon juniper berries, crushed
	a little milk

1. Roll out the pastry on a floured board, cutting off one-third and keeping it on one side to top the pudding. Use the teaspoon of butter to grease a 1.8 litre (3 pint) pudding basin and line it with the remaining two-thirds of the suet pastry, pressing it in to cover the basin completely and slightly overlap the edge of the basin.

2. Place the beef, game and onion in a bowl and sprinkle with the flour and season with salt and pepper. Add the rest of the ingredients, except the milk, and blend thoroughly. Place the meat mixture in the pastry-lined pudding basin. Moisten the edge of the pastry with a little milk and place the remaining third of the pastry on top of the pudding, pressing and sealing the circular edges together and trimming off any excess pastry. Cover the basin with generously greased greaseproof paper and tie it tightly with string.

3. Place the pudding in a large pan with enough boiling water to come two-thirds of the way up the sides of the basin. Bring to the boil for 15 minutes, then reduce the heat and steam gently for 3 hours.

4. Remove the greaseproof paper. Place a large serving plate on top of the pudding. Then, holding the pudding and plate, reverse the pudding onto the plate and serve.

Beef & Vegetable Roly Poly with Cheese Scone Pastry

SERVES 6

This is a wartime recipe from my grandmother's collection.

1 quantity Cheese Scone Pastry (p. 174)	450g (1lb) cooked minced beef
a little flour	1 teaspoon mixed herbs
2 large carrots, peeled and grated	1 tablespoon Worcester sauce
1 turnip, peeled and grated	2 tablespoons sweet chutney
1 onion, peeled and chopped	salt and freshly ground black pepper (to
4 large potatoes, peeled and grated	taste)
4 tablespoons fresh or frozen peas	

1. Roll out the cheese scone pastry on a floured board to a rectangular shape.

2. Put all the vegetables into a saucepan with the herbs and enough boiling water to just cover them and no more. Cook for 15 minutes, then strain until quite dry, keeping the liquid for the gravy.

3. Spread the beef and mixed vegetables onto the cheese pastry, seasoning with Worcester sauce and spreading over the chutney. Season and then roll the pastry up like a Swiss roll.

4. Grease a baking tray and line it with well-buttered greaseproof paper. Place the roly poly on the baking tray and bake in the centre of the oven at Gas Mark 6/200°C/400°F for 35 minutes until golden brown. This is tasty served hot or cold.

Christmas Beef and Chestnut Terrine

SERVES 6–8

To make a good beef terrine, you have to use the finest of ingredients and the best cut of British beef, which means fillet, this being the basis of all my beef terrines. Use a 900g (2lb) non-stick loaf tin coated with butter. It is then placed in a roasting tin half-filled with water (a bain-marie*), and covered with greased cooking foil. The baking time and temperature are virtually the same for all terrines and pâtés, 60–80 minutes at Gas Mark 4/180°C/350°F.*

Serve beef and chestnut terrine with blackcurrant jelly and toast fingers.

450g (1lb) beef fillet cut into 7.5cm (3 inch) × 1cm (½ inch) strips	400g (14oz) pre-cooked peeled chestnuts
2 tablespoons whisky	225g (8oz) minced fillet of beef
2 tablespoons port	275g (10oz) minced pork
3 tablespoons red wine	3 shallots, peeled and finely chopped
1 tablespoon freshly grated nutmeg	2 cloves garlic, peeled and crushed
25g (1oz) soft brown sugar	1 teaspoon ground cinnamon
25g (1oz) butter	

1. Preheat the oven to Gas Mark 4/180°C/350°F.

2. Place the strips of fillet and minced beef in a bowl with the whisky, port, red wine and freshly grated nutmeg.

3. Melt the sugar and butter together in a saucepan, add 100g (4oz) of the whole chestnuts to the pan and cook for 3 minutes. Meanwhile crush the remaining chestnuts. Mix all the ingredients together in the bowl with the beef fillet, adding all the remaining ingredients and blending together thoroughly.

4. Place the mixture in a buttered loaf tin, place it in a roasting tin half-filled with water, cover with greased cooking foil and bake in the centre of the oven for 80 minutes.

5. Remove from the oven and leave to cool naturally for 4 hours. Place the terrine in the refrigerator for at least 24 hours before serving.

Beef & Hazelnut Terrine

SERVES 6–8

This terrine should be served with rowan jelly, warm toast fingers and a glass of robust red wine.

450g (1lb) beef fillet cut into 7.5cm (3 inch) × 1cm (½ inch) strips
2 tablespoons brandy
2 tablespoons port
1 tablespoon freshly grated nutmeg
25g (1oz) soft brown sugar
25g (1oz) butter

25g (1oz) freshly grated ginger
275g (10oz) chopped hazelnuts
225g (8oz) minced fillet of beef
275g (10oz) minced chicken
3 shallots, peeled and finely chopped
2 cloves garlic, peeled and crushed
1 teaspoon ground cinnamon

1. Preheat the oven to Gas Mark 4/180°C/350°F.

2. Place the strips of fillet in a bowl with the brandy, port and freshly grated nutmeg.

3. Heat the sugar, butter and ginger together in a saucepan, add 100g (4oz) of the hazelnuts to the pan and cook for 3 minutes. Mix all the ingredients together in the bowl with the beef fillet, adding all the remaining ingredients and blending together thoroughly.

4. Place the mixture in a buttered loaf tin, place it in a roasting tin half-filled with water, cover with greased cooking foil and bake in the centre of the oven for 60 minutes.

5. Remove from the oven and leave to cool naturally for 4 hours. Place the terrine in the refrigerator for at least 24 hours before serving.

Steve Johnson's Potted Beef Terrine with Red Onion Marmalade

SERVES 8

*S*teve contributed to my last cookery book Bridge Over Britain *with a selection of recipes from Scotland, and the combination of flavours from Stewart Macphie's Glenbervie Aberdeen Angus fillet and the red onion marmalade makes this one of my favourite recipes from this cookery book.*

Arrange the marmalade in the centre of the plate with slices of terrine around it, garnished with a watercress and beetroot salad.

50g (2oz) best butter
450g (1lb) Glenbervie Aberdeen Angus
 fillet steak, diced
225g (8oz) lamb's liver, chopped
salt and freshly ground black pepper (to
 taste)
100g (4oz) smoked rindless back bacon,
 chopped
2 onions, peeled and finely chopped
100g (4oz) button mushrooms, wiped
 and finely chopped
2 tablespoons chopped fresh parsley
8 tablespoons single cream

2 eggs, beaten
a pinch of marjoram
2 tablespoons whisky

For the marmalade
560g (1¼lb) red onions, peeled and
 finely sliced
275ml (10fl oz) red wine
salt and freshly ground black pepper (to
 taste)
1 tablespoon orange zest
1 tablespoon clear honey

1. Preheat the oven to Gas Mark 4/180°C/350°F.

2. Heat the butter in a large, deep non-stick saucepan. Add the steak, liver, seasoning and bacon, and cook for 5 minutes to seal the steak. Add the onions, mushrooms, parsley, cream and eggs, cook for 1 minute, remove from the heat and blend thoroughly. Add the marjoram and whisky

3. Place the mixture in a buttered loaf tin, place it in a roasting tin half-filled with water, cover with cooking foil and bake in the centre of the oven for 90 minutes.

4. Remove from the oven and leave to cool naturally for 4 hours. Place the terrine in the refrigerator for at least 24 hours before serving.

5. To make the marmalade, place the onions and red wine in a saucepan, season lightly with salt and pepper and simmer for about 6 minutes until soft and transparent. Add the orange zest and honey and simmer for a further 6 minutes. Remove from the heat and let the marmalade cool with the terrine.

Addresses

✦

The addresses given on the next few pages range from recommended meat suppliers to companies supplying specialist kitchen equipment by mail order. (Kitchen Master, for example, will send you a catalogue of their professional cook's knives, boards and other essential kitchen equipment.) I have also listed organisations like The British Meat Information Service, British Organic Farmers and The Meat and Livestock Commission. Many companies will supply by mail order. Contact them first for details.

Recommended Meat Suppliers

I list here top-quality butchers and wholesalers who have helped me throughout this book, who I know and can personally recommend. I can also recommend any butcher who is a member of **The Guild of Q Butchers** (see page 9). This is an amalgamation of the meat trade's three quality assurance schemes – Q Guild Ltd., Shop with Assurance and Shop with Confidence. It is not possible to list all 500 Q Butchers here but you can obtain a list of Q Butchers in your area by contacting the Secretary on 01908 235018.

Orkney Meat supply their Orkney Gold Beef to butchers all over the country. They also supply David Jones in Llandudno, which was the Top Butcher's Shop finalist in 1996. To find a shop near you selling Island Gold Beef ring Edgar Balfour on 01856 874326.

You can buy your beef with confidence from Sainsbury's as their meat is supplied by ABP Ellsmere, a very well respected beef wholesaler. Tesco and other supermarkets also use reliable wholesalers and suppliers.

From Scotland, Ian Simpson's Scotch Premier brand represents uniquely assured premium quality beef which has been produced by Scotland's specialist livestock producers

BUTCHERS

Robert Anderson
Rosewell
Midlothian

Buccleuch Scotch Beef Ltd
27 Gate Central Markets
Smithfield
London EC1A 9ND
0171 236 1191

Buccleuch Scotch Beef Ltd
185 Caledonian Road
Wishaw
Lanarkshire ML2 0HT
01698 361707

James Chapman (Q)
35 Glasgow Road
Wishaw ML2 7PG

Craig Farm Organic Meat
Dolau
Llandrindod Wells
Powys LD1 5TL
01597 851655

Jim & D Cruickshank (Q)
1 The Square
Fochabers
Morayshire

Eastbrook Farm (Organic Meats)
Bishopstone
Swindon
Wiltshire SN6 8PW
01793 790460

England & Sons
810 Ormskirk Road
Pemberton, Wigan

T Firth
2A Station Road
Parbold Village
Parbold
Lancashire WN8 7NU
01257 463068

Glenbervie Aberdeen Angus Ltd
Glenbervie
Stonehaven
Kincardineshire AB39 3UA
01569 740540

C. Lidgate
110 Holland Park Avenue
London W11 4UA
0171 727 8243

Macbeth's
11 Tolbooth Street
Forres Moray
Scotland IV36 0PH
01309 672254

McCartney's Family Butchers
Main Street
Moira
Co Down
Northern Ireland

Orkney Meat Ltd
Grainshore Road
Hatston
Kirkwall
Orkney KW15 1FL
01856 874326

Pennys
Meats of Excellence
192 Whalley Road
Clayton le Moors
Accrington
Lancashire BB5 5HF
01254 389878

**St Marcus Fine Foods &
Butchers**
1 Rockingham Close
London SW15 5RW

Scotch Premier Meat
63 Woodend Place
Aberdeen
Scotland AB15 6AP
01224 311874

WHOLESALERS &
RESTAURANT
SUPPLIERS

A.B.P. Ellesmere
Hordley, Ellesmere
Shropshire SY12 9BL
01939 270333

Eastbrook (Organic Beef)
Eastbrook Farm
Bishopstone
Swindon SN6 8PW
01793 790460

Fairfax Meadow (Head Office)
6 Newmarket Drive
Osmaston Park Industrial Estate
Derby DE2 9SW
01332 757300

Fairfax Meadow (London)
24–27 Regis Road
London NW5 3EZ
0171 485 5115

Fairfax Meadow (Heathrow)
The Fulcrum Building
Horton Road, Colnbrook
Slough SL3 0AT
01753 790790

Fairfax Meadow (Newcastle)
353a Dukesway Court
Team Valley Trading Estate
Gateshead
Tyne & Wear
NE11 0PZ
0191 491 0595

**Fairfax Meadow (Great
Yarmouth)**
15 Bessemer Way
Harfrey's Industrial Estate
Great Yarmouth
Norfolk
01493 650611

Fairfax Meadow (Canterbury)
Wincheap Ind Estate
Cotton Road
Canterbury CT1 3RD
01227 763777

Lagan Meat Co Ltd
Duncrue Road
Belfast
Northern Ireland BT3 9BS
01232 749421 / 755811

Leeway (Wholesale) Meats Ltd
Unit 33
Leeway Trading Estate
Newport
Gwent NP9 0PT
01633 272645

Luddesdown Organic Farms Ltd
Court Lodge
Luddesdown
Cobham
Kent DA13 0XE
01474 813376

McGrath Meats
City of Belfast Meat Plant
Duncrue Pass
Belfast BT3 9BS
01232 749419

Makro Multi-Trade Centre
Emerson House
Albert Street
Eccles
Manchester M30 0LJ
0161 707 1585

Matthews Quality Meats
Units 8 & 9
Lingard Ind Estate
off Wood Street
Rochdale OL16 5QN
01706 41151

The Meat Centre
Unit 3
4a O'Hagan Street
Newry
Co Down BT34 1AP

Godfrey Meynell
Meynell Langley
Kirk Langley
Derby DE6 4NT
01332 824207

North Devon Meat Ltd
School Lane
Torrington
Devon EX38 7EX
01805 23371

Orkney Meat Ltd
Grainshore Road
Hatston, Kirkwall
Orkney KW14 1FL
01856 874 326

The Organic Food Club
7 Dudley Villas
Cleeve Road
Marlcliff
Bidford-on-Avon
Warks B50 4NR
01789 772870

Real Meat Co Ltd
East Hill Farm
Heylesbury, Warminster
Wiltshire BA12 0HR
01985 40436

Russel Hume
Sims House
Sims Food Park
Sherbourne Drive
Milton Keynes MK7 8BV
01908 375155 / 270061

Sandyford Foods Ltd
Sandyford
Prestwick
Ayrshire KA9 2SY
01292 520486

Miles Saunders (Organic Beef)
Willow Farm
Inglesham
Highworth
Wilts SN6 7QZ
01367 252163

Scotch Premier Meat
63 Woodend Place
Aberdeen
Scotland AB15 6AP
01244 311874

Sims Food Group PLC
Sims House
Sims Food Park
Sherbourne Drive
Tilbrook
Milton Keynes MK7 8BS
01908 270061

Sims of Carnaby
The Abattoir
Lancaster Road
Carnaby
East Yorkshire YO15 3QT
01262 670251

Stairs Farm Produce
Stairs Farmhouse
High Street
Hartfield
East Sussex TN7 4AB
01892 770793

Tordean Farm
Tordean
Dean Prior
Buckfastleigh
Devon TQ11 0LY
01364 43305

Woodhead Bros Meat Co
Junction Street, Colne
Lancashire BB8 8LH
01282 865704

OTHER USEFUL ADDRESSES

Bibendum Wine Ltd
113 Regents Park Road
London NW1 8UR
0171 722 5577

The British Meat
Information Service
59 Russell Square
London WC1 4HJ
0171 631 3434

British Organic Farmers
86 Colston Street
Bristol BS1 5BB
0117 9299666

British Standards Institution
2 Park Street
London W1A 2BS
0171 629 9000

Butchers & Drovers
Charitable Institution
Butchers Hall
87 Bartholomewe Close
London EC1A 9EA
0171 606 4106

Chartered Institute of
Environmental Health
Chadwick Court
15 Hatfield Road
London SE1 8DJ
0171 827 5868

The Chefs & Cooks Circle
PO Box 239
London N14 7NT
0181 368 3237

Department of Health
Richmond House
79 Whitehall
London SW1A 2NS
0171 210 3000

Euro-Toques (U.K. Chapter)
Winteringham Fields
Winteringham
North Lincolnshire DN15 9PF

Food Marketing &
Manufacturing Magazine
Yandell Publishing Ltd
8 Vermont Place
Tongwell
Milton Keynes MK15 8JA
01908 613323

Hart of England Deer Farm
Bakers Lane, Knowle
Warwickshire B93 8PR
01564 730199

The Humane Slaughter
Association
34 Blanche Lane
South Mimms
Potters Bar
Herts EN6 3PA
01707 659040

Kitchen Master
Quality Kitchens & Cook
   Shops
Trinity House, Unit 15
Trinity Court Industrial Estate
Warrington
Cheshire WA3 6QT
01704 834747

The Meat & Livestock
Commission
PO Box 44
Winterhill House
Snowdon Drive
Milton Keynes, MK6 1AX
01908 609826

Meat Training Council
PO Box 141
Winterhill House
Snowdon Drive
Milton Keynes, MK6 1YY
01908 231062

National Association of
Catering Butchers
217 Central Markets
Smithfield
London EC1A 9LH
0171 489 0005

National Federation of Meat
& Food Traders
1 Belgrove Road
Tunbridge Wells
Kent TN1 1YW
01892 541 412

Neff UK Ltd
Grand Union House
Old Wolverton Road
Old Wolverton
Milton Keynes, MK12 5PT
01908 328300

Red Velvet Beetroot
Kershaws Farm
Smithy Lane, Scarisbrick
Lancashire L40 8HN
01704 840392

Ricon
Ingredients & Technical
Systems For the Food Industry
Unit 4 Morris Green Business
   Park
Fearnhead Street
St Helens Road
Bolton, Lancashire BL3 3PE

The Yandell Food & Meat
Media Group
Tongwell
Milton Keynes MK15 8JA
01908 613323

Index

♦

after Christmas beef and turkey pie, 184
American beef, American, 153
American beefburgers, 130–1
American meatloaf, 24
anchovies, roulade of beef stuffed with, 28–9
apples: garlic beef curry with sultanas and, 116
  sirloin of beef Lady Jayne, 50
  Waldorf summer beef salad, 39
apricot and beef pie, 187
aubergine, Los Angeles steak with grilled, 137
AWT's pickled tongue, 108
AWT's spiced Mediterranean burgers, 129

bacon: beef casserole with bacon and beef rosti, 89
  smoked bacon, beef and oyster pudding, 203
baps, Tom's cheesy burger, 127
barbecue salsa, 147
barbecuing, 120–53
beans: beef with bean and beetroot casserole, 91
  Boston baked beans, 153
béarnaise sauce, 157–8
beef à la mode, 62
beef bourguignonne, 94
beef 'n' beer, 84
beef porcupine, 77
beef satay, 151
beef tails with fried vegetables, 167
beef teriyaki, 148–50
beef Wellington, 175–6
beefburgers, 126–33
beer: beef 'n' beer, 84
  beef steak and ale pudding, 201
  see also Guinness
beetroot: beef with bean and beetroot casserole, 91
  braised beef with chestnuts and, 110
  Bridge tournedos with red velvet sauce, 155
  curried dumplings with beetroot filling, 19
blackbean sauce, topside of beef with peppers and, 165
Bombay beef and potatoes, 58
Boston baked beans, 153
braises, 109–12
Brian Sack's traditional steak and kidney pudding or pie, 178–9
Bridge tournedos with red velvet sauce, 155
brisket, cold spiced beef, 106
brown stock, 13
burgers, 126–33
butters, herb, 124
buying beef, 4–5

cabbage and beef stuffed latkes, 26–7

Cajun spiced beef, 45
carbonnade of beef, 95
  marinade for, 122
carrots: Mrs Beeton's boiled beef and carrot pie, 182
casseroles, 74–104
champagne: champagne and beef curry, 118
  fillet of beef with truffles and champagne sauce, 85
Chateau Briand with Dijon mustard and herb crust, pot roasted, 72
Chateaubriand in garlic butter, 134
cheese: cheese scone pastry, 174
  Italian meat ball kebabs filled with mozzarella, 145
  Julian Groom's steak Waldorf with a pear and blue cheese salad, 160
  Lancashire pasties, 199
  prime beef fillet with Hramsa cheese, 61
  roast sirloin Stilton steaks garnished with pears, 59
  tatie pie with cheese scone topping, 200
  Tom's cheesy burger baps, 127
  TTB's beef Wellington with Lancashire cheese, 175
  TTB's cottage pie with Lancashire cheese and potato topping, 191
chestnuts: beef and chestnut pudding, 202
  braised beef with chestnuts and beetroot, 110
  Christmas beef and chestnut terrine, 206
chicken and beef teriyaki, 150
chillies: barbecue salsa, 147
  TTB's Mexican red hot pepper sauce, 142–3
Chinese egg noodles with beef, 162
choosing beef, 8–9
Christmas beef and chestnut terrine, 206
Cliveden fillet of Scotch beef poached in Madeira sauce, 102–3
coconut and beef curry, 114
consommés, 20–1
Cornish pasties, 195
cottage pie: traditional, 190
  TTB's cottage pie with Lancashire cheese and potato topping, 191
  with leek and potato topping, 192
creamed strips of sirloin, 29
Creole beef, pot roast rib of, 69
Creole noisettes of English beef H.R.H., 125
curries, 113–19
  beef and coconut curry, 114
  champagne and beef curry, 118
  creamy beef and wild mushroom curry, 115
  curried dumplings with beetroot filling, 19

garlic beef curry with apple and sultanas, 116
  hot beef curry with lime and rosemary, 117
  Persian royal beef korma with rice, 119
  red hot beef curry, 113
  roast Bombay beef and potatoes, 58
  roast rib of beef with curried rosemary and garlic stuffing balls, 57

daube of beef, 63
devilled steaks, 141
drunken beef Caribbean–style, 36–7
dumplings, 18
  curried dumplings with beetroot filling, 19
  Scottish beef sausage pot with scone dumplings, 97
  tarragon dumplings, 16–17

English fillet beefburgers, 132
espagnole sauce, 157

fennel sauce, ribs of beef in, 138–9
Forfar bridies, 196
Francis Coulson's suet pastry, 173
fritters, corn and rice, 152

game: beef and game pie, 189
  beef and game pudding, 204
garlic: Chateaubriand in garlic butter, 134
  garlic beef curry, 116
  ribs of Scottish beef with garlic sauce, 139
  San Francisco garlic beefburgers, 132–3
goulash 'my way', 80
gravy, 42–3
  onion gravy, 44
grilling, 120–53
guava sauce, Jamaican roast beef with, 49
Guinness: beef and Guinness pie, 186
  carbonnade of beef, 95

hanging beef, 5–6
Hannah Woolley's burger recipe, 127
haricot beans: Boston baked beans, 153
hazelnut and beef terrine, 207
herb butter, barbecued sirloin steaks with, 124
herb suet pastry, 173–4
Highland beef fillet, 168–9
honey, roast sirloin of English beef basted with mustard and, 46
horseradish: creamed horseradish, 26
  poached fillet of beef with horseradish and brandy sauce, 103
hot pot, Spanish, 98
hot water pastry, 172
hotchpotch, 100

hunter's beef, 64
  Tom Bridge's hunter's beef, 65
hutspot met klapstuck, 100

Indian fillet steak with corn and rice
    fritters, 152
Italian meat ball kebabs filled with moz-
    zarella, 145
Italian pot roast strips of beef, 70
Italian sauce, 34

Jamaican roast beef with guava sauce, 49
jambalaya with prawns and smoked oys-
    ters, 164
jugged steak, 81
Julian Groom's steak Waldorf with a
    pear and blue cheese salad, 160

kebabs, 143–52
kidney beans: drunken beef
    Caribbean–style, 36–7
kidneys: beef steak and ale pudding, 201
  Brian Sack's traditional steak and kid-
    ney pudding or pie, 178–9
Korean beef satay, 151–2

Lancashire pasties, 199
Lancashire sirloin of English beef roasted
    with a herb crust, 51
lasagne, 33
latkes, beef and cabbage stuffed, 26–7
leeks: beef and leek pasties, 196
  beef casserole with leeks in red wine
    sauce, 82
  beef, leek and horseradish pie, 185
  cottage pie with leek and potato top-
    ping, 192
lemon and chive marinade sauce, sirloins
    with, 123
lime: casserole of steak, peppers and
    onions in lime sauce, 90
  hot beef curry with rosemary and,
    117
  slow roast beef with coriander and, 71
lobster tail and beef teriyaki, 150
lombo de boeuf, 99
Los Angeles steak with grilled
    aubergine, 137

Macbeth's Aberdeen Angus beef special,
    133
Madeira: Cliveden fillet of Scotch beef
    poached in Madeira sauce,   102–3
  Madeira sauce, 43
mangetout, stroganoff with sliced roast
    potatoes and, 169
marinades, 75, 121–3
Mark Owen's `trade secret' Christmas
    pie, 183
marrow: baked field mushrooms with
    bone marrow and Taleggio, 38
  osso buco Tom Bridge–style, 96
meat balls: Italian meat ball kebabs filled
    with mozzarella, 145
  meat balls in red wine sauce, 32
  meat balls in tomato sauce, 31
meatloaf, American, 24
Mexican red hot pepper sauce, 142–3
Mexican T–bone steak supreme, 135

Milanese risotto with sirloin of beef,
    161
minced beef Parmentier, 105
mincemeat, 76
  Mark Owen's `trade secret' Christmas
    pie, 183
Mrs Beeton's boiled beef and carrot pie,
    182
Moroccan beef casserole, creamy, 78
mushrooms: baked field mushrooms
    with bone marrow and Taleggio,
    38
  beef, mushroom and potato pasties,
    197
  braised steak and shallots in wild
    mushroom and ginger sauce,   111
  creamed strips of sirloin, 29
  creamy beef and wild mushroom
    curry, 115
  creamy Moroccan beef casserole, 78
  fillet of beef in herb suet pastry, 179
  individual beef Wellingtons, 176
  TTB's beef Wellington with
    Lancashire cheese and mustard, 175
  twentieth–century beef, 88
mustard: beef fillet kebabs with English
    mustard, 146
  fillet of beef with German mustard
    and Asbach brandy, 134–5
  mustard seed Yorkshire pudding, 51
  pot roasted Chateau Briand with
    Dijon mustard and herb crust, 72
  roast sirloin of English beef basted
    with honey and mustard, 46

noodles: Chinese egg noodles with beef,
    162
nutrition, 9–11

Olde English potted beef, 22
olives, beef, 30
olives: braised silverside of beef with,
    112
  pot roast silverside of beef Portuguese,
    68
  pot roast silverside of beef Seville, 67
onions: beef 'n' onion pie, 181
  braised steak and onions in whisky
    sauce, 109
  onion gravy, 44
  red onion marmalade, 210
orange: beef and orange casserole, 87
  beef with thyme, orange and red
    wine, 107
osso buco Tom Bridge-style, 96
overcoat, roast sirloin of English beef in
    an, 46–7
oxtail: casserole of oxtails, 86
  oxtail and truffle sausage, 23
  oxtail soup with tarragon dumplings,
    16–17
  oxtail with sausages, 104
  ragout of British beef or oxtail, 101
oysters: beef jambalaya with prawns and
    smoked oysters, 164
  smoked bacon, beef and oyster pud-
    ding, 203
  surf and turf kebabs, 144–5

pan frying, 154–69
pasties, 195–9
pastry: cheese scone, 174
  Francis Coulson's suet, 173
  herb suet, 173–4
  hot water, 172
  puff, 171–2
  shortcrust, 171
patties: beef and cabbage stuffed latkes,
    26–7
  beef cakes cooked in dripping, 25
Paul Reed's red wine sauce, 73
peanuts: Korean beef satay, 151–2
pears: beef on skewers with pears and
    whisky, 148
  Julian Groom's steak Waldorf with a
    pear and blue cheese salad, 160
  rump steaks with pear rings, 140
peppercorns: pepper sauce, 156
  peppered steak, 136
  pink peppercorn steak, 125
  roast peppered rump steak, 45
  TTB's barbecued pepper ribs, 142
peppers: barbecue salsa, 147
  casserole of steak, peppers and onions
    in lime sauce, 90
  goulash `my way', 80
  lambo de boeuf, 99
  Polish cassolette, 83
  pot roast silverside of beef Portuguese,
    68
  pot roast silverside of beef Seville, 67
  topside of beef with peppers and
    blackbean sauce, 165
Persian royal beef korma, 119
pickled tongue, AWT's, 108
pies, 170–200
pigeon and beefsteak pie, 193
pineapple and sirloin kebabs, 144
pink peppercorn steak, 125
Polish cassolette, 83
pork: beef and pork pie, 180
port and coriander, sirloin of beef with,
    92
pot roasts, 41–2, 62–73
potatoes: beef and cabbage stuffed latkes,
    26–7
  beef cakes cooked in dripping, 25
  beef casserole with bacon and beef
    rosti, 89
  beef, mushroom and potato pasties,
    197
  cottage pie with leek and potato top-
    ping, 192
  minced beef Parmentier, 105
  perfect roast potatoes, 44–5
  roast Bombay beef and potatoes, 58
  roast rib of beef with rosemary pota-
    toes, 55
  stroganoff with sliced roast potatoes
    and mangetout, 169
  tatie pasties, 198
  tatie pie with cheese scone topping,
    200
  traditional cottage pie, 190
  TTB's cottage pie with Lancashire
    cheese and potato topping, 191
potted beef, Olde English, 22
potted hough, Victorian, 21

prawns: beef and tiger prawn teriyaki, 149
   beef jambalaya with smoked oysters and, 164
   surf and turf kebabs, 144–5
puddings, 177–9, 194, 201–4
puff pastry, 171–2

ragout of British beef or oxtail, 101
rare beef salad, 40
red hot beef curry, 113
rice: beef jambalaya with prawns and smoked oysters, 164
   drunken beef Caribbean–style, 36–7
   Indian fillet steak with corn and rice fritters, 152
   Milanese risotto with sirloin of beef, 161
rich beef stock, 14
risotto, Milanese, 161
roasts, 41–61
roly poly: beef and vegetable, 205
   with herb suet pastry, 177
rose petal sauce, roast sirloin of English beef with, 48
rosemary potatoes, roast rib of beef with, 55
rosti: beef casserole with bacon and beef rosti, 89
roulade of beef stuffed with anchovies and onions, 28–9
Ruth Pinch's beefsteak pudding, 194

salads: grilled sirloin with green salad, 138
   Julian Groom's steak Waldorf with a pear and blue cheese salad, 160
   rare beef salad, 40
   Waldorf summer beef salad, 39
salsa, barbecue, 147
salt and peppered fillet steak, 163
salt and peppered rump steak, roast, 60
San Francisco garlic beefburgers, 132–3
satay, beef, 151–2
sauces: barbecue salsa, 147
   béarnaise, 158
   espagnole, 157
   gravy, 42–3
   Italian, 34
   Madeira, 43
   onion gravy, 44
   Paul Reed's red wine, 73
   pepper, 156
   TTB's Mexican red hot pepper, 142–3
   velouté, 34–5
sausages: oxtail and truffle, 23

   oxtail with, 104
   Scottish beef sausage pot, 97
   TTB's homemade, 166
scallops: surf and turf kebabs, 144–5
scone dumplings, Scottish beef sausage pot with, 97
scone pastry, cheese, 174
Scottish beef sausage pot, 97
seventeenth–century spiced beef casserole, 79
shallots: braised steak and shallots in wild mushroom and ginger sauce, 111
   fillet of beef and shallot pie, 188
   Italian pot roast strips of beef with sweet shallots and brandy cream, 70
shortcrust pastry, 171
sirloin of beef Lady Jayne, 50
sirloin steaks in foil, 140–1
slow roast beef with lime and coriander, 71
soups, 15–21
Spanish beef kebabs, 143
Spanish hot pot, 98
spiced beef brisket, 106
spiced or hunter's beef, 64
spinach: fillet of beef in herb suet pastry, 179
spit roast, sirloin of beef, 147
steak and kidney pudding or pie, 178–9
steak Diane, 159
steaks: grilling and barbecuing, 120–5
   pan frying, 154–60
Steve Johnson's potted beef terrine, 209
stocks, 12–13
storing beef, 6–7
stroganoff with sliced roast potatoes and mangetout, 169
suet pastry: Francis Coulson's, 173
   herb, 173–4
surf and turf kebabs, 144–5
sweetcorn: Indian fillet steak with corn and rice fritters, 152

tarragon dumplings, 16–17
tatie pasties, 198
tatie pie with cheese scone topping, 200
teriyaki beef, 148–50
terrines, 206–9
Thai stir–fried beef with vegetables, 161–2
tomatoes: barbecue salsa, 147
   meat balls in tomato sauce, 31
Tom's cheesy burger baps, 127
Tom's ultimate whopper burger, 130

tongue, AWT's pickled, 108
tournedos à la Béarnaise, 158
tournedos Rossini, 156
traditional cottage pie, 190
traditional Scotch broth, 16
truffles: fillet of beef with champagne sauce and, 85
   oxtail and truffle sausage, 23
TTB's barbecued pepper ribs, 142
TTB's beef Wellington with Lancashire cheese and mustard, 175
TTB's cottage pie with Lancashire cheese and potato topping, 191
TTB's homemade sausages, 166
TTB's Mexican red hot pepper sauce, 142–3
turkey: after Christmas beef and turkey pie, 184
turnips: beef casserole with young turnips and cider, 93
twentieth–century beef, 88

vegetables: beef tails with fried vegetables, 167
   hutspot met klapstuck, 100
   Thai stir–fried beef with, 161–2
   traditional Scotch broth, 16
   Victorian pot roast beef, 66
velouté, 34–5
Veronica Shaw's seventeenth–century beefburgers, 128
Victorian pot roast beef, 66
Victorian potted hough, 21

Waldorf summer beef salad, 39
whisky: beef on skewers with pears and, 148
   braised steak and onions in whisky sauce, 109
wine: beef bourguignonne, 94
   beef casserole with leeks in red wine sauce, 82
   beef with thyme, orange and red wine, 107
   forerib and silverside marinade, 121–2
   marinade for carbonnade, 122
   meat balls in red wine sauce, 32
   Paul Reed's red wine sauce, 73
   wine marinade, 75

Yorkshire pudding, 53–4
   mustard seed, 51
   roast rib of English beef and, 52
   with minced beef and onion, 54